FROMM

WALKING TOURS

Venice

Robert Ullian
and Thomas Worthen

MACMILLAN • USA

MACMILLAN TRAVEL
A Simon & Schuster Macmillan Company
1633 Broadway
New York, NY 10019

ISBN 0-02-860467-9
ISSN 1081-342X

Editor: Alice Fellows
Map Editor: Douglas Stallings
Design by Amy Peppler Adams—designLab, Seattle
Maps by Ortelius Design and John Decamillis

CONTENTS

LIST OF MAPS

• • • • • • •

This book is dedicated to the talented, caring people who labor to save and preserve Venice.

• • • • • • •

About the Authors

Robert Ullian, who designed the neighborhood walks for this book, is also author of Frommer's *Israel on $45 A Day.* Educated at Amherst College and Columbia University, he is the recipient of a National Endowment for the Arts award for his short stories, and has taught writing and art at Hampshire College and the University of Massachusetts at Amherst.

Thomas Worthen, who is responsible for the walks describing the Piazza San Marco, the Accademia, and the San Michele cemetery, is an art historian of the Italian Renaissance. He recently completed a year's residence in Venice, studying various aspects of its art and architecture. He teaches at Drake University in Des Moines, Iowa.

Acknowledgements

With special gratitude to Claudia Rech of the Colleczione Peggy Guggenheim, Helene and Roberto Feruzzi, Marta Marie Lotti, and Amy Worthen for their very patient encouragement and advice.

An Invitation to the Reader

In researching this book, we discovered many wonderful places, sights, shops, restaurants, and more. We're sure you'll find others. Please share them with us, especially if you want to bring to our attention things that have changed since we researched this book. Please write to:

Robert Ullian and Thomas Worthen
Frommer's Walking Tours: Venice
Macmillan Travel
1633 Broadway
New York, NY 10019

An Additional Note

Please be advised that travel information is subject to change at any time—and this is especially true of prices. The authors, editors, and publisher cannot be held responsible for the experiences of readers while traveling. Your safety is important to us, however, so we encourage you to stay alert and be aware of your surroundings. Keep a close eye on cameras, purses, and wallets, all favorite targets of thieves and pickpockets.

Introducing Venice

When you visit Venice, you don't just visit another city—you visit a place that for a thousand years was an independent country and a world unto itself. While Europe struggled through centuries of feudal warlords and intellectual darkness, Venice flourished as a serene, well ordered republic. It had no fortifications or walls, and it was governed with a constitutional system of checks and balances that students of government marvel at to this day. Napoleon claimed he would be an Attila to Venice's exotic world of commerce and fantasy. Indeed, the unique, magical civilization that was Venice disappeared into thin air in 1797, when Napoleon's armies became the first in history to conquer the lagoon. Yet the physical structure of the city built by this extraordinary civilization remains almost completely intact—as fantastic as the Xanadu of Kublai Khan described by Venice's own native son, Marco Polo. Nowhere else in the world has the capital of an empire survived frozen in time at its moment of perfection. Waves lap at its doorsteps, tides flood its campos and churches, yet miraculously, we can still walk through the world of exotic architecture and delicate reflections, the carefully contrived illusion and reality that was Venice two, three, and four hundred years ago.

For centuries before the Christian era, the swampy lagoon of Venice supported small fishing communities of simple thatch-roofed buildings. Unlike Rome, Naples, Padua, and many other Italian cities, the history of Venice as a major city does not go back into antiquity. Inhabitants of the mainland cities of Padua, Altinum, and Aquileia, fleeing from the 5th-century barbarian invasions, sought temporary refuge in the lagoon, and in the chaotic centuries after the fall of Rome, these settlements became permanent. The refugees learned to survive and even thrive on the marshy tidal fields and islands. Salt was the first export commodity, and not long after, the lagoon became a way station for the sale of Slavic captives into the slave markets of North Africa.

Torcello, Malamocco, and Chioggia were among the first major settlements to emerge. Sometime between the years 697 and 726, these early settlements formed a protective confederation under the first elected doge, or leader. In these communities, something of the heritage of Roman Italy survived, almost within sight of the warring Gothic and Lombard kingdoms of the mainland. One of the city's oldest legends tells the story of the invasion of the lagoon by the armies and fleets of Pepin, son of Charlemagne, in A.D. 810. As Pepin's forces approached, the local population fled en masse from the exposed outer communities of the Lido and Malamocco to the swampy islets of the Riva Alto (the Rialto), in the heart of the lagoon, where Venice stands today. Only one woman, too old and crippled to flee, was found at Malamocco by Pepin's soldiers. She was brought before Pepin, and questioned under threat of death as to where the channel across the lagoon lay. Pointing across the water to Venice, the woman replied, "Sempre diretto"—"Always straight." Pepin's fleet followed the direction of her hand, and went disastrously aground. In the lagoon of Venice—as in the city of Venice today, the way is never straight. The concept of "sempre diretto" simply does not exist.

Unable to invade the lagoon, or to force its surrender by siege, the Franks agreed to a treaty giving nominal sovereignty over the lagoon to Byzantium. Now legally beyond the pale of feudal Italy, and only theoretically under the sway of distant Constantinople, Venice was free to develop its own unique ways. A palace was built for Agnolo Participazio, the doge who had led the resistance against Pepin, at the site of the present Doge's Palace. In 828, the body of the evangelist, St. Mark, was abducted from its burial place in Islamic-ruled Alexandria, and spirited away to Venice. Within a few years, a resting place for the relics of St. Mark was under construction beside the Doge's Palace, and in true Venetian fashion, an appropriate legend arose in conjunction with the new basilica: St. Mark, in his many travels, had supposedly come to the Venetian lagoon where an angel appeared to him and announced, "Pax tibi . . . Peace to you, Mark, my evangelist . . . here your body shall lie." The lion of St. Mark, with his paw on the page of a book opened to the words "Pax tibi" became the symbol of Venice, and "Viva San Marco" became its rallying cry. The upstart community on the mudflats now had a religious and patriotic tradition independent of either Byzantium or Rome.

In the next centuries, Venice waged a constant struggle to keep its trade routes to Constantinople free from Arab pirates and Slavic marauders along the Dalmatian coast; it also survived an attempt by the Magyars to overrun the lagoon. By the year 1000, the islands of the Rialto had emerged as the center of the Venetian world, and the coast of Dalmatia was secured by Venetian fleets.

In 1095, came Pope Urban II's call to Christendom to reclaim Jerusalem and the Holy Sepulcher from Islam. Venice, controlling the trade route from Western Europe to the Near East, and true to its nature as a mercantile state, was less touched by the religious fervor of the time than involved in the profitable logistics of transporting thousands of Crusaders and pilgrims to the Holy Land on Venetian ships. In addition to cash payments for shipping supplies and armies to the Near East, Venice demanded and received grants of property and trading rights in the Aegean, the Black Sea, and along the coasts of Syria and Palestine.

When Jerusalem was recaptured from the Crusaders in 1187, and a Fourth Crusade was proposed, Venice, for an enormous fee, was commissioned to provide shipping for the expedition. As the Crusader armies gathered in Venice, it became apparent that they were short of the transportation payment promised to the Republic. It was agreed that the armies could work off part of their payment by helping Venice to reconquer Zara, a port on the Dalmatian coast that the Venetians had recently lost to Hungary. After the capture of Zara, with the Crusaders still short of their fare to the Holy Land, it was not difficult for Venice to persuade them to intervene in Constantinople, where a crisis over the sucession to the throne of Byzantium had developed. In 1204, Crusader armies led by the wily ninety-year-old Doge Enrico Dandolo sacked Constantinople, the greatest repository of the ancient world's art, libraries, and treasures. Every object of value that could be found was smashed, burned, or carried off. Among the prizes shipped to Venice were the four magnificent bronze horses that used to ornament the facade of the Basilica of San Marco. Thousands were massacred; the destruction was so great that the Byzantine Empire was mortally wounded.

The 13th, 14th, and 15th centuries saw a steady rise of Venetian power, punctuated by wars with Genoa and other Italian cities for control of trade routes to the East. Under the great *condotierre*, or mercenary commander, Bartolomeo Colleoni (1400–1475), Venice reached the height of its military power. Wealth poured into the city. During the 1400s, the Doge's Palace took its final form, the Ca' d'Oro and other gothic palaces were built along the Grand Canal, and the great churches of San Giovanni e Paolo and the Frari were constructed. But even as Venetian power and magnificence reached its zenith, the seeds of Venice's fall were being planted. In 1453, Constantinople, which had never recovered from the sack of 1204, fell prey to the Ottoman Turks. Without the protection of the benign Byzantine Empire, Venice would be forced to spend the next three hundred years fighting Turkish expansion.

The voyage of Columbus to the New World in 1492 was another piece of bad news for Venice. It spelled an end to the Venetian stranglehold on Europe's fragile trade route to Asia. The centers of power and commerce in Europe moved to countries on its Atlantic and northern coasts. Despite these ominous developments, for a century, starting in the late 1400s, Venice glided serenely to new heights of splendor. It was an age graced by the greatest of Venice's artists. Vittore Carpaccio (c.1460–1525) depicted the world of early Renaissance Venice with poetry and lyricism. Giovanni Bellini (1430–1516) created paintings of sublime, contemplative spiritual intensity; the great Titian (c.1488–1576) and Giorgione (1578–1510) both studied under this master. It was the age of Tintoretto (1518–1594), whose dynamic, visionary masterpieces fill the Scuola Grande di San Rocco and the Madonna dell' Orto; it was also the age of Veronese (1528–1588), perhaps the most enchanting decorative painter of the High Renaissance.

Venice reveled in its riches and in the talent of its artists. The state visit to Venice of the newly crowned King Henry III of France in 1574 offers a glimpse of the Republic at the summation of its Golden Age. The king entered the lagoon at the Lido through a triumphal arch, designed by the great architect, Andrea Palladio, and painted by Tintoretto and Veronese. Accompanied by the doge and a fantastic ceremonial flotilla that included hundreds of gondolas, with orchestras playing from the decks of war galleys, the king sailed past San Marco and into the Grand Canal, where the palaces were hung with tapestries. His entourage landed at the lavish Palazzo Foscari (now part of the university) in Dorsoduro. As the bells of Venice tolled, Henry was taken to his private apartments in the palace, filled with paintings by Bellini, Titian, Tintoretto, and Veronese, all especially commissioned or acquired for his visit. On his bed, the sheets were of crimson silk with threads of gold. Among the many special delights in store for him, when the king entered his bedchamber, he found himself walking across a masterpiece mosaic floor designed by Veronese especially for the occasion.

The king was taken to the Piazza San Marco for a state banquet for three thousand guests. The entire Piazza was covered by a blue awning filled with stars; the pavement was covered with rare Oriental carpets. Under a golden canopy in the Great Hall of the Doge's Palace, Henry was offered a menu of twelve hundred different dishes and three hundred kinds of sweets, all served on gold and silver plate. The tables were decorated with enchanting spun-sugar figures and tableaux designed by the Republic's greatest artists and sculptors. Regattas, fireworks, choirs, pageants, and processions ornamented by giant sea creatures made of Murano glass accompanied the king's every activity. He was taken to meet the aged Titian, was painted by Tintoretto, and offered the pleasures of the most legendary courtesan in all Venetian history, the brilliant and exquisite Veronica Franco, who composed two sonnets in his honor. Venice's reputation for magical sumptuousness was beyond compare.

As the Republic declined, the physical splendor of Venice still continued to develop. Palladio's Redentore Church and the great baroque Church of Santa Maria della Salute mark two disastrous plagues that devastated the city in 1576 and in 1630.

Invisible to 20th-century visitors is the musical tapestry which for centuries must have adorned Venice. By the time of

Claudio Monteverdi (1567–1643), who became maestro di cappella at San Marco in 1613, the city resounded with 410 major processions a year. New music was constantly being commissioned for these pageants and for the processions that accompanied the saint's days of the more than seventy Venetian parish churches. World famous choirs and orchestras gave a steady stream of performances. Opera, which had previously been performed only in private residences, first went public in Venice.

As the economy of Venice stagnated in the 18th century, the Republic, once so efficiently organized and purposeful, fell into severe decay. One by one, Venetian trading posts and colonies throughout the eastern Mediterranean fell to other powers. Allowed to survive in a kind of ghostly twilight by extraordinary diplomatic luck, 18th-century Venice threw itself into fantasy and escapism. Carnival was extended for six months, during which time masked, costumed revelers of all classes could indulge in public behavior that would have been beyond scandal in other European societies. Married women of the patrician class considered a *cicisbeo*, or lover/gentlemen-in-waiting to be an indispensable companion in making their daily rounds. Gambling went on around the clock. Many of the convents of Venice, filled with daughters of patrician families, were rife with romance, and intrigue; when the nuns of San Lorenzo were once locked inside their convent, they rioted and burned down the gates in order to join the Carnival festivities. Giovanni Battista Tiepolo (1696–1770) and Pietro Longhi (1702–85), among others, often depicted the exotic, bizarre Carnival world of Venice in their paintings. Pleasure seekers from around the world descended on Venice (as they do to this day); money and treasures flowed away. It is symptomatic of this era that while you can buy postcards of famous Venetian landscapes by Antonio Canal, known as Canaletto (1697–1768), throughout Venice, almost all of the actual paintings are in collections far from both Venice and Italy.

With Napoleon's conquest of Venice in 1797, the facade of Carnival collapsed, and the inconsolably romantic decay of the city continued into the 19th century without benefit of masks and costumes. A foreign power, the Austrian Empire, ruled Venice from the end of the Napoleonic Wars in 1815 until 1866; to a large extent, the artists and writers who were inspired by Venice were also foreign. The most famous 19th- and early 20th century paintings of the city are by J. M. W. Turner, Monet,

Renoir, and Signac, all of whom were fascinated by Venice's plays of light, mist, and reflection. Venice became the home of writers such as Byron and Robert Browning; it hosted the tumultuous visits of George Eliot and George Sand. Richard Wagner composed here and died in a palazzo on the Grand Canal. There was a brief, heroic rebellion against Austria in 1848–49, led by Daniele Manin, but the city continued to sink into lethargy. The fin de siecle Hotel des Bains on the Lido, with its spectacle of "civilized people getting sensuous enjoyment at the very

Finding Your Way

A few Italian and Venetian words are useful to know as you wander about Venice. Piazza is a square, and in most Italian cities there are numerous piazzas. In Venice, however, there is only one—the Piazza San Marco. All other squares are called *campos,* or if they are very small, *campiellos.* A *salizada* is a main street leading away from a campo; *rua* (a cognate of the French word *rue*) is another word meaning a major thoroughfare. *Calle* is the word used to refer to most streets. A covered passageway is a *sotoportego.* The word for bridge is *ponte.* A canal is a *rio*; a walkway along a rio is a *fondamenta*; a broad paved walkway along a major waterfront is a *riva.*

Finally, when you look at the palaces and great houses of Venice, it is useful to know that the *piano nobile* refers to the second or third floor, which contains the most impressive rooms of the building. You can identify the piano nobile by the windows of the *portego* or central hallway, which are usually located in the center of the piano nobile, and are the most elaborate windows on the facade of a *palazzo,* or palace. Until the fall of the Republic, in 1797, there was only one palazzo—the Doge's Palace. The great houses of the city were designated by the word *ca'*; a few landmarks such as the Ca' Pesaro or the Ca' d'Oro are still referred to in this way. After the fall of the Republic, however, most great houses came gradually to be called *palazzi* (plural of *palazzo*), and most of the great houses you'll see in Venice, such as the Palazzo Grassi or the Palazzo Labia, are now officially so classified.

edge of the elements," provided the resigned, elegiac setting for Thomas Mann's *Death in Venice*. The title of Mann's book became a state of mind.

With the end of the Austrian occupation, Venice voted to become part of the newly established kingdom of Italy, and in the 20th century, the city began to stir, with efforts designed to bring the once magical and Serene Republic into the contemporary world. A modern industrial complex, begun in 1917 at Mestre and Marghera on the mainland, brought hopes of an economic revival; it also brought a nightmare of pollution-causing decay, and a drain on the local water table that accelerated the rate at which Venice is sinking into the sea. The Venice Biennale was founded in 1895 and has developed into a famous international exposition of contemporary art that takes place every two years; the modern permanent pavilions that various nations have built for the Biennale fill the Public Gardens. In 1932, the Venice Film Festival, now the doyenne of international film festivals, was organized (the centerpiece of the opening festival was *Grand Hotel*, with Greta Garbo, Lionel Barrymore, and Joan Crawford). Held at the Lido each summer, the festival is known for its prestigious Golden Lion Award, but for onlookers, the real prize is often a glimpse of the cinematic superstars who fill the the outrageously romantic beachside Hotel Excelsior (the Excelsior was the inspiration for Hollywood's interpretations of the once-elegant Lido, such as the set for the 1935 film, *Top Hat*, with Fred Astaire and Ginger Rogers).

Fantasy came crashing down on Venice, however, with the ever increasing flood tides that inundate the city. The most dramatic *aqua alta* to sweep Venice occurred on November 3 and 4, l966, and launched an initially slow program of efforts to preserve and restore the city that has developed into a turning point in Venetian history. As you explore Venice, you will be amazed by the brilliant restorations of buildings and works of art across the city. The scope of this international effort is enormous. It reflects both faith in the master plans for the protection of Venice from the sea, and a determination that Venice will not merely survive, but will shine. The city has become a center for the many organizations and individuals that are working with great devotion to save Venice, for its inhabitants and for the world. It has also become home to an increasing number of Venetians-by-choice, who have come from all over the world to share the experience of living in what is perhaps the most fantastical community ever to arise in Europe.

Venice is a place where you must lose yourself. Remember the words of the old woman at Malamocco whose directions across the lagoon caused the fleet of Pepin to go aground in A.D. 810. Over the centuries, "Sempre diretto!" ("Always straight ahead!") has become the wry, sardonic watchword of those visitors who dare to explore the labyrinthine mysteries of the city.

There are many anecdotes about lost travelers in Venice. In one, a courtly Venetian is stopped by tourists and asked the way to a specific site in the city. He responds by asking if they want to know the fastest way, or the most beautiful way. In these walks through Venice, we try to show you the most beautiful way. At times the routes twist and turn so that you will come upon a major site from the direction that shows off its greatest perfection. As you explore Venice, you'll come to understand that the entire city is a communal work of art, filled with surprises and treasures where you least expect them.

We were often tempted to add just one more nearby church, museum, or vista to a walk. However, Venice is meant for pleasure—it should never be experienced on the far side of overload. The walks in this book are not meant to be an encyclopedic, connect-the-dot tour of everything worth seeing in Venice, although we do try to touch base with many important sites. In Venice, you must wander and choose.

Many truly marvelous sites did not fit into these walks. Among them are the Scuola San Giorgio degli Schiavoni, a Dalmatian traders' guildhall in Castello, that contains a cycle of nine masterpiece canvasses painted by Vittore Carpaccio illustrating episodes from the lives of St. George, St. Tryphon, and St. Jerome; the lovely gothic Madonna dell'Orto Church in Cannaregio, the parish church of Tintoretto, which is filled with his paintings; the Greek Orthodox Church of San Giorgio dei Greci in Castello, with its accompanying museum of Byzantine art; and the Church of San Sebastiano in Dorsoduro, a treasure house of paintings by Veronese.

The islands of the Venetian lagoon that could not be included here also offer more extraordinary pleasures. The overgrown, haunting island of Torcello, with its Byzantine cathedral and church can be combined with a visit and a walk around the neighboring island of Burano. Burano was once

The Tours at a Glance

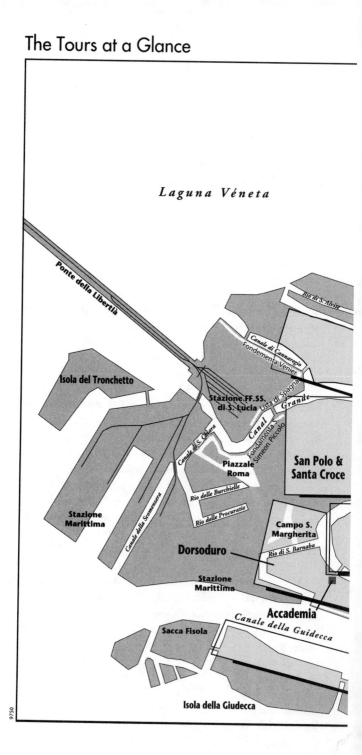

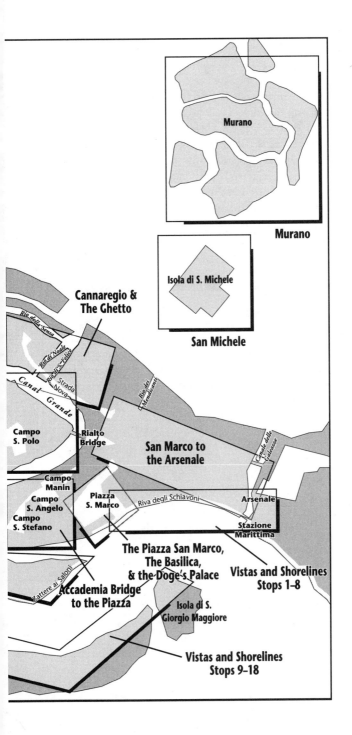

Murano

Murano

Isola di S. Michele

San Michele

Cannaregio &
The Ghetto

Rio della Sensa

Rio di Noale

Rio di S. Felix

Canal Grande

Strada
Nova

Rio dei Mendicanti

Canale delle Galeazze

Campo
S. Polo

Rialto
Bridge

San Marco to
the Arsenale

Campo
Manin

Campo
S. Angelo

Piazza
S. Marco

Riva degli Schiavoni

Arsenale

Campo
S. Stefano

Stazione
Marittima

The Piazza San Marco,
The Basilica,
& the Doge's Palace

Vistas and Shorelines
Stops 1–8

Zattere ai Saloni

Accademia Bridge
to the Piazza

Isola di S.
Giorgio Maggiore

Vistas and Shorelines
Stops 9–18

famous for its master lacemakers, and lace fills the island's shops (much of it is now made in China). For many, however, the real masterpiece of Burano is its canal-laced village, with brightly colored fishermen's houses reflecting in the glassy waters. From Burano, you can hire a small boat to take you to the island of San Francesco del Deserto where St. Francis of Assisi is believed to have been briefly marooned in the year 1220. Here you'll find a Franciscan monastery with paradisical gardens. Another worthwhile excursion is a boat tour to the great Renaissance villas on the mainland in the Brenta region.

Surveys indicate that over half the visitors to Venice come on day trips or stay only one or two nights. If these walks help you decide to spend a longer time there, and lead you to wander on your own, they will have performed their greatest service.

Reading the Signs

Most street signs and markers in Venice are written in Venetian dialect, which is slightly different from standard Italian. Our text generally conforms to Venetian spelling, but readers should be aware that they may encounter variant spellings on signs throughout the city.

THE PIAZZA SAN MARCO, THE BASILICA & THE DOGE'S PALACE

Start: Basilica of San Marco.

Finish: Basilica of San Marco.

Time: About three hours or more.

Best Time: Mornings (9 or 9:30am).

Worst Time: Afternoons, when crowds gather.

This is the heart of Venice, and there's enough to keep you busy for a week. Here you find the Basilica of San Marco, which was the spiritual heart of Venice, and the Doge's Palace, which was its political center. These are two of the world's great cultural treasures. The other buildings that surround the Piazza have much to offer as well.

The Piazza San Marco may be the most beautiful square in the world. It has always been Venice's ceremonial gathering place. Napoleon pronounced it "the most elegant drawing room in Europe." It has become the major gathering place of tourists, and it's a wonderful place to stroll, to window shop, to listen to the cafe orchestras, and to watch pigeons attack tourists. The one thing you won't find is a rock concert. After Pink Floyd performed here in 1989, the Piazza was so thoroughly trashed that the authorities have said, "Never again!"

In the height of the tourist season you may want to ignore our itinerary and just go to what is open and available, since there can be a line just to get into the Basilica of San Marco.

• • • • • • • • • • • • • • • • •

1. **The Basilica of San Marco** was built in 832 to house the relics of St. Mark, brought here from Alexandria in Egypt by two Venetian merchants—or grave robbers, depending on your point of view. According to the legend, they took the holy body from its shrine in Alexandria with the help of some local Christians to prevent the precious relic being desecrated by the Muslim rulers of Egypt. St. Mark himself was said to have made a few timely appearances to bless and abet the enterprise. The legend inspired many wonderful works of art but it is at least as likely that the doge, Giustiniano Participazio, actually commissioned the theft to enhance his own prestige, and that of Venice. In any event, relics could not be owned but merely possessed, so "robbery" would certainly be too strong a word for this trans-location of a spiritual treasure.

The Venetians based the design of their new church on that of the Church of the Apostles in Constantinople—then the richest city in Christendom—in order to announce architecturally that Venice was one of the great cities of the world with one of the really great relics. The church built to honor St. Mark has remained the most magnificent in Venice. The basic church structure you see today is mainly the result of a rebuilding that took place from around 1063 to 1094. The process of clothing the building in marble and mosaic was to take more than two additional centuries.

The greatest influx of riches for the church began in 1204, when Doge Enrico Dandolo's manipulation of the

The Piazza San Marco

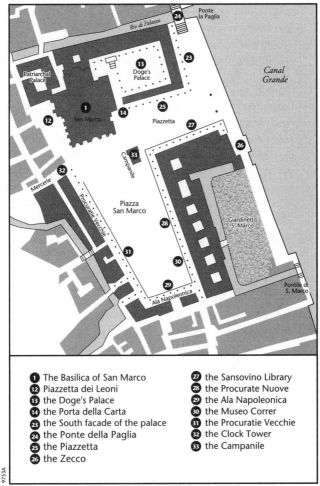

- **1** The Basilica of San Marco
- **12** Piazzetta dei Leoni
- **13** the Doge's Palace
- **14** the Porta della Carta
- **23** the South facade of the palace
- **24** the Ponte della Paglia
- **25** the Piazzetta
- **26** the Zecco
- **27** the Sansovino Library
- **28** the Procurate Nuove
- **29** the Ala Napoleonica
- **30** the Museo Correr
- **31** the Procuratie Vecchie
- **32** the Clock Tower
- **33** the Campanile

Fourth Crusade contributed to the sack of Constantinople. Repair and restoration is ongoing. You will be very, very lucky if you don't find some part of the building hidden behind the restorers' scaffolding.

2. **The principal facade** was originally plain brick. The columns, sculpture, and sheets of marble that cover it now are pure show. Since they are mainly spoils from elsewhere, they have a slightly hodgepodge quality, but because of careful attention to symmetry, the variety of colors and shapes is a

delight. Venetian sculptors made free copies of some of the imported (or stolen) reliefs to maintain this symmetry. The large Byzantine relief of Hercules carrying a boar on the far left, just past the leftmost portal, is balanced by a Venetian carving of Hercules with a stag, on the far right. The Venetian imitation is less dignified and less classical, but it is also sharper, more energetic, and more decorative, like Venice itself.

Now stand just in front of the central doorway, and look up at **the three stone arches** above the central doorway, two below and one above the large mosaic of the Last Judgment. Here the sculptors were at their most original. The inner arch was carved first and has the simplest figures in the lowest relief. As the sculptors proceeded to the second and third arches they became progressively more confident, and the relief of the carving projects more and becomes more complex and naturalistic.

The outer faces of the upper two arches show such pious subjects as virtues and prophets. The insides of the arches—the parts you have to get underneath to see—are most interesting for the scenes they give us of 13th-century Venetian life. In the the second arch, the inner face depicts the months, each illustrated with the appropriate zodiac sign and a typical seasonal labor. The inside of the third arch, the one surrounding the mosaic, shows a number of specifically Venetian occupations, such as fishing (in the lower right) and shipbuilding (in the lower left), just above the seated man with crutches. According to tradition, that seated man was the architect of San Marco; however, he probably represents old age, when men can no longer practice their occupations.

Only around the year 1400 were the standing saints added to the very top of the facade, together with their airy tabernacles rising from the rambunctious stone leaves, slathered across the top of the uppermost arches.

Above the central portal, in front of the large window, are **four horses.** These were the most spectacular of the trophies sent from Constantinople by Doge Enrico Dandolo, and when they were installed here they were the only free-standing works of sculpture on the facade. As one of Venice's greatest treasures, they became something of a

The Basilica of San Marco

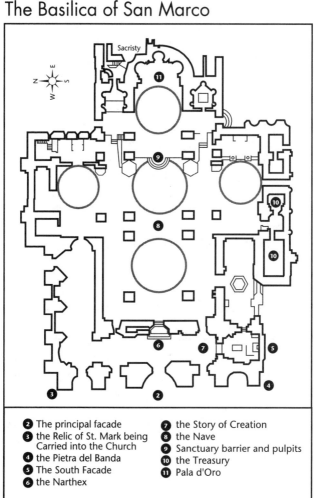

Sacristy

2 The principal facade
3 the Relic of St. Mark being Carried into the Church
4 the Pietra del Banda
5 The South Facade
6 the Narthex

7 the Story of Creation
8 the Nave
9 Sanctuary barrier and pulpits
10 the Treasury
11 Pala d'Oro

9753B

symbol of the Republic's greatness. The Four Horses of St. Mark's once stood at the hippodrome in Constantinople, and before that, they may have decorated Nero's arch in Rome. Napoleon had them carted off to Paris after he seized Venice in 1797. In Paris, they graced the Triumphal Arch of the Carousel for 18 years, but they were returned to Venice after Waterloo. What you see today are actually copies, made in 1982. The originals are in the church's museum.

The four semicircular mosaics above the side doors illustrate the story of the theft of the body of St. Mark, while the four large mosaics on the second story depict the death and resurrection of Jesus Christ. Most of them were made in the 17th century as replacements for the original Byzantine-style mosaics, which were then totally out of fashion.

One 13th-century mosaic mercifully escaped destruction, the one above the doorway on the far left, showing:

3. **the relic of St. Mark being carried into the church.** This lovely mosaic depicts San Marco as it was around 1260 when the mosaic was laid, and when the topmost part of the facade was much simpler.

Go to the other end of the main facade, where you'll find the:

4. **Pietra del Banda,** a short red column, really no more than a platform, which was probably brought from Acre late in the period of the Crusades. Decrees were publicly announced by an official who stood upon it. It was severely battered in 1902 when the belltower collapsed and a lot of the rubble slid onto it.

Now go around the corner to the side of the church facing the Doge's Palace and the lagoon:

5. **the south facade,** a showcase for some of the finest loot. The most distinctive piece is the dark red porphyry relief carving with four grim men, at the corner adjacent to the Palace. These four are the Tetrarchs, who ruled the Roman Empire around A.D. 300; they too were brought from Constantinople. A Venetian legend accounts for their presence here in a more appealing way—these are four Muslims who were turned to stone as they tried to carry off the treasury of San Marco, the exterior of which they adorn.

Fifteen feet from the south facade are two highly decorated squared shafts. It had always been thought that they were trophies taken from the Genoese at Acre, but recently it has been proved that they came from a 6th-century church in Constantinople, destroyed by the crusaders.

Return to the principal facade and enter the church through the main door. As you do so, admire the 6th-century bronze doors with the lion's heads. (No prizes for guessing where the doors came from.) Within the doorway is:

6. **the narthex,** the porch of the church. It's a different world, dimmer, more delicately adorned, and with a soft, uncanny glow of golden light coming from the mosaics in the vaults overhead. The low late afternoon sun shining into the narthex can turn this effect into a glittering blaze. On either side of the entryway into the church are miniature columns framing mosaic niches. These mosaics, of around 1100, the oldest surviving in San Marco, present us with austere but colorful Byzantine saints.

The larger mosaic in the half-dome above the door shows *St. Mark in Ecstasy* (1545). Here is a very different, boldly Renaissance, conception of a saint, three-dimensional and energetic. It was designed by Titian, who wisely left the time-consuming and demanding job of inserting little cubes of stone and glass in wet mortar to a professional mosaicist.

The mosaics in the vaults that cap the narthex to the right and left depict scenes from the Old Testament. In the Christian view, as the Old Testament prepares the way for the New Testament, so this porch prepares for the church proper.

Now go to to your right (as you entered the narthex), and stand beneath the dome. When you look up into the dome you will see:

7. **the Story of Creation,** according to the book of Genesis. Each of the six days of creation is represented by the appropriate number of dainty little winged women. The reason for this odd bit of symbolism is made clear if, while standing beneath the dome, you face 45° to the right of the door leading back into the piazza and look up at the middle row of scenes in the dome. There you will see the Lord blessing the Sabbath Day and making her holy.

A number of thread-like red lines run through the mosaics (you can see them clearly in the scene closest to the door to the church). The red lines outline sections of the mosaic that, because of their ruinous condition, had to be filled in by the restorers. You can see similarly outlined areas in many of the other older mosaics.

Now return to the part of the narthex just before the main entrance to the church. If you are up for climbing

44 steep steps, then, with the soft glow of the narthex mosaics fresh in your mind, enter the small door just to the side of the central portal and climb up to **the museum** above the narthex (admission fee), which contains ancient paintings, manuscripts, and fabrics that were used in the church services. The unfinished brick vaults in the smaller rooms will help you imagine what the entire building must have looked like before it was covered with mosaics. The museum is especially worthwhile for the views you will have of the Piazza and the interior of the church.

In the room near the top of the stairs you can study fragments of 14th-century mosaics close up. The faces are lined with small squares of reds, greens, and blues as intense as in a Matisse. When seen from across the room, the brilliant colors make the faces vivid, but blend together in such a way that they are hardly visible individually.

Continue still farther into the museum and you'll come to the originals of the four magnificent horses brought from Constantinople in 1204, that were once on the facade of the building. In ancient Rome they had been harnessed to a bronze chariot carrying a bronze Roman emperor holding the reins. The horses are so magnificent that it's hard to regret the loss of the chariot.

If the church is extremely crowded, you might begin your tour from the balcony; otherwise descend the stairs and enter the main door into the church proper.

8. **The nave.** If you come in the dead of winter and are very lucky, you may have the entire place to yourself, but more likely you will find yourself in a dense throng with rather too many guides. Don't abandon hope or the building. Find a place to sit (you may have to go well into the church to find an empty bench), and take time to gaze about.

The church is cross-shaped, covered by five domes. Three of the domes march in succession from the main door to the high altar. Another dome is above each of the arms of the cross (the transepts). The lower part of the church is covered with stone that is flatter and simpler than that in the porch. The alabaster columns are all functional. The walls are covered with sheets of marble, so cut and arranged that their veining creates symmetrical patterns.

When we look up into the vaults and mosaics, we enter (at least visually) a realm where everything massive and sharp is avoided. Even the edges of the arches are softened by the golden mosaics. In these vaults the Venetian mosaicists created their greatest masterpieces, all surrounded by a golden aura that W. B. Yeats called "God's holy fire." Light is important mainly to illumine and reflect off the mosaics, therefore the windows were placed at the very bottom of the domes to be as unobtrusive as possible. There is a large circular gothic rose window in the south transept that seems very out-of-place in this Byzantine-style building; it was added to provide light for ducal ceremonies and for the display of relics.

The three major domes between door and altar depict three forms of interaction between God and humanity. In the large dome immediately above as you enter the church is the Descent of the Holy Spirit, in the form of a dove, on Jesus' disciples. The great dome in the center of the church shows the Ascension of Christ into heaven. In the dome above the sanctuary is still another image of Christ, this time with the prophets who foretold his coming.

The arches between the domes have scenes from the life of Christ. On the arch between the first and second domes are some of the most beautiful narrative scenes in San Marco, illustrating Christ's death and resurrection with Byzantine restraint. On the right is the Crucifixion. On the top is the holy women visiting the empty tomb on Easter morning. On the left, opposite the Crucifixion, is Christ's journey to hell to liberate the souls of the righteous of the Old Testament. This last scene was the usual way of illustrating Christ's resurrection in Byzantine art.

The lesser domes, arches, and walls depict various saints, and stories connected with St. Mark.

Many of the original mosaics have been replaced in the last five hundred years. Sometimes the mosaicist simply copied the composition that had been there before. The apse above the high altar is Renaissance in date (1506) but very Byzantine in style. More often an artist was commissioned to design a new composition of the same subject, and these changes were generally for the worse.

9. **Sanctuary barrier and pulpits.** The culmination of any church is its sanctuary, the place around the altar reserved for the priests and choir. The rest of the church, where the congregation would stand is focused on it. The sanctuary is architecturally separated by being raised up and enclosed by a screen. The stone slabs that form the parapet of the screen have, however, been put on hinges so that they can be opened for services.

Beneath the sanctuary is a many-columned crypt designed to contain the shrine of St. Mark. It's well below water level and was generally flooded until an impressive job of sealing, completed in 1993, rendered it dry for the first time in centuries. The crypt is accessible only for prayer.

On top of the screen, in the center, is a silver crucifix flanked by statues of Mary and John the Evangelist, and flanking this group are the twelve apostles. These handsome gothic figures, installed in 1396, may seem as inappropriate as the rose window, since there are usually no free-standing statues in a Byzantine-style church.

Immediately in front of the screen on either side is a pulpit. The one on the left, the green stone wedding-cake topped with a bulging parapet and a canopy, was for reading the bible. The reddish pulpit on the right was for the presentation of the doge to the people and the display of holy relics. In the 18th century, when the choir of San Marco was world famous, musicians would crowd into it to play for services.

Walk into the transept and, beneath the dome, turn right between the columns. In front of you is:

10. **the Treasury** (admission fee), which has the world's best collection of Byzantine treasures, together with a number of masterpieces made in Venice itself.

The very best treasure, however, is in the sanctuary, and requires still another admission fee. As you leave the museum move toward your right and toward the sanctuary, following the signs that say PALA D'ORO. The turnstile just beyond the ticket seller is more or less where the doge's throne would have been placed when the doge attended the service. After you pay, go around to the back of the high altar to see:

11. **Pala d'Oro** (Golden Altarpiece), a stunning conglomeration of Byzantine enameling, gold, and jewels.
According to a 1796 inventory, its decorations include 1,300
pearls, 400 garnets, 300 sapphires, 300 emeralds, 90 am-
ethysts, 75 balases, 15 rubies, 4 topazes, and 2 cameos.
Begun around 1105, it reached its present appearance only
in 1342—it was enlarged and enriched through several
centuries. It was made to face into the nave, and still does
on the major feast days. Generally, however, it is turned
around in the opposite direction so that you can't look for
free.

While you're in the sanctuary, admire the four richly
carved alabaster columns that support the stone canopy
above the altar. The figures within the arches illustrate the
life of Christ. Scholars have argued about whether the columns were made in Constantinople in the 6th century or
Venice in the 13th. The latter date is probably correct, but
it hardly matters. Like so much else in San Marco, they are
unique.

You will probably leave the church on the side opposite
the Doge's Palace, which will bring you to the:

12. **Piazzetta dei Leoni** (Small Square of the Lions) named
for the two battered red Verona stone beasts (1722) that
guard the well. Facing it, beneath the large arch (to your
right if you left the church through the side door), is the
noble tomb of Venice's 19th-century hero, Daniele Manin,
who led the short-lived revival of the Venetian Republic
from 1848 to 1849.

Now it is time to circle back to the other chief treasure
of Venice:

13. **the Doge's Palace.** It was begun in or shortly after 811
as a castle for the first duke, Agnolo Participazio. The palace has undergone several rebuildings and expansions, so
no traces of the original structure are visible. The gracious
gothic structure we see today was not begun till around
1340, and was constructed in various stages over the next
hundred years

This palace remained the home of the doges for almost
a millennium, until the fall of the Venetian Republic in
1797; but the doge's actual living quarters were effectively

reduced to four rooms. The purpose of the 14th-century rebuilding was to accommodate the various councils, offices, courts, prisons, and armories that were needed to make the palace not merely the town hall of the city of Venice but capital of the Venetian Empire as well. Unlike other medieval Italian governmental buildings, it is not a fortress. Its open loggias, picturesque decorations, and graceful structure bear witness to the security that the Venetian rulers felt here in the center of their stable, prosperous state.

There is sculpture at each corner of the building. On the level of the upper loggia is a protecting archangel. On the lower level are symbolic biblical scenes: *The Judgment of Solomon* is nearest the basilica church and *Adam and Eve* is at the opposite end of the facade near the Piazzetta. There are delicate bits of symbolic sculpture on the capitals. Look for the ninth arch from the left on the upper loggia. Between these columns of red stone, death sentences were read.

The principal entrance to the palace is between the palace and the basilica:

14. **the Porta della Carta** (Paper Door, perhaps named from the professional scribes who set up shop near here). It was built under Doge Francesco Foscari (in office 1423–57). Doge Foscari liked glory. He began the series of conquests of the mainland of Venice—conquests that ultimately turned Venice from an aggressive city of merchant-gentlemen, in the 14th century, into a conservative city dominated by a landed aristocracy, in the 18th. Foscari built this impressive and elaborate late gothic entrance to the Doge's Palace, with a statue of himself kneeling before a winged lion, the symbol of St. Mark and of Venice itself.

Napoleon liked glory too. After he conquered Venice in 1797, the French paid the chief stonemason, Giacomo Gallini, 982 ducats to destroy all the lions of St. Mark in Venice. Though Giacomo took the money, this was one of the few lions his masons got around to chiseling off. It seems appropriate that the effigy of the man who began Venice's mainland empire should have been effaced by order of the man who destroyed it. The lion and the statue of the doge that you see today are 19th-century replacements.

Go through the entrance to the enormous stairway you see before you:

The Doge's Palace

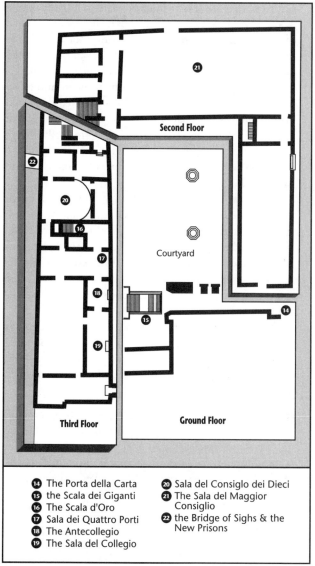

Second Floor

Courtyard

Third Floor

Ground Floor

- ⑭ The Porta della Carta
- ⑮ the Scala dei Giganti
- ⑯ The Scala d'Oro
- ⑰ Sala dei Quattro Porti
- ⑱ The Antecollegio
- ⑲ The Sala del Collegio
- ⑳ Sala del Consiglio dei Dieci
- ㉑ The Sala del Maggior Consiglio
- ㉒ the Bridge of Sighs & the New Prisons

15. **Scala dei Giganti** (Stairway of the Giants). The stairway and the facade of the courtyard on that side were constructed to designs by Antonio Rizzo after a fire gutted the east wing of the palace in 1483. The project was finished in 1501, but Rizzo didn't get to see it through—he had to flee Venice

in 1489 when his overseers suspected that he was keeping about 15% of the construction funds for himself. The carved decoration here is derived from ancient Rome; but it is as delicate and charming—and as expensive and overdone—as the late-gothic entryway that leads to it.

The magnificent stairway takes its name from the two oversized statues of Neptune and Mars, carved by Jacopo Sansovino in 1554, that symbolize Venice's domination of the sea and the land. The stairway was principally a stage for such ceremonies as the coronation of the doge and the reception of important foreign dignitaries. Curiously, there is a jail cell beneath the stairs.

To go any farther you'll need to pay, but it's well worth it. The council rooms are decorated with some of the best art that Venice produced. The tickets are sold under the arcade on the left (the side closest to the church).There is also a guided tour in Italian (at 10am and at 2pm), the *itinerari segreti,* that takes you to parts of the palace most tourists never get to see. You can book it at the ticket window marked INFORMAZIONE.

Your tour through the Palazzo Ducale will have to follow the path laid out for you. The following are some of the highlights and are (probably) in the order that you will encounter them; but be warned that the mandatory path can be changed.

16. **The Scala d'Oro** (Golden Stairs), the white-and-gold stairway that rises from the second floor, was designed by Jacopo Sansovino (1554–58) to give important dignitaries a splendid access to the major reception and council rooms.

    At the top of the stairs turn right and you will be in the:

17. **Sala dei Quattro Porti** (Room of the Four Doors), really a staging area for three of the most important meeting rooms. The best thing in it is the painting on the long wall immediately to your right as you enter, *Doge Antonio Grimani Kneeling Before Faith,* begun by Titian around 1555.

    The next room on the itinerary is the:

18. **Antecollegio,** which has perhaps the loveliest collection of paintings in the palace. On the the walls before you and

behind you as you enter the room are four allegories by Tintoretto, filled with spiraling figures that are at once austere and sensuous (1577). Each allegory combines pagan gods (symbolic of properties particularly propitious for Venice) with the four seasons to suggest that Venice is favored under all seasons and circumstances. If you face the door you came through you'll see on your left, in winter, Vulcan, god of craftsmen. On your right are the three Graces in spring. Facing the opposite direction on your right is Ceres, goddess of prosperity, harvest, and summertime, separated by Wisdom (Minerva) from the harms of War (Mars). On your left, Bacchus, god of wine and of fall, is married to Ariadne, even as Venice was wed to the sea.

On the wall opposite the windows, on your right, is Jacopo Bassano's *Return of Jacob into Canaan*. To the left of it is Veronese's stunningly elegant and beautiful *Rape of Europa* (1580). We see the Phoenician princess, Europa, climbing in all innocence on the back of a white bull, who is Jupiter in disguise. Then, in several more distant scenes, we see him carrying her to the shore and across the Mediterranean, towards Crete, one of Venice's major possessions.

19. **The Sala del Collegio** with its richly decorated ceiling and walls may well be the single most beautiful room in the palace. On the walls are glorifications of the virtues and piety of various 16th-century doges. Though there is a certain redundancy of virgins and Christs, each work separately is quite handsome. As you enter, all the paintings to your right and behind you are by Tintoretto. The painting facing you is by Veronese, celebrating Doge Sebastian Falier and the Battle of Lepanto (1581–82). Veronese also painted the allegorical scenes in the ceiling (1575–78); the large painting above the raised tribune is *Venice Enthroned, Honored by Justice and Peace*. The smaller figures in the ceiling represent the virtues of Venice. The woman knitting a spider web on your right, in the second ceiling panel from the entrance wall, for instance, is Dialectic, weaving (allegorically) a web of words.

The next room is a larger hall for the senate. The paintings (1585–95) are more extensive, if not necessarily of higher quality.

The exit returns you to the Room of the Four Doors. The painting on the easel is *Venice Honored by Neptune*, by Tiepolo (1745–50), one of the more recent paintings in the palace; the version above the windows is a copy. Next follows the:

20. **Sala del Consiglio dei Dieci** (Room of the Council of Ten), the meeting place of the most powerful committee in Venice. This council actually consisted of 17 people, the Council of Ten itself, the doge, and the doge's six counselors. The room's ceiling would be even more spectacular if the central painting by Veronese hadn't been carted off to Paris during the Napoleonic occupation, and replaced by a copy.

After this room the tour can vary. You'll probably pass through the armory, and you may see fragments of some of the older works of art in the building, if that section is open. The two following sites are among the most memorable parts of the palace, though you may or may not see them in this order.

21. **The Sala del Maggior Consiglio** (Room of the Great Council), originally constructed between 1340 and 1355, after being gutted by fire in 1577, it was completely rebuilt. It had to be big, since it had to seat every enfranchised citizen of Venice, namely noblemen over 25. Their average number was around 1,500, and their major function was to elect the officials in the other councils. There were nine double rows of seats, arranged back-to-back and running lengthwise down the hall. (The specific arrangement of seats can be seen in a display at the far end of the room.)

The ensemble of the decoration may be more spectacular than its parts, but two of the paintings are wonderful. The enormous scene on the end wall is *Paradise*, by Tintoretto (1588–94), one of the largest paintings on canvas in the world. The oval painting on the ceiling above it is the *Apotheosis of Venice*, by Paolo Veronese, the perfect embodiment of Venice's self-conception—elegant, wealthy, aristocratic, and most serene.

On the walls immediately beneath the ceiling are portraits of the doges. The most famous is the one who isn't there. On the wall opposite the *Paradise*, on the left, one of the portraits seems to be covered with a veil, and a text reads: "Here is the place of Marin Falier, beheaded for his crimes." In 1355, after one year in office, Doge Marin Falier attempted to overthrow the Republic in an effort to replace his ceremonial power with real power, but underestimated the efficiency of the Venetian bureaucrats.

After passing through small barren corridors, you'll come to:

22. **the Bridge of Sighs and the New Prisons** (1566–1614). The bridge served as the link between the court and torture rooms in the Doge's Palace and the prisons on the other side of a small canal. The name "Bridge of Sighs" was a 19th-century romantic invention, but it is certainly appropriate and evocative.

The prisons continued to be used until 1919. The most famous prisoner here was Daniele Manin, the Venetian patriot, who was imprisoned here by the Austrians, and later released in the 1848 rebellion. The famous and daring escape of another prisoner, Casanova, was made from an older prison, under the roof of the palace.

Much has been written about the evils of the Venetian judicial system, its use of secret denunciations and trials, political imprisonment and torture. It had its faults (see the story of Antonio Foscarini in Walk 5). The Piazzetta, in front of the Doge's Palace was the traditional spot for state executions, and even in the Republic's eminently civilized later centuries, these spectacles were gruesome. In 1595, Fynes Moryson, an Elizabethan traveler, witnessed the execution of two young men who were the sons of senators. Their hands were cut off, and their tongues ripped from their throats before they were beheaded. Their crime had been a night of public drunkenness and wild behavior—their sentence may have had as much to do with their failure to uphold standards expected of patricians as with their actual crime. William Lithgow, a Scottish visitor to Venice in 1610, reported seeing a friar "burning quick [i.e., alive] at St. Mark's pillars for begetting 15 young noble nuns with child, and all within one year."

Still, similar methods were standard for the period, and the rulers of Venice instinctively avoided fanaticism; for its time it had one of the more equitable judicial systems. In the 18th century the Republic became the second country in the world to outlaw judicial torture.

At the end of your tour of the palace, you'll find yourself in the large courtyard. Note the two fantastically elaborate well heads (1556 and 1559), made of expensive bronze.

After you leave the palace you'll be beside:

23. **the south façade of the palace.** This was built before the facade near the San Marco, and the sculptural details are even better. Each capital is elaborately carved and each is different.

The bridge next to this corner is the:

24. **Ponte della Paglia** (Bridge of Straw). It was named not for the building material but for the cargo that was brought here. It offers a fine view of the Bridge of Sighs. Drowned bodies used to be placed nearby for relatives to claim, or, if unclaimed, to be buried by a charitable institution.

The sculpture at this corner of the Doge's Palace is the *Drunkenness of Noah*, whose three sons are just around the corner. Since those sons were supposed to have been the ancestors of all the races on the earth, this scene may suggest the breadth of Venetian trading enterprises.

Now go to the opposite end of the palace, to the two enormous columns, and you'll be in:

25. **the Piazzetta,** the sea-entrance to San Marco and the palace with the two columns forming its gateway. This was the site of a variety of ceremonies and celebrations. From here the doge entered his ceremonial boat, the Bucentaur, for his annual Marriage with the Sea on Ascension Day (see Walk 2). During Carnival acrobats used to form huge human pyramids and some daredevil would slide down a rope to the Piazzetta from the top of the campanile.

The enormous monolithic columns were trophies, brought from the eastern Mediterranean in the 12th century, and dedicated to Venice's patron saints. The one with the winged lion on the top is the Column of St. Mark. The lion was probably made around 300 B.C. in what is today southeast Turkey, but the wings are Venetian additions. The other column supports St. Theodore, the pre-Mark patron saint of Venice; it is a hodgepodge of antique fragments standing on a Venetian dragon. Executions took place between the two columns, and to this day some Venetians are reluctant to walk between them.

The large building opposite the Doge's Palace is the library designed by Jacopo Sansovino, beginning in 1536, and called, appropriately, the Sansovino Library (see below). It's a glorious building, "above envy," as Aretino said. Using nothing but white stone and shadows, Sansovino achieved an effect as rich and lush as that of its polychromed neighbors. No surprise that it was influential; and you'll see echoes of it along the Grand Canal.

If you go around the library, along the water and away from the Doge's Palace, the next building you'll come to is:

26. **the Zecco, or mint.** The shiny gold coins minted here were called zecchini, which gives us our word "sequin." The facade of this knobby building is radically different from that of the library; strangely, the two were designed by the same man, Sansovino. The ponderous and rough stones suggest the building is so strong that the gold within is safe. Originally it had only two stories, but because the furnaces made it intolerably hot, a third story was added in 1554 to help with ventilation.

The next part of the tour is a stroll alongside and through the porticoes that surround the Piazzetta and the Piazza of San Marco. Begin in the nearest one, the portico beneath the:

27. **Sansovino Library** (also called Biblioteca Marciana— Library of St. Mark). At no. 7 is the entrance to the library itself. Probably its greatest treasure is its collections of books printed in Venice; for, until the end of the Republic, Venice was the most important book-printing center in Italy, at one time producing more books than the rest of the world combined. Its most famous press was that of Aldus Manutius, known especially for his beautiful and scrupu- lously correct editions of Greek and Latin classics.

No. 13A is the entrance to the **old library,** generally opened only for special exhibits. If the door is open, by all means go up, if only to see the richly decorated rooms with paintings by Veronese, Tintoretto, and Titian, among others. With a place this beautiful for study, it's surprising that Venice didn't produce more great writers.

No. 17 is the entrance to the **Museo Archeologico,** which has an excellent collection of sculpture from ancient Greece (remember the Venetian empire included many possessions in what is today Greece!) and Rome.

Shortly after, the portico takes a left-hand turn, you'll be in the:

28. **Procuratie Nuove.** Built after 1586, its design was conceived as a sort of extension of the Sansovino Library, with one floor too many. It served as the residence for the procurators, the most honored officials in Venice after the doge. Today it houses some of the city's more elegant shops and, in the upper floors, the Correr Museum.

No. 52 leads into a courtyard with the best collection of well heads in Venice and with an excellent explanatory text in English, just inside the door from the portico. If a doorkeeper should question your purpose, indicate that you want to see the *vere da pozzo* (well heads).

Take a Break   A few doors down is the **Caffè Florian,** a coffeehouse that has been here since the middle of the 18th century. Casanova claimed to have stopped there for coffee after breaking out of his cell in the Doge's Palace, before fleeing Venice. From 1815 to 1866, during the years of the Austrian occupation, Caffè Florian was a bastion of Venetian patriots. During the 1848–49 rebellion against Austria, Florian for a time called itself Manin, in honor of the leader of the insurrection. Later in the century, according to Ruskin, it was a place where "the idle Venetians of the middle classes lounge, and read empty journals." It is a real pleasure to sit at an outdoor table or in one of the hyperdecorated rooms (1858) and while away an hour conversing or reading an "empty journal," but it's a pleasure that doesn't come cheap.

On your left, at the very end of the portico and a little past the piazza, is the Venice Tourist Information Bureau, which has helpful people and much information.

Now turn into the portico that runs at a right angle to the one you've been in:

29. **the Ala Napoleonica** (the Napoleonic Wing), opposite San Marco. It was rebuilt under Napoleon (1808–14) to

make a formal entrance and a ballroom for the royal residence that he had built into the Procuratie Nuove. In the middle of this wing is a large passageway named for the Church of San Geminiano, torn down in 1808 for the greater glory of the French ruler. A representation of the facade of the church is set in the pavement in the middle of the passageway.

A grand though chilly neoclassical stairway rises from the passageway to the second floor and:

30. **Museo Correr,** which is really several connected museums. There are temporary exhibition galleries (tickets are sold at the foot of the stairs in the tourist season) which are almost always worthwhile since the Correr hosts some of the finest temporary exhibitions in Venice. The first room of the exhibition hall is a magnificent neoclassical ballroom of 1822, designed by Lorenzo Santi, with pieces of sculpture by Venice's great neoclassical sculptor, Antonio Canova.

Tickets for the museum proper are sold in the room just past the top of the stairway. The main floor of the Correr Museum is dedicated to Venetian civilization, in both its more stately and its more intimate forms. Objects range from battle standards to *zoccoli*, the foot-high shoes that many upper-class women and prostitutes once tottered about on. Painted scenes range from dogal processions to battles between rival Venetian mobs at a parapetless bridge, with losers cascading into the canal (see Walk 7, Stop 29).

The museum continues on the next floor with the **Picture Gallery** (Quadreria), which features an excellent collection of earlier Venetian art, including what may be the earliest surviving Venetian panel painting (on a chest of around 1250). It is especially strong in paintings of the 14th and 15th centuries, and includes not only works by such Venetian artists as the Bellini (Jacopo, Gentile, and Giovanni) and Carpaccio, but also some small masterpieces by their northern European contemporaries.

The same ticket gets you into the **Museo del Risorgimento** (Museum of the Unification of Italy— follow the signs near the entrance to the Picture Gallery), which has a number of delightful political cartoons from the first half of the 19th century.

The last wing, bordering the piazza is the:

31. **Procuratie Vecchie** (the older residence of the procurators), built between 1514 and 1526, again with elegant shops on the ground floor.

Shortly after you turn into this wing you'll come upon two arches on your left that open into the **Bacino Orseolo,** which has probably the largest conglomeration of gondolas in the city (that is to say, in the world); and if you're interested in hiring one—and can afford it—this is a good staging point.

Take a Break   Continuing down the portico of the Procuratie Vecchie, you will pass several cafés with their orchestras, including **Quadri's,** which the Austrians patronized in the first half of the 19th century, while Venetian patriots were at Florian's, across the piazza. Now the bands occasionally seem at loggerheads, but not the clientele.

At the end of the portico is:

32. **the Clock Tower** (Torre dell' Orologio), designed by Mauro Coducci and constructed between 1496 and 1499 with the two side wings added at a later time. It tells the time to within five minutes, the phases of the moon, and the place of the sun in the zodiac. The clock is the city's most wondrous and beloved timepiece. At the top of the tower is a balustraded terrace from which two mechanical bronze statues, called "moors" because of the dark color of the bronze, faithfully strike the hour on a massive bell. Just below, against a field of golden stars, a winged Lion of St. Mark looks out over the piazza and lagoon with his book open to the words, "Peace unto you . . . " Below the lion, a niche contains a statue of the Madonna and Child. On Epiphany and during the Feast of Ascension, the clock's hourly pageant expands to include the Magi, led by an angel, who emerge from the doors on either side of the niche and bow before the figure of the Madonna. Legend has it that the eyes of the creators of the clock, Paolo and Carlo Rainieri, were put out to prevent them from ever matching this achievement for other patrons, but in actuality, the two master clockmakers received only solid praise and very solid pensions.

The arch beneath the tower marks the beginning of the Merceria, the main shopping drag that connects San Marco and the Rialto (see Walk 2).

Now that you've seen the piazza from the ground, you may want to see it from above. Return to:

33. **the Campanile** (Bell Tower). It collapsed on July 14, 1902, harming no one, apparently, but the watchman's cat. In the reconstruction, the original design (of 1511–14, by Bartolomeo Bon) was followed faithfully, but with a much more sophisticated understanding of building principles. It's unlikely to fall again soon.

At the base of the tower is a loggia that was begun in 1538 by Jacopo Sansovino, flattened in 1902, and carefully reconstructed by piecing together the original fragments as much as possible. It is a real jewel box, and is decorated with some of Sansovino's finest statues. Originally it was a sort of clubhouse for nobles; now it's the entrance to the elevator going up the tower.

This is one of the two great tower views in Venice (the other is across the water at San Giorgio Maggiore—see Walk 3, Stop 9). If the line here isn't too long you can complete your tour of the piazza with a different perspective on what you have seen.

San Marco to the Arsenale: Landmarks and Labyrinths

Start: Piazza San Marco.

Finish: The Arsenale.

Time: Three or more hours, depending on time allotted at sights.

Best Time: Mornings (9am or earlier) when churches are open.

Worst Time: Midday, when churches and the Arsenal Museum are closed.

This is a walk through a network of calles, campos, and churches as intricate and amazing as a masterpiece of Burano lace. It leads through the oldest and most densely structured part of Venice, and will introduce you to a number of the city's most important landmarks, including the campo and Renaissance church of Santa Maria Formosa, the marble poetry of Venice's beloved Miracoli Church and the monumental civic ensemble of the gothic church of SS. Giovanni and Paolo and the Scuola Grande di San Marco. The walk ends at the Arsenale, with its naval museum that is filled with remarkable models of the ships that created Venetian pre-eminence on the seas.

On this tour, the major sites and the beauty of the areas you'll pass will fill most of your time. You should start early and keep a steady pace if you want to include the interiors of the churches. These are generally open from 9am to 11:45 or noon, and again from 4pm to 6pm (a bit later in summer). The Arsenale Museum, the last stop on the tour, is open until 1pm, but ticket sales stop at 12:30pm. You may want to concentrate on the churches and not try to race to the Arsenale. The Actv stop at the Arsenale is the terminus for this walk, and you can take a vaporetto there to wherever you plan to go next in the city.

Because of the time constraints, you might decide not to take a break until the end of the walk, where you'll find a choice of less expensive restaurants and cafes as well as one of Venice's best middle-to-upper range restaurants, hidden in the labyrinth of small streets near the Arsenale.

● ● ● ● ● ● ● ● ● ● ● ● ● ● ● ●

As you face the front of the Basilica of San Marco, turn to your left and walk toward the:

1. **Clock Tower** (Torre dell' Orologio), built between 1496 and 1499, and the city's most wondrous and beloved time-piece. It's fully described in Walk 1, Stop 32. The 24-hour clock and zodiac rise above the portal, which forms a tri-umphal arch leading into the Mercerio, the great shopping street of Venice connecting Piazza San Marco with the Rialto Bridge.

Proceed through the Clock Tower portal. A few steps into the Mercerio on the left, you'll pass the:

2. **Sotoportego del Capello.** Above the entrance to the sotoportego is a carved relief of an old woman that com-memorates the spot where the most serious rebellion against the Venetian Republic was turned back in the year 1310. On the night of June 10, as the rebel army led by Bajamante Tiepolo marched from the Rialto down the Mercerio toward

San Marco to the Arsenale

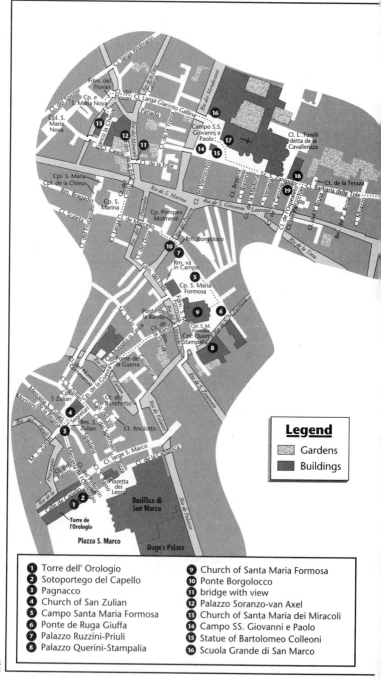

Legend

- Gardens
- Buildings

1. Torre dell' Orologio
2. Sotoportego del Capello
3. Pagnacco
4. Church of San Zulian
5. Campo Santa Maria Formosa
6. Ponte de Ruga Giuffa
7. Palazzo Ruzzini-Priuli
8. Palazzo Querini-Stampalia
9. Church of Santa Maria Formosa
10. Ponte Borgolocco
11. bridge with view
12. Palazzo Soranzo-van Axel
13. Church of Santa Maria dei Miracoli
14. Campo SS. Giovanni e Paolo
15. Statue of Bartolomeo Colleoni
16. Scuola Grande di San Marco

17	Church of SS. Giovanni e Paolo
18	Church of the Ospedaletto
19	Laboratorio Artegiano Maschere
20	The Church of San Francesco della Vigna
21	Campo Due Pozzi
22	Church of San Martino
23	Spazio Legno
24	Renaissance brick palazzetti
25	Gate of the Arsenale
26	Naval Museum

0 ____ 90 m
____ 98 yds.

N

Cn. Massa
Cl. de la Moschete
Cp. de S. Giustina detto de Barbaria
Stp. del Boter
Cl. del Cafetier
Cl. Cavalle
Cl. Zen
Cl. S. Francesco della Vigna
Fdm. S. Giustina
Cl. de le Deum
Cl. de la Pietà
Cp. S. Francesco de la Vigna
Cl. de la Nunziatura
Ct. de la Do Porte
Cp. S. Giustina
Cp. de la Confraternita
Cl. drio la Chiesa

20

Rio del
Rio de S. Giustina
Rm. al Ponte Francesco
Cpl. de la Chiesa
Rio de S. Francesco de la Vigna

Sz. S. Giustina
S. Lorenzo
Cl. del Murion

Cl. Sacca
Sz. de la Gata
Rio de S. Francesco
Cl. de l'Ogio
Cl. va al P. dei Scudi
P. dei Scudi
Cl. Magno

Cp. de la Gata
Rielo dei Furlani
Cl. del Magazen Vechio
Cp. Do Pozzi
Rio de la Gorna
Ct. Peschiera
Fdm. de le Gorne

21

Cl. dei Mandoli
Cl. del Forno Municipio
Piscina S. Martino
Cp. de la Gorne

Darsena Vecchia

Rio de S. Martino
Ct. Vener
Fond. dei Penini

Cp. S. Martino

23

22

Cpl. de la Scarestia
Fdm. de Fazza Arsenal
Fdm. dei Arsenalotti

24 **25**

Cp. de l'Arsenal

Arsenal

Rio de l'Arsenal
Fdm. de l'Arsenal
Cp. de la Tana

Riva degli Schiavoni
Rio de la Ca' di Dio
P. de la Ca' di Dio
Riva de la Ca' di Dio

Bacino S. Marco
Actv.

26

Cp. S. Biagio

the Doge's Palace, an old woman named Giustina Rossi opened her window to see what the noise was all about. According to some sources, she accidentally knocked a stone mortar off her window ledge (others claim her action was more purposeful). The mortar brained Tiepolo's standard bearer and killed him; the rebels panicked and fled. When invited by the Republic to name her own reward, the modest Giustina Rossi asked only to be allowed to hang the Venetian flag from her window on feast days, and a promise that her rent would never be raised. The carving (with the mortar on its ledge) marks Giustina's fateful window.

Continue up the Merceria to:

3. **Pagnacco** (no. 231), one of the two most interesting places in the city for miniature glass collectibles (the other is Amadi, Walk 5, Stop 29). Here you'll find tiny orchestras of glass musicians, period battalions of soldiers, glass insects, and other fantasies. Venice has always been fascinated with illusion, be it life-size or miniature, and Venetians as well as tourists have loved this genre for centuries.

From the front of Pagnacco, turn right onto Merceria San Zulian (San Julian), and you'll face:

4. the mid-16th-century **Church of San Zulian** (St. Julian), its facade newly restored with the aid of funding from the British-based Venice In Peril. The interior of the church, a cool oasis from the bustling Merceria, contains Veronese's *Pieta with SS. Roch, Jerome and Mark*, above the first altar to the right. In the central panel of the ceiling is Palma il Giovane's *St. Julian in Glory*.

Exit the church and take a left onto Calle dei Segreteri, which runs alongside the church. Then take a left at the end of the calle, and the first right onto Campo de la Guerra. Continue over Ponte de la Guerra, and straight onward. Here tourist shops begin to give way to quieter businesses. Cross Ponte de la Banda, and you will face the first of the two great facades of the Church of Santa Maria Formosa surrounded by:

5. **Campo Santa Maria Formosa,** a large campo with a personality that is both patrician yet also very popular. The Renaissance facade of the church, facing the canal, was built

in 1542 to honor Vincenzo Capello, one of the Republic's naval heroes: it is notable for its lack of religious imagery. The unusual campanile, to the left of the facade, is faced with pale rose-colored stone patterned in graceful geometric motifs. At the foot of the campanile, guarding a low, rustic wooden door, you can't miss the grotesque face which the 19th-century British writer John Ruskin decried as "too foul to be either pictured or described." Charles Laughton, in his role as the Hunchback of Notre Dame, would have been green with envy.

Take a Break   Across from the campanile door is a small inviting canalside building that houses the **Orchedia Snack Bar,** which serves coffees, gelatos, and other quick tidbits.

Before entering the church, walk around to the graceful Renaissance facade that fronts on the larger part of the campo; this area usually hosts a small outdoor market and a jumble of moveable green shrubbery. This second facade, built in 1604, is adorned with a figure of the Virgin as well as three portrait busts of members of Admiral Capello's family. Continue around to the back of the church, with its triple apse. Here, you'll discover the far side of the campo, where four small bridges cross the Rio Sta. Maria Formosa canal, three of them leading to private entrances of the impressive Renaissance palaces that line this hidden part of the campo. The small bridge in the left corner is:

6. **Ponte de Ruga Giuffa.** Climb to the top, turn back, and take in the vista of the campo. The church breaks up the space of the campo into different areas and views. Check the views up and down the canal with its wonderful network of traversing bridges. As you look directly across to the far side of the campo from the bridge, the large rose colored building is:

7. **Palazzo Ruzzini-Priuli,** built in 1580, one of the most beautiful late Renaissance houses in the city, with white pilasters and lacy carved balconies that have been attributed to one of the architects of the Doge's Palace. The long-shuttered windows of Palazzo Ruzzini-Priuli give it the mysterious air of a mansion in a William Faulkner novel.

Descend the bridge, step back onto the campo, and continue your walk around the church, going through the sotoportego on the side, and emerging into the Campiello Querini-Stampalia, which is an even more hidden part of the Santa Maria Formosa complex. A short bridge across the canal leads directly to the:

8. **Palazzo Querini-Stampalia,** the upper floors of which were the residence of the Patriarch of Venice during the first half of the 19th century. During the great rebellion against Austrian rule in 1848–49, the palazzo was sacked by an angry mob when it was rumored (correctly) that the Patriarch favored capitulation to Austria. In 1868, the last of the ancient Querini family (a number of whose ancestors had been part of the notorious plot to overthrow the Republic in 1310) bequeathed the palazzo, along with a vast library and collection of art to the city of Venice. Now a museum, with its emphasis on the final twilight century of the Venetian Republic, the art on display here includes works by Gabriel Bella, who conscientiously depicted the street scenes, customs, and rituals of 18th-century Venice in an un-Venetian style that almost touches on the naive. The paintings of Pietro and Alessandro Longhi, more perceptive and mysterious, detail a dreamlike, decadent Venetian world. The palazzo also hides a contemporary garden with water channels filled with lilies and papyrus, designed by the noted architect, Carlo Scarpa. The museum is open Tuesday to Sunday from 10am to 12:30 pm, and there is an admission fee of about $3.

Retrace your steps back to the church's canalside facade and enter the main door.

9. **The Church of Santa Maria Formosa** was originally built to commemorate a 7th century vision of the Virgin that appeared to St. Magnus, Bishop of Oderzo. St. Magnus described the Virgin in his vision as "formosa," a word carrying the connotation of beautiful in a very buxom way. An unusual later legend is also attached to the church. In 944 A.D., the confraternity of wedding-chest builders, which had its oratory in this church, rescued a group of Venetian maidens who were being carried off by Slavic pirates. (As the maidens were potential customers for the wedding-chest

builders, good Venetian business sense, rather than chivalry, may have motivated this act of bravery.) As a reward, the artisans of the wedding-chest guild requested that the doge make a ceremonial visit to the church each year on Candlemas, the anniversary of the rescue.

"But what if it is raining?" the elderly doge asked his petitioners. "We will give you a hat," the artisans replied. "But what if I am thirsty?" the doge questioned. "We will give you wine," they answered. For almost nine centuries, until the fall of the Republic in 1797, the doge visited the church each year and participated in a ritual in which he was ceremonially offered a gilded straw hat and wine. The last of the ceremonial hats is now displayed at the Correr Museum in Piazza San Marco.

Although the church was reconstructed in 1492 by Mauro Coducci (who designed the Clock Tower where our walk began), the interior space of the church still betrays a Byzantine complexity not usually found in churches of Renaissance design. Immediately to the right of the entrance is Palma del Vecchio's *St. Barbara*, painted approximately in 1524, and described by the British novelist, George Eliot, as "an almost unique presentation of a hero-woman." An early Christian, St. Barbara was so devout that she added a third window to her two-windowed bathing chamber to symbolize the Trinity; she was murdered by her understandably exasperated father, a pagan, who in turn was promptly struck dead by lightning. By this act of celestial vengeance, St. Barbara became the patron saint of soldiers and bombardiers, who unleash and are exposed to sudden, violent death—naturally, the painting of St. Barbara stands in the former chapel of the Scuola dei Bombardieri. Ironically, the church was severely damaged during the Austrian bombardments of 1916, and required heavy rebuilding.

The church's 15th-century former high altarpiece, Bartolomeo Vivarini's triptych of the Madonna of the Misericordia (with portraits of members of the congregation sheltered by the Madonna's cloak) is now in a nave chapel on the same side of the church as St. Barbara.

Exit the church, and head toward the far right corner of the main part of the campo. On the right side of the campo are a number of palazzos with fine gothic detailing. As you pass the gothic palaces on your right, just before you exit the campo, note the Othello-the-Moor face on the door at number 6121.

Exit the campo. As you cross the:

10. **Ponte Borgolocco,** look back across the narrow canal at the waterfront facade of the Palazzo Ruzzini-Priuli, so different from its campo facade.

Continue past the narrow Campiello Pompeo Molmenti, and go straight until you reach Campo Santa Marina. Turn right at the entrance to the campo (past the shop at no. 6098 that sells an assortment of 1950s-style bronze souvenir gondolas). Exit the Campo Santa Marina and cross the Ponte del Cristo, from which, on the far side of the canal to your left, you'll see a tiny upper story corner balcony framed by a motif of arabesques. To the right, there's a view of the impressive gothic Palazzo Pisani-Contarini. Continue straight on the picturesque Fondamenta de la Erbe with its canalside gardens, and climb onto:

11. **the second small bridge on the right;** then turn around. Looking back across the canal to the right, you get a view of:

12. the gothic **Palazzo Soranzo–van Axel,** at the end of the Fondamenta de la Erbe. This is one of the most beautiful palaces in the city, with facades on two canals, two inner courtyards, and a beautiful, overgrown walled garden (the umbrella-shaded Madonna on the wall of the garden was once a street lamp). Despite the palazzo's seemingly secluded location in the midst of a tangled Venetian labyrinth, the bridge we're standing on crosses the Rio della Panada, once a direct shipping route into Venice from the north. Perhaps because it is located on this strategic trade route, the palazzo was bought in 1652 by the van Axels, a family of Flemish merchants from the Brabant region who were among the few non-Italian families admitted to the Venetian patriciate. Descendants of the van Axel family lived here until the 1920s. The house is not open to the public, but you can walk up to the majestic gothic land entrance to the palazzo at the end of the fondamenta and check out the original 15th-century carved larchwood door with a spyhole and a *bataor*, or knocker in the form of a fish.

From the doorway of the Palazzo Soranzo-van Axel, backtrack a few steps down the Fondamenta de la Erbe, and turn right onto Calle Caselli, which frames another beautiful gothic door at its terminus. Turn right at the end of the calle, and you come face to face with Venice's much loved:

13. **Church of Santa Maria dei Miracoli,** a masterpiece in marble inlay design and delicate ornamental carvings, rated by many as one of the most exquisite buildings in the world. Created during the 1480s by Pietro Lombardo and his sons, Antonio and Tullio, the Miracoli rises from the waters of the canal to house a miracle-working image of the *Madonna and Child and Two Saints* that was believed to have brought a drowning victim and a stabbing victim back to life. Originally in a votive niche outside a house in the neighborhood, as the fame of the image grew, money was contributed by rich and poor alike to create an appropriate sanctuary for it. According to legend, sumptuous marble, earmarked for the Basilica of San Marco, was somehow diverted to the Miracoli. The Miracoli was the Lombardo family's first building commission. They created a carved stonework song of inlaid marble panels, filigree, mermaids, flowers, and child-creatures that was like nothing else Venice had seen. Over the centuries, the Miracoli's location and its sheer loveliness have made it a favorite for weddings in which the bride and groom arrive and depart directly by gondola, gliding past the church in true Venetian style. Although the Miracoli is actually a small, intimate church, its unusual design makes it appear to be much larger, and at the same time, the delicacy of its ornamentation brings to mind a finely carved ivory box.

The Miracoli was one of Venice's most seriously threatened treasures. Salt water from the canals had worked its way into the brick core of the marble-faced walls, destroying the structure of the church from within, while at their lower levels, the carved bas-reliefs and carefully matched marble panels had deteriorated to the consistency of waterlogged sugar. Through the efforts of Save Venice, an ongoing project of preservation is bringing the Miracoli back from danger, and a careful cleaning of the exterior has restored it to its original beauty.

Give yourself time to experience this remarkable building. The interior, which you enter beneath a galleried choir supported by beautifully carved pillars, is faced with gray and rose marble. The gilded barrel-vaulted ceiling of the nave contains fifty panels by Pier Maria Pennacchi depicting the heads of prophets and saints. The balustrade at the altar end of the nave is adorned with a carved *Annunciation*, and half-length figures of the Archangel Gabriel, St. Francis, and St. Clare. Ruskin was appalled by the carved children's faces to the side of the steps because he felt, ". . . the man who could carve a child's head so perfectly must have been wanting in all human feeling to cut it off, and tie it by the hair to a vine leaf."

Exit the Miracoli, and take the calle that runs along the right side of the church (examining the decorative carvings that adorn the walls as you walk by) to the little campiello at the rear; from there take the little bridge across to the Campo Santa Maria Nova, from which you can look back for a last view of the Miracoli. At the foot of the bridge into this campo, turn right onto the Fondamenta dei Piovan, and continue onto the Ponte dei Piovan. There's a wonderful confluence of canals here, lined with fabulous old buildings. Continue straight: after the next bridge, the way soon becomes the major thoroughfare, Calle Larga Giacinto Gallina. At the other side of the next bridge is:

14. **Campo SS. Giovanni e Paolo** (merged together in Venetian dialect as SS. Zanipolo). The campo is a strong, monumental civic space defined by three elements: the enormous gothic brick **Church of SS. Giovanni e Paolo** directly before you, the lavish facade of the **Scuola Grande di San Marco** to the left, and:

15. **the equestrian statue of Bartolomeo Colleoni,** the great *condottiere,* or mercenary military leader, which is called upon to counterpoint the massive weight of the Scuola Grande and the church. Designed in 1481 by Andrea Verrocchio (the pre-eminent Florentine sculptor of his time, and teacher of Leonardo Da Vinci), the statue is regarded as one of the greatest equestrian monuments in the world.

Bartolomeo Colleoni

Bartolomeo Colleoni (1400–75) was born in Bergamo. For forty years, Colleoni defended Venice's interests with a combination of skill, savagery, and audacity (minus occasional well-paid intervals of service to Milan and other Italian cities). During his last twenty years of service, from 1455–75, he presided over a strategic situation in which Venetian military supremacy reached its greatest height. On his deathbed, Colleoni warned the rulers of Venice not to depend on foreign mercenaries or allow them to accumulate the powers he had been granted. "You do not know the harm I could have done . . ." He also left an immense sum of money to the Venetian state on the condition that an equestrian monument be erected to him "in the square of San Marco." The Republic had a long-standing tradition of suppressing cults of personality and of never erecting public monuments to anyone. It was not inclined to commemorate a paid outsider who was both vulgar and brutal with a statue in front of San Marco. On the other hand, Venice was not a fanatic society and was certainly not in the habit of turning away money. With typical guile, the Senate decided it could compromise, but still remain within the terms of the bequest by placing the statue before the Scuola Grande di San Marco. Not intended as a physical portrait (Verrocchio had never seen Colleoni) the statue holds its own as brilliantly as the condottiere it honors.

16. **The Scuola Grande di San Marco** was founded in 1260 and rebuilt between 1487 and 1490 by Pietro Lombardo and his sons (who had just finished their tour de force at the Miracoli) in collaboration with Giovanni Buora. It has housed the Civic Hospital since 1819 and its interior has been completely altered. The Lombardos clearly loved working with stone, and their approach to this august commission was playfully inventive, but totally different from the

Miracoli. The trompe l'oeil panels on the lowest course of the facade were executed by Tullio (and perhaps also by Antonio) Lombardo. Despite the skill required to produce these remarkable tricks of perspective, the idea of creating such panels for this site is somewhat naive, because the illusion of depth only works from one viewpoint; in the large campo, however, the facade can be viewed from any number of angles. We'll never know the full extent of what the Lombardos had planned: Perhaps the facade would have been a maze of through-the-looking-glass tricks of perspective. However because of disagreements with the Scuola, the commission was taken away from them. The upper courses of the facade were designed by Mauro Coducci, who gave the top course its multiple curved crownings, which may have been meant to echo the domes and crownings of the Basilica of San Marco. Transparent screens have been erected to protect the magical Lombardo lions from the soccer balls which are always being kicked about the campo by youngsters.

Dominating the campo is the:

17. **Church of SS. Giovanni e Paolo,** one of the city's two monumental gothic houses of worship (the other being the Frari). Founded in 1246 by the Dominicans, the present building was consecrated in 1430; its facade is marked by a rose window and a 15th-century doorway (attributed to Bartolomeo Bon), which is flanked by Byzantine reliefs of the Annunciation and by columns salvaged from the nearby island of Torcello. The vast interior of the church is a pantheon of Venice's leaders and patrician families. Twenty-five doges are buried inside and for centuries, the state funerals of all doges were conducted here.

The interior is dominated by a lofty gothic nave and slender double-lancet tracery windows in the apse. There are eight side chapels. The interior wall surrounding the main entrance to the church is filled with tombs and monuments to the Mocenigo family, the most famous of which (as you face back toward the door and look to the left) is the Renaissance tomb of Doge Pietro Mocenigo, with its statues representing the *Three Ages of Man*, created from 1476 to 1481 by Pietro Lombardo and his sons, Tullio and Antonio, just before their commission to do the Miracoli.

Over the main doorway to the church is the massive tomb of Doge Alvise Mocenigo I and his wife (1477) by Pietro Lombardo, and to the right of the door is Tullio Lombardo's tomb of Doge Giovanni Mocenigo (after 1485), ornamented with a relief of *St. Mark Baptizing Annianus*. You can follow the career of the Lombardos as you browse through the church. Just after the second altar on the left aisle is their classical tomb of Doge Nicolo Marcello (1475); farther down the left aisle, just before the door to the sacristy is the tomb of Doge Pasquale Maliero (1460s), a delicate early work by Pietro Lombardo before his sons were old enough to assist him. In the central apse to the left of the high altar is the Renaissance tomb of Doge Andrea Vendramin (1492–95) by Tullio and Antonio Lombardo (the baroque high altar is by Baldassare Longhena, architect of the Salute Church). At the end of the left transept, you'll find the Cappella del Rosario, built in 1582, and dedicated to the naval victory over the Turks at Lepanto. A fire in 1867 destroyed parts of the chapel, including the church's two greatest masterpieces, Bellini's *Madonna*, and Titian's *Martyrdom of St. Peter Martyr*. During 20th-century restorations of the chapel, ceiling panels of *The Annunciation*, *The Assumption*, and *The Adoration of the Shepherds*, by Veronese were installed. Another wonderful *Adoration* by Veronese is to the left of the door.

In the right transept is one of the finest paintings in the church: Lorenzo Lotto's *St. Antonine Giving Alms to the Poor* (1542), with its graceful grouping of women's faces at the bottom of the composition. Above this painting you'll see a rare example of a Murano stained glass window. It depicts personages from the Bible.

The large Chapel of St. Dominic, the first one to your left as you head back towards the entrance, is one of the most sumptuous baroque ensembles in Venice. The walls are lined with bronze reliefs of the life of the saint (1715–20, by G. M. Mazza), but the greatest work in the chapel is the ceiling painting, Piazzetta's spectacular *St. Dominic in Glory* (1725–27), in which the saint rises to heaven in a rich golden light.

Filling the wall in the next bay of the aisle, over the entrance to the Cappella della Madonna della Pace, is a monument remarkably baroque (in both style and senti-ment) to the Doge Bertucci Valier, who died in 1658, his son, Doge Silvestro Valier, who died in 1700, and Silvestro Valier's wife, Elizabetta Querini, who died in 1708: The three are depicted almost like actors emerging for a curtain call. Silvestro Valier was a constant gambler who always carried a deck of cards, in case the chance for a quick game might arise. His term as doge ushered in the final and deca-dent century of the Republic. When he greeted the Infanta of Spain, who stopped in Venice on her way to marry Em-peror Leopold I, Valier wore a cloth-of-gold robe lined with small diamonds and the Infanta presented him with a large diamond which the Senate permitted him to keep. This was a far cry from the scrupulous days earlier in the history of the Republic, when the dress of all Venetians, including the doge, was regulated by strict sumptuary laws, and a doge could only accept gifts of sweetmeats or scented balm.

Next to the last altar on the right aisle is the monument to the heroic Marcantonio Bragadin, commander of the Venetian garrison in Cyprus during the eleven-month Turk-ish siege in 1571. With 90 percent of his troops dead, Bragadin and his officers sued for peace, and under a guar-antee of safety, met with the Turks, who hacked all except Bragadin to pieces. Bragadin's ears and nose were cut off, and he was slowly flayed alive before the pasha; what was left of his body was publically desecrated for months. Nine years later, a Venetian prisoner of war managed to steal Bragadin's skin, which had been stuffed and given to the Sultan as a trophy. The skin was returned to Venice, where it rests in an urn high on the wall above a fresco depicting Bragadin's martyrdom. The chapel just before the Bragadin monument contains Giovanni Bellini's polyptych of St. Vincent Ferrer (whose fiery sermons helped incite Spain into waves of religious persecution), St. Christopher, and a famed portrayal of St. Sebastian, all recently restored.

Guidebooks, pamphlets, and postcards are sold at a table near the entrance to the sacristy. The church is open daily from 7:30am to 12:30pm and from 3:30pm to 7:30pm.

Exit the church, turn to the left, and to the left again. Along the right flank of the church you can see the apses of the chapels that open onto the right aisle of the nave inside the church. Notice the beautiful brickwork patternings around the gothic windows and the cornice of the largest apse.

Take a Break On the side of the campo facing the Scuola Grande di San Marco and the side of the Church of SS. Giovanni e Paolo, you'll notice two cafe/bars (one with outdoor tables that offer a pleasant view of the campo). Here you can pick up a quick *tremezzino*, coffee, or glass of wine.

Exit the campo onto Salizada San Zanipolo, which begins at the far corner of the square to the side of the church. Very soon, on the left, you will come upon the:

18. **Church of the Ospedaletto,** with a riotously baroque facade by Baldassare Longhena. It's worth taking a while to enjoy the many sculpted faces that adorn this building. Also known as Santa Maria dei Derelitti (of the orphans or abandoned children), the church belonged to an orphanage complex founded in 1527. Sixteenth-century Venice, with more than 11,000 registered courtesans and prostitutes out of a population of slightly more than 100,000, was awash with abandoned children. At the Ospedaletto, a music school was developed to train children with musical ability and the school became internationally famous for its performances. The Ospedaletto now is a rest home for senior citizens, but upon request, you may be allowed to visit the elegant 18th-century frescoed concert chamber, to the side of the church, which is still used for musical performances. The interior of the church is far more refined than you'd suspect from its facade: Look for the three-dimensional trompe l'oeil organ over the altar.

Across the street from the Ospedaletto, you'll find:

19. **Laboratorio Artegiano Maschere,** at no. 6657, probably one of the three most interesting mask shops in Venice (the others are the wonderfully inventive Mondo Novo, near Campo Santa Margharita in Dorsoduro, and Tragicomica, in San Polo, just across from the house of the playwright, Carlo Goldoni). Founded by a puppet maker who had done much research into the history of mask making and its techniques, this shop has now branched out into all kinds of

papier-mâché creations, including architectural details, ancient Greek vases, and bowls of imitation fruit.

Continue straight on this calle, which changes its name to Barbaria delle Tole, and then to Calle del Cafetier. It ends at small Campo de Santa Giustina with a tiny free-standing chapel on the right side of the square. Exit the campo on Calle Zen, on the far right corner of the campo, and continue straight, crossing the Santa Giustina bridge. At the foot of the bridge, turn left onto the Fondamenta Santa Giustina and walk along the canal; then take the first right onto Calle San Francesco della Vigna. Proceed along this calle, which passes the looming gasworks on the left, and you'll soon arrive at Campo San Francesco della Vigna (of the vineyard). At the far end of the campo, half hidden by buildings, is the:

20. **Church of San Francesco della Vigna,** with its facade (1568–72) by Andrea Palladio. This is the earliest Palladian church facade in Venice, but partly because of its cramped surroundings, the church does not appear to be as majestic as the master architect might have hoped. At the time of the facade's construction, few Venetian churches would have been faced with white Istrian stone; the most dazzling of these was Mauro Coducci's San Michele on the shores of the lagoon just north of Venice. Palladio's later and more successful churches, San Giorgio Maggiore, Il Redentore, and the Zitelle, all sited along the water, profit from the interplays of light and the lagoon against their white classic Renaissance facades. The site of San Francesco della Vigna is hallowed by ancient legend: It was here, on the marshy northern shore of what would later become Venice, that an angel appeared to St. Mark as he passed by on a boat. The angel's message was the famous "Pax tibi . . . " (Peace unto you, Mark, my Evangelist), which foretold that St. Mark's body would one day rest in Venice. Over the centuries that message, coupled with the Lion of Venice, has been made into the emblem of the city. The vineyard on which the church is built was given to the Franciscans in 1253; the original church was reconstructed into the present Renais-sance building in 1534, according to a design by Sansovino. Inside the church, one of the most interesting elements is the Giustiniani Chapel, a survivor of the original pre-

Sansovino church, to the left of the chancel. It is lined with a beautiful cycle of sculpture by Pietro Lombardo and assistants, including reliefs of prophets and evangelists, placed above scenes from the life of Christ, all attributed to Tullio and Antonio Lombardo. From the left transept, you can enter a beautiful, flower-filled 15th-century cloister. The Cappella Santa, a chapel near the entrance to the cloister, contains an especially gentle *Madonna and Child*, by Giovanni Bellini and assistants (you'll need change for illumination). From this garden, you can continue into a second, larger cloister, which now contains a vineyard and a nursery. The church is open from 7am to 11:45am and from 4:45pm to 7pm.

Exit the church, turn left, and continue straight, passing under the 19th-century colonnaded portico. Continue straight across the bridge of San Francesco, and onto Ramo al Ponte San Francesco. The calle widens, and eventually ends; jog slightly to the left onto Salizada de la Gata; at the end of this calle, jog slightly to the right, and continue straight onto Calle dei Scudi, which quickly crosses a bridge. After the bridge, take the second left onto Calle del Mandolin, which leads into the:

21. **Campo Due Pozzi,** today a quiet square, but once a busy center for this medieval neighborhood that not many tourists get to see. The square is lined with small houses that were once inhabited by members of trade guilds and shopkeepers (many of the ground floors were originally built as shops). The small two-story house with gothic windows at the far end of the campo has real charm; look for second and third floor windows around the campo that show signs of Byzantine and gothic origins.

Exit the campo on the Calle de la Muneghete, and follow it straight to the end, where it meets Campo de le Gorne, which runs along a canal and faces the blank walls of the Arsenale. Turn right at the canal onto the Fondamenta dei Penini and follow it as it turns toward the left. After crossing a bridge, you'll find yourself in a small campo facing:

22. **the Church of San Martino** (c. 1540) designed by Sansovino with a Greek cross interior. On the right side of the facade is a 15th-century relief of St. Martin on horse-

back, looking much like the ornate, sculpted San Martino cookies for sale in local bakeries during the week before the festival of San Martino on November 10. Inside there is a 17th-century trompe l'oeil octagonal cupola by Domenico Bruno on the ceiling; unfortunately, if you want to get the full impact of the illusion, you may have to lie on the floor of the church. This architectural embellishment frames an 18th-century central fresco of *St. Martin in Glory* by Jacopo Guarana. The church was recently restored with help from the Australian Venice Committee.

Exit the church, turn left, and take the bridge on the left side of the campo. Just across the bridge, at no. 3855, a building to the left, you'll see:

23. **Spazio Legno, the workshop of Saverio Pastor,** a real find for anyone interested in boats in general, and Venetian gondolas in particular. Sig. Pastor is a specialist in the *forcola*, or wooden oarlock traditionally made of carved walnut that is crucial to the gondola's propulsion and maneuverability. No two forcola designs are ever exactly alike, but their fluid, abstract form has been recognized as a work of art, an example of functional sculpture that captures the twist of the gondolier's complicated oar movements. There have been exhibitions of forcola design at the Museum of Modern Art in New York, as well as in museums and galleries in Europe. Prices range from hundreds of thousands to millions of lire, and examples from this workshop are bought not only by professional gondoliers but also by art collectors.

Retrace your steps across the bridge and continue straight alongside the canal in front of Campo San Martino, passing the church; exit the campo onto the Fondamenta de Fazza l'Arsenale, which continues along the canal. Bridges span this picturesque waterway and lead directly to the doorways of the:

24. **Renaissance brick palazzetti** (small palaces) which are just across the narrow canal. Most likely these comfortable homes were built for managerial level personnel at the Arsenale. Today, the Dante Alighieri Society, an international Italian cultural institute, has offices in these buildings. If you plan to stay in Venice for some time, you can

arrange to take classes in Italian under their auspices or attend English-language lectures on art, architecture, history, and culture that are often given here.

The fondamenta leads right into the Campo de l'Arsenale, and you'll find yourself in front of the:

25. **Gate of the Arsenale,** which is as far as you are allowed to go by foot, as the area is a military base. You can, however cruise through the empty dockyards of the Arsenale complex aboard the No. 52 vaporetto, which travels the canal just to the right of the land gate on its way from the San Zaccaria Actv stop toward the Fondamente Nuove.

The triumphal arch which forms the main land portal into the Arsenale was built in 1460 and is considered to be the first example of Renaissance architecture in Venice. Like many Venetian landmarks, the gate is made of booty from other times and places. The four marble columns were brought from Greece; their capitals and decorative floral reliefs are Byzantine. The wonderful menagerie of ancient lions is also Greek. The next-to-last of the smaller statues on the right dates from the 6th century B.C., and is believed to have been filched from the Lion Terrace on the sacred Aegean island of Delos (it arrived in Venice in 1718). The small lion on the far right may also be from Delos, but its pedigree is less certain. The two large lions on either side of the entrance were sent to Venice by Francesco Morosini in 1687 (his troops scored a direct hit on the Parthenon, which the Turks had been using to store gunpowder). The one on the left was once the famous Lion of Pireaus, and bears 11th-century Norse graffiti (in runic letters) that may have been inscribed by a Viking mercenary commander working for the Byzantine empire; according to one theory, this medieval Viking vandal went on to become a Norwegian king. The goofiest lion in all of Venice stands over the main portal. Venice's traditional emblem is the lion with its paw on a book open to the words, "Pax tibi . . ." This particular lion, guarding a place of war, rests his paw on a page without this text. The Dante Alighieri Society was a major sponsor of the project that restored the entrance to the Arsenale in the 1970s.

The campo in front of the gate was built in 1682, replacing a canal and a drawbridge that were once part of the

Arsenale's line of defenses. Of course, the fleets produced at the Arsenale guaranteed that Venice would never be touched by war or invading armies.

The Arsenale was founded in 1104, and its name seems to derive from the Arabic *dar sina'a* or "house of industry." Encircled by a two-mile-long protective wall, it was here that the Venetian military and merchant fleets were built as well as repaired and refitted. By the early 15th century, at the height of Venice's power, the Arsenale employed 16,000 men, and was the largest industrial complex ever seen in the world until modern times. Here, with an assembly-line system that predated Henry Ford's by 600 years, completely outfitted vessels could be turned out at maximum efficiency. One hundred ships could be built or repaired inside the Arsenale at one time, and although the secrets of the Arsenale were carefully guarded, on occasion the Republic would

The Marriage to the Sea

So crucial was supremacy on the seas to Venice, that early in its history, a symbolic annual ceremony of the "Marriage to the Sea" developed. Each year on Ascension Day, the doge, in his lavish gilded Bucentaur (ceremonial barge) would depart from the Riva degli Schiavoni to the accompaniment of trumpets and choirs, followed by a flotilla that included the members of the Council of Ten and all Venice's patricians and foreign ambassadors in their gondolas. At the Porto di Lido, where the lagoon meets the Adriatic, the doge would stand at the stern of his fantastic vessel, and cast a gold ring into the waters as he proclaimed, "O sea, we wed thee in sign of our true and everlasting dominion." By the 15th century, the wedding of Venice to the Adriatic had become the most famous and dazzling pageant in Europe, with more than 500 splendidly outfitted vessels accompanying the Bucentaur; feasts and celebrations continued for four days. The last of the Bucentaurs was burned by Napoleon when he conquered Venice in 1797, but salvaged fragments and a model can be seen at the Naval Museum of the Arsenale.

treat a visiting foreign V.I.P. to the spectacle of a complete galley being built from scratch and ready to launch in the time it took for a state dinner. Dante, visiting the Arsenale in 1312, took away the images of molten metal, boiling pitch, and frenzied, half-naked workers that become part of his *Inferno*. The Arsenale was part of the Republic's system of authoritarian state capitalism, in which all the facilities needed to promote commerce, such as docks, loading equipment, trading galleys, warehouses, and shipyards were owned by the state (only incoming and outgoing cargos were owned by private citizens, and these were heavily taxed). In exchange for the efficient and harmonious functioning of these facilities, workers had job security and guarantees of good wages, which, in turn, contributed to the general prosperity of Venice. As Venice fell into decline in the 17th century, the number of workers at the Arsenale fell to 2,400 by 1645; by 1766 the number had dropped to less than 1,500, and most of these merely showed up to collect their wages—there were no longer any contracts or commissions. In 1780, Doge Paolo Renier reported, "We have no forces on land or sea. We have no alliances. We live wholly by luck." After Venice became part of the Kingdom of Italy in 1866, the Arsenale, though antiquated and in ill repair, enjoyed a small revival. During World War I, however, Venice came within range of both Austrian bombardment and the threat of advancing Austrian armies; the Arsenale was evacuated and the Italian goverment concentrated on developing shipbuilding facilities in safer areas to the south. There are currently many ideas afloat about converting the Arsenale into a marina, a cultural center, or a tourist and exhibition center.

You now have a few choices about the final leg of this walk.

If you have enough time and energy, you can take in the Naval Museum just across the canal. It stops selling tickets at 12:30pm and closes at 1pm. Exit the Campo de l'Arsenale via the wooden bridge to the other side of the canal and turn right onto the Fondamenta de l'Arsenale. Continue straight along the canal. On your right, as you approach the lagoon, you'll see the Actv stop for the No. 52 vaporetto. Just beyond, on the left, is the:

26. **Naval History Museum,** which is the first stop of the next walking tour. For information, see Walk 3, Stop 1.

If you're absolutely exhausted, let your walk end here, relax at one of the cafe/restaurants around the Campo de l'Arsenale, and then take the No. 52 vaporetto from the Arsenale Actv stop across the canal. The vaporetto makes a circle around Venice in both directions, and if it doesn't take you close to your hotel, it will take you to San Zaccaria, near San Marco. From there, you can pick up a vaporetto to any place in the city.

If you've missed the Naval Museum, but still want to go on, you can begin the the next tour which includes a walk back to San Marco along the Riva degli Schiavoni. The spacious, open vistas of this walk will offer a nice contrast to the complicated, twisting neighborhoods from which you've just emerged.

If you want to break for lunch or dinner, this is a good opportunity to try some of the restaurants in this off-the-beaten track part of town.

Take a Break   There are a number of inexpensive places for a meal at the beginning of Via Garibaldi. First you'll see **Toscana,** with a simple but good menu. For a more stylish meal in the rustic Venetian tradition, try **Ristorante Corte Sconta** (Hidden Courtyard) on Calle del Pestrin one of the best upper-middle-priced places in Venice, located in an out-of-the-way neighborhood near the Arsenale. Specialties are Venetian seafood dishes, each prepared with real style (and fresh local ingredients). From the Gates of the Arsenale, retrace your steps back to Campo San Martino and continue straight across the campo to the Ponte Storto, which leads back to the forcola workshop. Across the bridge, turn right onto Fondamenta del Tintor, and at the end of the short fondamenta, turn left onto Calle del Pestrin. The Corte Sconta is on the left at no. 3886 (tel. 522-7024). Open Tuesday to Saturday from 12:30pm to 2:30 pm and 7:30 to 9:30pm; closed January 7 to February 7 and July 15 to August 15. Reservations are advisable.

VISTAS AND SHORELINES

Start: The Arsenale.

Finish: La Giudecca Island.

Time: Two to four hours, depending on time spent at sites.

Best Time: The walk is designed to pick up where Walk 1 left off. Start out around 1pm, and you'll get to San Giorgio Maggiore at its 2pm opening time.

Worst Time: Noon to 2:30pm and after 5pm when the campanile of San Giorgio, with its wonder view, is closed.

This is a walk of open vistas and spaces, an unusual experience amid the intricate, labyrinthine structure of Venice. It takes you down the Riva degli Schiavoni to San Marco, and by boat to San Giorgio Maggiore and the Giudecca. The Riva degli Schiavoni is one of the sunniest places in the city. People come there to get the chill out of their bones in winter, but be warned that there is no shade for a hot summer day. The most dramatic part of this tour is an absolute must trip across the Basin of San Marco to the island of San Giorgio

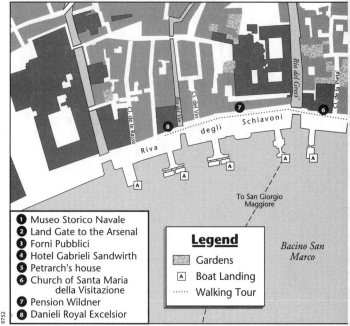

Legend

Gardens
Boat Landing
Walking Tour

Bacino San Marco

To San Giorgio Maggiore

1. Museo Storico Navale
2. Land Gate to the Arsenal
3. Forni Pubblici
4. Hotel Gabrieli Sandwirth
5. Petrarch's house
6. Church of Santa Maria della Visitazione
7. Pension Wildner
8. Danieli Royal Excelsior

Maggiore, where you can take in Palladio's masterpiece church and the view of Venice from the top of the island's campanile. From there you can take another vaporetto to the island of Giudecca, a nearly rustic district, with hidden gardens and sweeping views across the wide Giudecca Canal to Venice.

• • • • • • • • • • • • • • • •

This walk ideally begins around noon at the:

1. **Museo Storico Navale** (Naval History Museum) occupies a building that was originally a granary for the Venetian fleet. The most fascinating exhibit in this museum is the extraordinarily beautiful collection of model ships. It was once common practice for vessels to be built, not from blueprints, but rather from meticulously made models; the scale models of Venetian vessels are those from which real ships were built. There are models of Far Eastern vessels and more recent ships as well. The prize of the collection is a model of the legendary Bucentaur. A second section of the museum, closer to the Arsenale, contains an array of historic vessels. The Museum is open Monday to Saturday

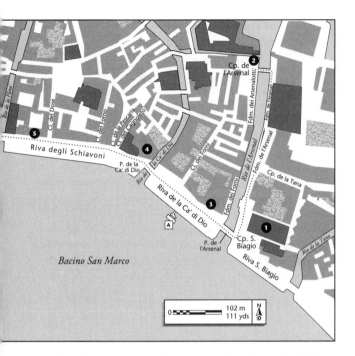

from 9am to 1pm; tickets are sold only until 12:30pm. Admission is approximately $1.50.

From the museum, walk up the Arsenale Canal, and cross the wooden bridge to the Campo de l'Arsenale and the:

2. **Land Gate to the Arsenale** (for description, see Walk 2, Stop 25).

☕ **Take a Break** Around the Campo de l'Arsenale, you'll find a number of cafe/bars, some with outdoor tables. These are a good bet for *tremezzini,* or other light snacks and a drink before the next leg of the walk.

Walk down to the lagoon, turn right (in the direction of San Marco) and cross Ponte dell'Arsenale. From the top of this bridge, the vista of the Riva degli Schiavoni and entrance to the Grand Canal is truly magnificent. You descend from the bridge onto the short stretch of waterfront known as the Riva de la Ca' de Dio, which takes its name from a hospice built for pilgrims and crusaders in the 13th century (the last building on the right before you cross the next bridge). The first building you pass on the riva is:

3. **the Forni Pubblici,** or Public Military Bakery (1473), which supplied ships departing from the Arsenale and the Riva degli Schiavoni with a long-lasting type of hardtack biscuit. (A cache of such hardtack, discovered in Crete more than a century after it was baked, was reportedly still edible.)

Cross the Ponte de la Ca' de Dio, onto the Riva degli Schiavoni. The first group of buildings on the right comprise the:

4. **Hotel Gabrieli Sandwirth,** which has been featured in a number of films. The lobby was used in filming *Don't Look Now*, an atmospheric 1973 psychological thriller starring Julie Christie and Donald Sutherland. While the luxurious room Julie Christie and Donald Sutherland shared was merely a set, the rambling Gabrieli Sandwirth is a wonderful place, with a private canalside garden (you can see it from the Ponte de la Ca' de Dio), and a rooftop sun terrace with dramatic, sweeping views.

Since the 19th century, the sunny, south-facing Riva degli Schiavoni has been lined with hotels for tourists. In the 1870s, both Baedeker and Murray's *British Handbook for Travellers in Northern Italy* recommended swimming at "the floating baths moored opposite the Riva degli Schiavoni." They also noted two up-and-coming bathing beaches on the Lido belonging to the owners of the Albergo Danieli; however the British guidebook felt, "the line of demarcation between the baths of the two sexes is not sufficiently observed to make bathing pleasant for English ladies . . ."

Continue up the Riva degli Schiavoni. The word *schiavoni* denotes Slavic traders from Dalmatia, and the name of this broad promenade refers to the time when Dalmatian ships docked here. Venice has had a long relationship with Dalmatia, going back to the 9th century when the Venetians sold Slavic captives as slaves. After the Christianization of the Slavic areas of the Balkans in the 11th century, however, such activity was not considered sporting, and the Venetian slave markets turned to other sources. The guildhall of the Dalmatians, San Georgio degli Schiavoni, a treasure-house of paintings by Vittore Carpaccio, is just a few calles inland.

Just before the next bridge is:

5. **Petrarch's house** in which the poet, humanist, and scholar, lived from 1362 to 1367 (the building is now marked no. 4142 to 4145). Petrarch came to Venice to escape the plague in Padua; the Republic conferred this palazzo on him with the understanding that he would bequeath his library to Venice. Petrarch's marvelous collection was indeed given to the Venetian state, but apparently it was lost while in storage for two centuries, awaiting the construction of the Marciana Library in Piazza San Marco.

Across the next bridge is the imposing classical facade of the:

6. **Church of Santa Maria della Visitazione,** known as the Pieta. The orphanage attached to the Pieta, like others throughout the city, trained its wards in the musical arts (the word *conservatory* originally meant a place where

---

Antonio Vivaldi

Antonio Vivaldi (1678–1741) was the son of a violinist in the orchestra at the Basilica of San Marco, and was trained as a musician before being ordained as a priest in 1703. In addition to his position as violin master at the Pieta, Vivaldi served as resident composer, and many of his religious works (of which sixty have survived into the 20th century) were written for the Pieta. As time went on, Vivaldi became less active in the church and devoted his time to composition. He was the author of approximately 250 violin concertos, 53 sonatas, and 40 operas; in 1714 he became director of the Teatro Sant' Angelo, where twenty of his operas were produced between 1714 and 1739. In 1740, after a scandal involving one of his pupils, he went to Vienna to offer his services to King Charles VI, but the king died before Vivaldi's arrival; Vivaldi, unknown and poverty-stricken, died in Vienna the following year. His work was neglected and forgotten until he was rediscovered in the 20th century, and his popularity revived.

orphans were kept); the Pieta became unrivalled as a music school under the direction of Antonio Vivaldi, who was violin master from 1704 to 1718 and choirmaster from 1735 to 1738. Concert programs at the Pieta became world famous. The present church does not look the way it would have appeared when Vivaldi served here. Giorgio Massari, the architect who also designed the post-baroque Palazzo Grassi, won a competition in the 1730s to redesign the Pieta; the facade was not completed until 1906, but the interior was in place by 1760. It is likely that Massari would have consulted with Vivaldi on acoustic requirements and on problems such as the positioning of the double choir. The Pieta is still used as a concert hall more often than as a church; the best way to see the interior (freshly restored by the Kress Foundation) is at a performance. When the box office is open, you may be able to look in at the elegant oval nave, crowned by G. B. Tiepolo's masterpiece fresco, *The Triumph of Faith* (1775).

Continue along the Riva Schiavoni. After the next bridge, the promenade becomes noticeably thicker with tourists. Before the monument to Victor Emmanuel, look for:

7. **no. 4161 (now Pension Wildner),** where the 37-year-old novelist Henry James stayed on his first visit to Venice in 1881. From his windows, James could see ". . . the far-shining lagoon, the downward curve of the Riva, the distant islands, the movement of the quay." To James, who returned to Venice many times, the city's spirit changed according to the weather or the hour. "It is always interesting, and almost always sad, but it has a thousand occasional graces and is always liable to happy accidents . . ."

Just over the next bridge is the most famous luxury hotel in Venice, the:

8. **Danieli Royal Excelsior,** the oldest part of which is housed in the gothic 14th-century Palazzo Dandolo. In the years after the fall of the Venetian Republic in 1797, the Palazzo Dandolo was divided among a number of families. One of the tenants, a man named Da Niel, turned his apartment into a pensione in 1822; as his establishment grew in popularity, he slowly bought up the other floors of the building. The Danieli's guest list is without equal: from Dickens and Ruskin, to Wagner, Proust, Cocteau, and Tina Turner. George Sand and her lover Alfred de Musset stayed

Vistas and Shorelines: Stop 9

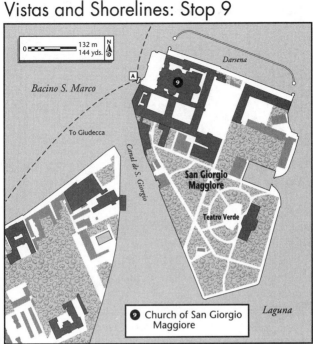

here and had a violent confrontation when Sand discovered de Musset with another woman. He fell ill, and George Sand fell in love with Pietro Pagello, the Venetian physician summoned in by the hotel to treat de Musset. When de Musset returned to Paris, Sand remained in Venice, promenading in the Piazza each evening on her new lover's arm. The two moved to France, but almost immediately Dr. Pagello returned to Venice, where he married and lived to the age of ninety without ever publicly mentioning his affair with the tumultuous French novelist. Don't hesitate to check out the hotel lobby and grand staircase, a lavish 19th-century interpretation of Venetian gothic. After World War II, a modern wing was added to the original structure.

From the Riva degli Schiavoni near the Danieli Hotel, take the No. 82 vaporetto to the island of San Giorgio Maggiore with its white Palladian church, just across the Basin of San Marco. The island has been home to a Benedictine community since the 10th century. The brief vaporetto ride provides wonderful views of the island as well as of the Piazzetta of San Marco and the Doge's Palace behind you. You will disembark right in front of the:

Vistas and Shorelines: Stops 10–12

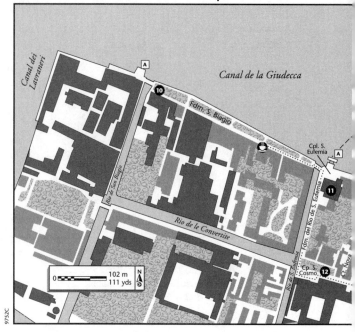

9. **Church of San Giorgio Maggiore,** the great
Andrea Palladio's masterpiece, designed in 1565 and completed in 1610, 30 years after Palladio's death. The church
is open from 9am to 12:30pm and from 2pm to 6pm, with
slightly shorter hours for visiting the campanile, with its
dazzling views.

In order to mount a classical facade on the traditional
structure of a church, which calls for a high central nave
and two lower side aisles, Palladio imposed two interlock-
ing facades onto each other. (Think of the two side wings
as part of one facade topped by a broad, low, triangular
pediment over which a second, taller facade has been placed.)
The repeating triangles, rectangles, and columns within the
facade are carefully proportioned according to natural, harmonious ratios derived from measuring the expansion of
sound and music; the same principles guided the design of
the interior. The monumental size of the facade's classical
elements, and the shadows they cast on the white stone surface help to keep the lines of the church crisp and clearly
outlined when viewed across the water from San Marco.

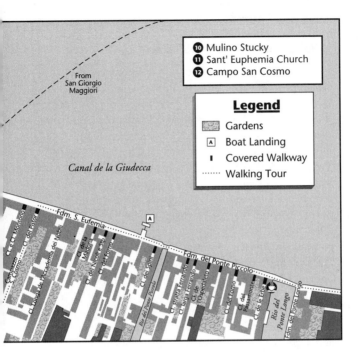

From
San Giorgio
Maggiori

10 Mulino Stucky
11 Sant' Euphemia Church
12 Campo San Cosmo

Legend

Gardens
A Boat Landing
▮ Covered Walkway
······ Walking Tour

Canal de la Giudecca

Fdm. S. Eufemia

A

Fdm. del Ponte Piccolo

Campazzo
Cl de Ch Monastero
Cl del Pistor
Sottoportego
Cl del Cosmo
Cl Longa de l'Academia dei Nobili
Cl de la
Madona
Cl del Nicole Sopa
Cl del Forno
Cl del Spini
Rio del Ponte Piccolo
Cl strata Ferando
Cl Larga Ferrando
Cl de l'Ospedaletto
Cl del Forno
Cl del Passamonte
Cl de le Erbe
Rio del Ponte Longo
Fdm. del Ponte Longo

The interior of the church is cruciform, its whitewashed surfaces encompassing a pure, luminous area of space. The chancel walls are flanked by two late Tintorettos: *The Last Supper* and *The Shower of Manna*, painted between 1592 and 1594. Behind the altar, the stalls of the monastic choir, a masterpiece of woodworking, depict scenes from the life of St. Benedict. Through the doorway to the right of the choir is the Cappella dei Morti (Chapel of the Dead), where you will find Tintoretto's *Deposition*, believed to be his last painting, and probably completed with the assistance of his son, Domenico. Beside this painting is a photograph of Carpaccio's *St. George and the Dragon* (the fragile original is now kept elsewhere in the San Giorgio Maggiore complex), painted in 1516, a few years after his more famous version in the Scuola di San Giorgio degli Schiavoni. The Benedictines practice Gregorian chant in this chapel at 11am on Sundays, and visitors are welcome to listen.

To the left of the choir, you'll find the elevator to the campanile (open from 9am to noon, and 2:30pm to 5pm). There is an admission fee, but the view of Venice is

Count Cini and the Cini Foundation

In 1917, a group of important industrialists led by Count Giuseppe Volpi (who brought electricity to Venice) and Count Vittorio Cini formed a consortium of investors to develop a modern port, refineries, and factories on the mainland at Mestre and Marghera. It was hoped that this industrial complex would provide jobs for the people of Venice, where the economic base and the population count were both in serious decline. The consortium was also instrumental in constructing a highway beside the rail link to the mainland that the Austrians had built in the mid-19th century. During the 1930s Count Volpi became Mussolini's Minister of Finance, and Count Cini served as a senator; both men continued to work for the development of Venice, and both were important patrons of the Venice Biennale and founders of the Venice Film Festival. In September 1943, when Victor Emmanuel III placed his prime minister, Benito Mussolini, under arrest and surrendered to the Allies, Cini and Volpi both declared their loyalty to the king. Unfortunately, the Nazis occupied Italy before the Allies could arrive. The king fled to Cairo, and Volpi, Cini, and other government members who had conspired against Mussolini, were hunted down. Volpi escaped to Switzerland, but Count Cini was sent to Dachau. His son, Giorgio, risked his life to go to Berlin in an attempt to ransom Cini from the Gestapo; after handing over a fortune, Giorgio Cini secured his father's release. In 1949, Count Cini saw his son die in an airplane crash at Cannes Airport.

In memory of his son, Cini devoted his fortune and the rest of his life to the restoration of San Giorgio Maggiore and the creation of the Giorgio Cini Foundation of Venetian Culture and Civilization. Cini's was the first major effort to save and preserve the deteriorating physical structure of Venice. Cini was acutely aware of the damage the Mestre-Marghera complex on the mainland had caused to Venice, and before his death he declared that he wished he could demolish with his own hands the bridge to the modern world he had helped to create.

magnificent. The campanile also offers a bird's eye view into the cloisters, gardens, and monastery, which, along with the church, were closed and stripped of their possessions under the Napoleonic occupation, and later used as a military barracks by the Austrians. The entire complex of San Giorgio Maggiore was carefully restored in the early 1950s by the Cini Foundation.

The restored monastery is truly magnificent, with two adjoining cloisters at the center of the complex: the Cloister of the Cypresses, designed by Palladio, and the Cloister of the Laurel Trees, planned by Giovanni Buora. Adjacent to the latter is the Refectory (1559–1563), Palladio's first project for the Benedictines. Veronese's *Marriage at Cana* hung here until Napoleon had it carted off to the Louvre. There is also a sweeping double grand staircase and a sumptuous, light-filled library designed by the baroque architect, Baldassare Longhena. The Cini Foundation also created paradisical gardens and an outdoor amphitheater, the Teatro Verde (now rarely used) on land behind the church. It's best to phone ahead (tel. 528-9200) for an appointment to see the monastery, which accommodates visitors, but is not open on a regular basis.

From the San Giorgio Maggiore Actv stop, take No. 82 vaporetto in the direction of the Giudecca, and get off at the Sant' Euphemia Actv stop, the fourth after San Giorgio Maggiore, on the island of Giudecca. After you disembark from the vaporetto, go to your right and walk along the fondamenta toward a large, gloomy 19th-century factory building in the far distance. This is:

10. **Mulino Stucky,** a flour mill built in 1897 by Giovanni Stucky, whose mother was Venetian, and father, Swiss. This massive building, a late attempt to bring the Industrial Revolution to Venice, was unpopular with many Venetians. Stucky bought the Palazzo Grassi on the Grand Canal, but did not long enjoy his 18th-century palace; he was murdered by one of his workers in 1910. The mill was plagued by poor labor-management relations and closed in 1954. Although it's now a near ruin, there are many proposals to renew the site.

We'll walk in this direction along the broad Giudecca Canal only as far as Harry's Dolci:

Vistas and Shorelines: Stops 13 – 18

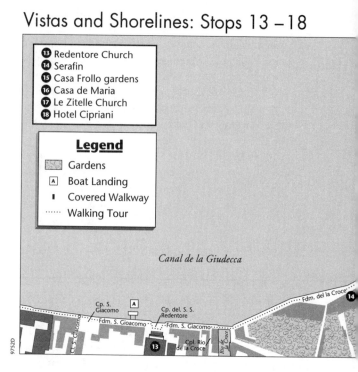

13 Redentore Church
14 Serafin
15 Casa Frollo gardens
16 Casa de Maria
17 Le Zitelle Church
18 Hotel Cipriani

Legend

Gardens

A Boat Landing

I Covered Walkway

...... Walking Tour

Canal de la Giudecca

Fdm. del la Croce

Cp. S.
Giacomo   A   Cp. del. S. S.
Redentore

Fdm. S. Gioacomo   Fdm. S. Giacomo

Cpl. Rio
de la Croce

9752D

Take a Break If you've reached this point between
12:30 and 3:30pm, you have the option of luxu-
riating at **Harry's Dolci,** 774 Fondamenta San Biagio
(tel. 522-4844), one of the most delicious and reasonably
priced restaurant splurges in Venice. Founded by the
Cipriani family of the famed Harry's Bar near San Marco,
Harry's Dolci is less expensive, less overrun, and offers fabulous views from its window tables or its outdoor waterfront
dining area; it also offers much of the same elegant menu as
its namesake. Desserts, as the name "Dolci" implies, are
spectacular, especially anything chocolate (you can come
just for coffee and cake). Harry's is open from April through
October. Evening hours are from 7:30pm to 10pm, but the
No. 82 vaporetto runs less frequently after 8pm. Closed
Mondays and Sunday evenings. Telephone ahead for reservations. Not too far away we'll come to another refueling
choice: an excellent, less expensive neighborhood trattoria.

Backtrack on the fondamenta to:

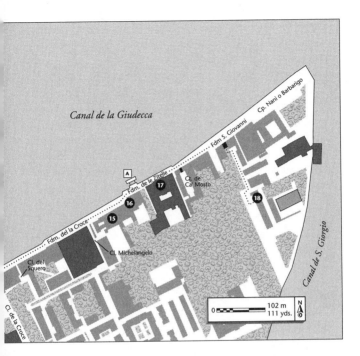

11. **Sant' Euphemia,** an 11th-century Veneto-Byzantine
church with an almost rustic doric portico (added in 1596)
on the side facing the Giudecca Canal. The church is only
open from 9am to noon, and 6pm to 7pm, but if you
get inside, you'll find a vague coexistence of 10th-century
columns, late Byzantine capitals, and rococo renovations
from the 18th century. The nave walls above the columns
have frescoes by Giambattista Canal (not to be confused
with the older Antonio Canal, called Canaletto), commissioned in 1764 when the artist was only 19. At the first
altar on the right as you enter is the church's strongest painting, *St. Roch and the Angel,* by Bartolomeo Vivarini (1480).

    Exit the church, and turn down the Fondamenta del
Rio de Sant' Eufemia which runs perpendicular to the
Giudecca Canal. On your left, you'll soon come to:

12. the overgrown, weedy, **Campo San Cosmo,** with its abandoned church and convent, closed during the Napoleonic
occupation. The campo has a romantic, derelict feel unlike

any other place in Venice. In early times, most campos were unpaved and used for gardens: San Cosmo seems never to have progressed beyond that state.

From the Fondamenta, turn into the campo, continue straight across past the church and convent, and turn left onto Campazzo San Cosmo, a neighborhood of 19th-century workers' houses. At the far end of the Campazzo, you'll enter a narrow calle. Continue straight down the calle, which ends at the fondamenta along the Giudecca canal. Turn right onto the fondamenta, and continue straight, with the view of Dorsoduro across the Giudecca Canal. In summer, you'll find this north-facing quay is shady and cool. As the civic numbers reach the low 280s, look for a sotoportego on the right called Calle de la Erbe (it's the last right before the fondamenta crosses the wide Rio del Ponte Longo). Turn down this calle if you'd like to try the neighborhood trattoria.

Take a Break **Altanella,** 268 Calle de la Erbe, offers outdoor waterside dining in summer, and a menu of authentic Venetian seafood and pasta dishes, as well as good house wine. Closed Monday evenings and Tuesdays.

Continue along the Giudecca Canal, across the Ponte Longo and beyond. Just beyond the Redentore Actv stop, you'll come to another Palladian masterpiece:

13. **the Redentore Church,** commissioned in 1577 by order of the senate in thanks for the city's deliverance from a plague that took almost 50,000 lives in 1575–76. Each year on the Feast of the Redeemer (the third Sunday in July), the doge and the senate made a pilgrimage to the Redentore over a pontoon bridge that stretched across the Giudecca Canal from the Zattere on Dorsoduro to the front door of the church. To this day, the tradition of the pontoon bridge continues, and thousands of Venetians take to their boats and picnic on the water. By day there are regattas, and by night flotillas of small boats are illuminated by Chinese lanterns that reflect onto the waters of Venice, while extraordinary fireworks illuminate the skies.

The Redentore, like Palladio's Church of San Giorgio Maggiore, was meant to be viewed from across the water; it was created as the terminal point for an almost miraculous religious procession across the Giudecca Canal. It was designed a decade after San Giorgio Maggiore, and many believe it to be a finely tuned improvement of the theories of harmony and proportion Palladio used in his design for the earlier church. The most important of the Redentore's paintings is in the sacristy: a *Madonna and Child and Angels* by Alvise Vivarini. The sacristy also contains a gallery of 18th-century wax effigies of notable Franciscans, depicted in various states of agony and ecstasy.

Exit the Redentore, and turn right onto the fondamenta. Not far beyond the church, on Fondamenta de la Croce, look for:

14. **Serafin,** a venerable second-hand shop run by the same family for generations. All kinds of interesting treasures turn up here.

Continue along the fondamenta. At no. 86 is the vast Venice Youth Hostel; at no. 50, walk into:

15. the overgrown gardens of the **Casa Frollo,** long one of the most wonderful, secluded little hotels in Venice. For years, the Casa Frollo has been threatened with closure, and it may finally be out of business when you pass by; vested interests want to turn this enchanting site into something more lucrative, and no wonder. From here you have dramatic views of San Marco across the water at sunset. There's an international movement to keep the Casa Frollo afloat.

Farther along the fondamenta, at nos. 42 to 47 is:

16. **the Casa de Maria,** also known as the "Tre Oci," or "Three Eyes," a very noticeable landmark when seen from the Dorsoduro side of the Giudecca Canal. Built from 1910 to 1913 by the painter, Mario de Maria as a house/studio, according to his own custom design, the facade is a late Victorian goulash of gothic details you've probably seen on centuries-old buildings elsewhere in Venice. Notice the *merlatura,* or lacy roofline ornamentation, in the tradition of the Ca' d'Oro, and the brickwork patterning, which brings to mind the Doge's Palace. The "eyes" were meant to flood the artist's studio with northern light.

By now, the view across the Giudecca Canal has begun to include more of the Basin of San Marco. A bit beyond the Casa de Maria, you'll come to:

17. **Le Zitelle** ("The Maidens" or "Spinsters"), a small church designed by Palladio, originally for another site, and built here from 1582 to1586, just after his death. The square interior plan, with rounded corners, was known for its acoustics; the famed choir of the Pieta orphanage performed here regularly. On either side of the church there are wings which broaden the effect of the whole complex. They housed the hostel of Le Zitelle, a shelter for indigent women and children who had fled from, or did not wish to try, prostitution as a means of support. The women of Le Zitelle were known for their delicate *punto in aria* lace, which was sold to support the hostel. For many years, Le Zitelle was rarely open, but recently the residential parts were renovated and are now used as a space for exhibitions. The church is open only for services on Sunday morning.

   From the Zitelle, continue down the fondamenta almost to the end. At No. 10, turn right under the sotoportego, and continue straight until you come to a metal gate leading to the:

18. **Hotel Cipriani,** Venice's most luxurious hotel (the only hotel in Venice with a pool), surrounded by magnificent gardens and with views of the lagoon and the neighboring medieval gardens of San Giorgio Maggiore. In order to see this enclave and its lyrical views, ring the bell at the gate, and request permission to visit. If you are allowed to enter, the gate will be buzzed electrically. Take the first turning on the right, for a look at one of the large, hidden gardens that cover the interior of the Giudecca; then backtrack to the central pathway, which will lead to the hotel. The hotel was established in 1958 by the owner of Harry's Bar; the buildings are modern, but the setting is a fantasy, with private boat service for guests every fifteen minutes or upon request across the lagoon to San Marco. You might want to look into the luncheon buffet, which is expensive, but excellent (all the more so because of the setting). The Cipriani is now owned by Orient Express Hotels, and with special package arrangements, it can be the final stop on the recently revived Venice-Simplon Orient Express.

   Retrace your steps back to the sotoportego and turn left onto the fondamenta. The No. 82 vaporetto will take you back to San Zaccaria.

ACCADEMIA BRIDGE TO THE PIAZZA

Start: Accademia Bridge.

Finish: Piazza San Marco.

Time: Two or more hours, depending on time spent in shops.

Vaporetto: No. 1.

Best Time: Weekday mornings or late afternoon, when shops and galleries are open.

Worst Time: Midday or Sunday when most shops are closed.

For most visitors to Venice, the sestiere of San Marco means the plush central part of the city. It's the lavish Basilica and the Ducal Palace; the elegance of the Piazza, lined with exorbitant cafes and shops; the Merceria, invaded by Benetton, Foot Locker, Gucci, Armani, and such dense hordes of tourists in summer that a one-way pedestrian traffic system has to be enforced. For savvy travelers, San Marco is also the world famous Harry's Bar, at the foot of Calle Vallaresso, a block west of the Piazza, as well as the sleek Via 22 Marzo and the sequence of shopping streets and luxury hotels that contin-ues onward to the west. Much of this walk will studiously avoid the parts of San Marco that visitors generally see anyway; in-stead, it leads down side streets that take you into hidden neighborhoods and enclaves of interesting shop windows and galleries. The walk includes a visit to one church with a wonder-ful interior, and a quick look at the exterior of another, but basically this is an odyssey of twisting explorations and small, unusual discoveries.

● ● ● ● ● ● ● ● ● ● ● ● ● ● ● ● ●

To start this tour, climb to the top of the:

1. **Accademia Bridge** (Actv Accademia Stop on the No. 1 vaporetto line), a wooden structure built in the 1930s (and re-done in the 1980s) to replace the first Accademia Bridge, an iron span constructed by the Austrians in 1854. Both for patriotic and aesthetic reasons, Venetians seem not to have fond memories of the original, which was demolished when traffic on the Grand Canal needed higher clearance. Most Venetians envision a permanent stone bridge here someday; there has even been a proposal for a transparent plastic bridge that would not obstruct the vistas.

If you're coming from the Accademia side of the bridge, the view to the right is spectacular. Looking back to the Dorsoduro side of the Grand Canal, the vista includes the white domes and towers of Longhena's baroque masterpiece, Santa Maria della Salute (completed in 1681). Ahead, on the San Marco side of the Grand Canal, the first building to the right of the bridge is the 15th-century:

2. **Palazzo Franchetti,** adorned with lavish gothic tracery and a large, beautifully tended canal-side garden created by the demolition of a squero (gondola building yard), in the 19th century. Heavily renovated in 1896 by the same Baron Franchetti who restored the Ca' d'Oro. The Palazzo Franchetti, though sumptuous, is not admired by purists. The next two buildings to the right of the palazzo, sepa-rated from it by a narrow side canal, compose the:

3. **Palazzo Barbaro.** The older, closer part dates from 1425. The second part of the house, added in 1694, included a

much-needed ballroom. By the mid-19th century, the beautiful apartments of the palazzo were being rented out to foreigners, and the last of the Barbaro line, two elderly gentlemen, had retreated to the attic. The international glory of Palazzo Barbaro began in 1882, when the upper two floors were bought by Mr. and Mrs. Daniel Curtis of Boston, noted patrons of the arts. Browning was invited to give recitations in the library; Henry James stayed while writing *The Aspern Papers* (he also used the palazzo as a setting for *The Wings of the Dove*); Claude Monet and John Singer Sargent each had a studio in the palazzo and Whistler had a residence there; Cole Porter visited in 1923 before he moved to a floating nightclub moored outside the Salute. The Curtis's fellow Bostonian, Isabella Stewart Gardiner, was so taken with the place that she built her own version of a Venetian palazzo back home; it is now one of Boston's most delightful museums.

From the left side of the Accademia Bridge, the first house on the San Marco side of the Grand Canal is:

4. **Palazzo Marcello,** now the German Consulate, with a lush, overgrown garden to its side. The large white palazzo immediately beyond is:

5. **Palazzo Giustiniani-Lolin,** an early work by Longhena, completed in 1623, when the architect was in his early twenties. The sculptural baroque extravagances (like those on the Salute Church) that later became Longhena's hallmark are scarcely evident in this restrained, classic facade. Note the delicately carved stone draperies looped between the capitals of the upper *piano nobile.* The next house to the left (if you stretch your neck to look and step back a bit toward the Dorsoduro side of the bridge) is the:

6. **Palazzo Falier** (early 15th century), with its two roofed terrace wings. Though they might seem to be a modern addition, they are really rare surviving examples of an old architectural form the Venetians called a *liago.* Such structures appear in Carpaccio's *Miracle of the Holy Cross,* (in the Accademia) which depicts the busy area of the Rialto Bridge as it looked approximately 500 years ago. During the early 1860s, the American writer, William Dean Howells, who was United States Consul in Venice, rented an apartment

The Accademia to San Marco

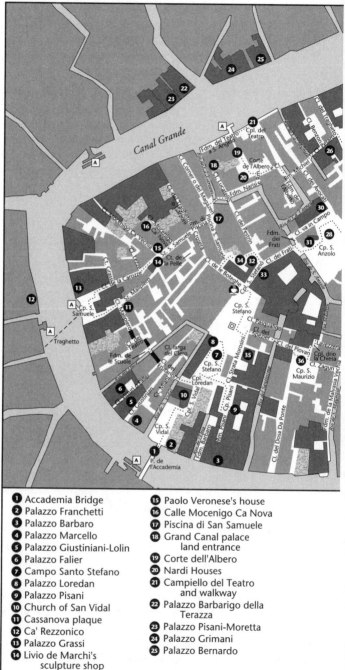

1 Accademia Bridge
2 Palazzo Franchetti
3 Palazzo Barbaro
4 Palazzo Marcello
5 Palazzo Giustiniani-Lolin
6 Palazzo Falier
7 Campo Santo Stefano
8 Palazzo Loredan
9 Palazzo Pisani
10 Church of San Vidal
11 Cassanova plaque
12 Ca' Rezzonico
13 Palazzo Grassi
14 Livio de Marchi's sculpture shop
15 Paolo Veronese's house
16 Calle Mocenigo Ca Nova
17 Piscina di San Samuele
18 Grand Canal palace land entrance
19 Corte dell'Albero
20 Nardi Houses
21 Campiello del Teatro and walkway
22 Palazzo Barbarigo della Terazza
23 Palazzo Pisani-Moretta
24 Palazzo Grimani
25 Palazzo Bernardo

9755

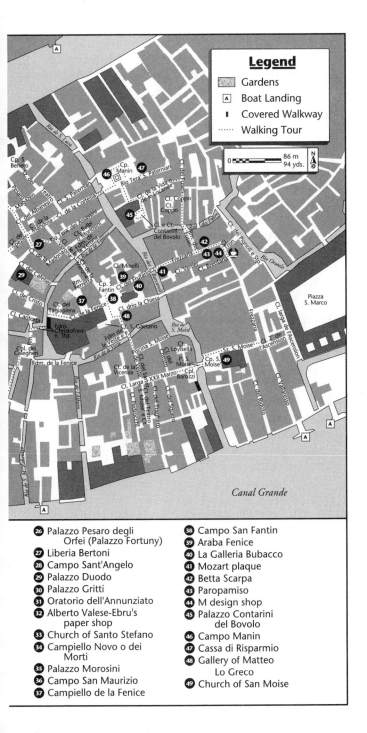

Legend

Gardens	
A	Boat Landing
▮	Covered Walkway
·····	Walking Tour

0 ————— 86 m
94 yds.

N

Piazza S. Marco

Canal Grande

26 Palazzo Pesaro degli Orfei (Palazzo Fortuny)
27 Liberia Bertoni
28 Campo Sant'Angelo
29 Palazzo Duodo
30 Palazzo Gritti
31 Oratorio dell'Annunziato
32 Alberto Valese-Ebru's paper shop
33 Church of Santo Stefano
34 Campiello Novo o dei Morti
35 Palazzo Morosini
36 Campo San Maurizio
37 Campiello de la Fenice
38 Campo San Fantin
39 Araba Fenice
40 La Galleria Bubacco
41 Mozart plaque
42 Betta Scarpa
43 Paropamiso
44 M design shop
45 Palazzo Contarini del Bovolo
46 Campo Manin
47 Cassa di Risparmio
48 Gallery of Matteo Lo Greco
49 Church of San Moise

on the mezzanine floor of the house. A branch of the Falier family produced Marin Falier, who, in 1355, became the only doge in the history of the Republic to be executed (he plotted to overthrow the Republic and seize power). If you've visited the Doge's Palace, you'll remember that the space where his portrait would have hung among all the other leaders of the Republic, has been filled with a black square.

Directly ahead as you proceed across the bridge, you'll see the campanile of the Church of San Vidal, the parish church originally built in the 9th century by the Falier family, whose connection to this part of town is very ancient. As you descend from the bridge onto the San Marco side, you may hear strands of folk music—refugee musicians from the former Yugoslavia have staked out this area. Follow the way around to the right and then left, past the imposing, pseudo-Palladian facade of the deconsecrated Church of San Vidal, and enter the spacious, sunny:

7. **Campo Santo Stefano** (also called Campo Francesco Morosini), the heart of the area this walk will explore. For now, we'll stay near the well head at the end of the campo closest to the Accademia Bridge.

This fashionable campo, surrounded by a number of Venice's most unusual palazzi, was inhabited by some of the Republic's great families. It was also the address of some notable courtesans. For centuries, one of Venice's main tourist attractions was its vast community of prostitutes. In the late 16th century, a directory for visitors was published, listing the names, addresses, and specialties of over 11,000 such professionals (a copy can be seen at the Marciana Library). Three or four hundred years ago, travelers to Venice visited this campo (among others) in hope of catching a glimpse of one or more of the most beautiful, cultured, and renowned courtesans as they walked in the sun with servants on either side to help them balance in their impossibly high platform shoes. The campo was also the scene of many bull-baiting spectacles; in 1802 the collapse of a grandstand here caused many injuries and led to the banning of this sport throughout Venice. A statue in the center of the campo commemorates Nicolo Tommaseo, who, along with Daniele Manin, led the Insurrection Against Austria in 1848–49.

From the well head, you are opposite:

8. the very long, low-slung Renaissance facade of **Palazzo Loredan.** After the fall of the Republic in 1797, the palazzo was used to house a number of public institutions. Since 1892, it has been the home of the Veneto Institute of Science, Letters, and Arts. Check out the lavish Neptune door knocker on the main entrance, just beneath the central second-story row of eight balconied windows.

In the corner of the campo opposite Palazzo Loredan, is the immense:

9. **Palazzo Pisani,** which was begun in 1614, and continued to grow until the mid-18th century, at which time the Republic virtually put an end to further additions. With its formal, Roman-baroque style, this palazzo is unusual because its principal facade has always faced the campo rather than a canal, and because of its interior arcades, courtyards, and vast wings, which threatened to slowly encompass the entire neighborhood. Note the palazzo's own entrance campiello, sometimes used for outdoor performances, and the few small houses nearby that did not get swallowed up as the palazzo grew. The last member of this enormously wealthy branch of the Pisani died in 1880, and the palazzo now houses the Venice Conservatory of Music, as well as a banking house. Visitors are not generally welcome, but at times, it is possible to see a bit of the interior during recitals, or, with luck, by slinking in and asking about the school or concert programs when you're stopped.

From this side of the campo, look across to the:

10. **Church of San Vidal** (San Vitale), which now houses an art gallery. Notice how the monumental facade, an imitation of Palladio's San Giorgio Maggiore, seems misplaced against a buiding with so little depth. Inside, Carpaccio's *San Vitale and Other Saints* survives from earlier times. The woodworking and furniture restoration shop at the side of the church is highly regarded.

Take a Break At the far end of the campo you'll see the austere wall of the side of the Church of Santo Stefano; to the left, across the calle from the entrance to the church, you'll find **Gelateria Pausin,** one of the best ice cream places in Venice, with flavors that are very rich and alive. You may not be in the mood to carry a cone or sherbet now, but we will cross this campo a number of times, and especially on a hot day, this is an option to keep in mind. Pausin is open Tuesday through Sunday from 7:30am to 8pm (later in summer) and is closed Mondays and December 15 to January 31.

We'll leave the palaces and facades behind for a while and enter another world via the narrow Calle de Frutariol, which starts between the side of the Church of San Vidal and Palazzo Loredan. Follow this narrow passageway as it continues relatively straight (though changing names), under a sotoportego and over a canal (check the view each way as you cross the small bridge). Just after the end of the second sotoportego, turn left onto Calle dei Teatro, and then immediately onto the first right (Calle Malpiero), which goes under another sotoportego. It was on this medieval street, once called Calle della Commedia, that Giovanni Giacomo Casanova (1725–1798), the son of two actors in the nearby Teatro San Samuele, was born.

11. **A plaque at the end of the street,** just before the intersection with Salizada Malpiero, conforms to the information in Casanova's autobiography, although no one can be certain in which house he was born, or even if the events he recorded in his picaresque memoirs are in any way close to the truth. Libertine, spy, economist, philosopher, satirist, tax expert, and iconoclast, we can only assume that Casanova's early years were spent planning how to escape to the glittering palaces and ballrooms only meters away from the world of his childhood.

At Salizada Malpiero, look right at the flowerboxes that adorn the buildings, but turn left, past the little-used Church of San Samuele, with its 12th-century campanile, and pass the Actv stop at Campo San Samuele, where you have a good view across the canal to the:

12. **Ca' Rezzonico** (the large white palazzo to the right of the Ca' Rezzonico Actv stop). Designed by the baroque master, Baldassare Longhena in 1657, though more reserved than his other landmark palazzo on the Grand Canal, Ca' Pesaro, the Ca' Rezzonico was not completed until 1750—its top

two floors were designed by Giorgio Massari. The Rezzonico family was legendary for lavish entertainments; in 1758 they reached new heights of prestige when one of their members became Pope Clement XIII. He was the fifth Venetian to serve as Pope.

In 1889, Robert Barrett Browning (known as "Pen"), the son of the poet Robert Browning, bought Ca' Rezzonico with the help of his wife, an American heiress, and together they refurbished the interior and built a chapel dedicated to Pen's mother, Elizabeth Barrett. They also installed a central heating system. Pen and his wife invited the 77-year-old Robert Browning, who had already spent much time in Venice, to join them in the palazzo, which the poet modestly described as "a quiet corner for my old age." Despite the heating system, Browning caught a chill and died there in December 1889. Ca' Rezzonico is now a museum of 18th-century Venetian art and furnishings (culled from many palaces) that gives you a wonderful sense of being in a still-functioning late baroque palazzo. Among the Ca' Rezzonico's treasures are the pastels of Rosalba Carriera, Tiepolo frescoes, and paintings by Guardi and Longhi that reflect the decadent, dreamlike Carnival society of the Republic's last decades. The attic houses a puppet theater and a period pharmacy. Ca' Rezzonico is open Monday to Thursday and Saturday from 10am to 4pm; Sunday from 9am to 12:30pm; closed Fridays.

If you'd like to add a visit to the Ca' Rezzonico to this walk (it is part of a walk through Dorsoduro, on the other side of the canal), a traghetto ferry service at Campo San Samuele runs Monday through Saturday from 8am to 2pm, and will take you directly across the Grand Canal in a gondola-like vessel (passengers traditionally stand for the 1-minute ride, which costs about 500 lire, or 30¢ each way). The traghetto deposits you on the far side of the canal, next to the charming 19th-century neo-gothic Palazzo Stern. Take Calle dei Traghetto to Campo San Barnaba, turn right at the San Barnaba Church, cross the little San Barnaba Bridge, and make a right onto the Fondamenta Rezzonico, which will take you to the land entrance of the museum. *Note:* Reconfirm the hours of the traghetto if you plan this addition to the walk.

In case you have not already noticed the vast palazzo overpowering the far side of Campo San Samuele, we are facing:

13. Giorgio Massari's restrained, neoclassical **Palazzo Grassi,** built between 1748 and 1772. This was the last of the great houses to be built on the Grand Canal; the Grassi family, latecomers to Venetian high society did not buy their way into patrician status until 1718. After the fall of the Republic, the palazzo became a hotel for a time, and later a public bathhouse. In 1984, Fiat bought and refurbished the palazzo and converted it into a dazzling center for cultural and art exhibitions. The Palazzo Grassi's exhibits are beautifully mounted, often mobbed, and almost always worthwhile.

From Campo San Samuele, turn right onto Calle de le Carroze, and continue straight until it becomes the wider Salizada San Samuele, which contains a number of interesting shops and galleries, some good for a quick glance, others worth further inspection. My favorite is:

14. the first shop on the right (3157A Salizada San Samuele), which displays the creations of **wood sculptor Livio de Marchi,** who, like many Venetian artists before him, loves to work with illusion. His small shopfront gallery is usually ascatter with amusing wooden fedoras, umbrellas, ties, and rumpled blue jeans, as well as clotheslines of wooden undershorts and socks hanging out to dry, and an occasional magnum opus, like a wooden nude standing under the spray of a wooden bathroom shower, or an occasional exuberantly carved traditional carousel horse.

By coincidence, across the street, a bit farther up, at no. 3338, is:

15. the comfortable but non-palatial **house of Paolo Veronese** (1528–1588), the last great painter of the Venetian Renaissance, and a master of the use of illusion in decorative art. Among Veronese's early triumphs are the lighthearted trompe l'oeil wall paintings of Villa Barbaro at Maser that create optical illusions of servants coming through non-existent doorways, children peering through elaborate windows, and beautiful women gazing down from balconies. Venice adored his magic and showered him with commissions. For a Dominican friars' refectory, Veronese

painted a Last Supper in the form of a lively and lavish banqueting scene that some inside the church regarded as irreverent. Summoned before the Inquisition and ordered to change the painting, Veronese quickly complied by re-naming the work, *Feast in the House of Levi.* Although (as his name indicates) Veronese was not a native Venetian, his work embodied the spirit of Venice at the height of its power—serenely joyful, poetic, and materially splendid.

Just past the house of Veronese, you might care to wan-der down the:

16. narrow **Calle Mocenigo Ca' Nova.** It doesn't look very interesting, but this was the land entrance to Palazzo Mocenigo, a quadruple palace on the Grand Canal that the British poet, Lord Byron, rented in 1817, two years after the final defeat of Napoleon. Byron's more spectacular en-trances would have been made directly from the Grand Canal, and not merely by gondola. At times the romantic Byron would swim from the Lido up the Grand Canal to his house, with members of the foreign community perched at various locations en route to admire his sagging but still heroic spirit and figure. The comings and goings at the land entrance were probably interesting as well. Byron's house-hold consisted of a wolf, a fox, a number of dogs, cats, birds, and monkeys; it also included a mistress who was the wife of a Venetian draper, and later an additional mistress called La Fornarina ("the little oven") because she was the wife of a baker. The fiery La Fornarina, whom he described as "en-ergetic as a python" attacked Byron with a knife, and threw herself into the Grand Canal after being banished from the palazzo. Another important British poet, Percy Bysshe Shelley, would also have trod this alleyway. He and his wife, Mary (author of *Frankenstein*), visited Byron in 1818, accompanied by Mary Shelley's stepsister, Claire Clairmont, who was Byron's former mistress. The 19-month-old Clara Allegra, Byron's daughter by Claire Clairmont, had already been in residence for some time, under the care of La Fornarina, but with La Fornarina's departure, she had been placed elsewhere. There's much more (when Byron finally decamped from the palazzo, he did so in the company of a new 19-year-old mistress, Countess Teresa Guiccioli), but perhaps this will be enough to entice you to detour down

this alleyway with its walled gardens and hidden mysteries. Byron completed several cantos of *Don Juan* while in Venice; he died in 1824 at the age of 36.

The next part of this walk will explore the beauty and eccentricity of this hidden part of San Marco. Continue straight up Salizada San Samuele, which narrows to become Ramo di Piscina, and ends at:

17. **Piscina di San Samuele,** a long, picturesque courtyard. The name "piscina" indicates this was once a pool or sleeve of water leading into a canal that has long since been filled in with earth. In earlier times, a piscina would have been used for bathing, or for sheltering boats.

    Walk to the left. At the end of the Piscina San Samuele, the way diverges into three possibilities. Take the small stairway with the iron banister on the extreme right. Follow the narrow bridgeway to the first cross passageway, and turn left into the Corte Lucatello, which is a worthwhile dead end leading to:

18. **the land entrance** of one of the many elegantly renovated Grand Canal palaces. Now that private gondolas are history, this is the kind of daily route most palazzo dwellers must take, though not every palazzo is so pleasantly landscaped. Look through the gate into a secret garden, and beyond that, the *androne*, or water-level lobby. In this palazzo, you can see straight through the *androne* to the Grand Canal at the front of the building.

    Retrace your steps and walk a bit past the sotoportego on the left; then turn and look back. Roof gardens abound in this neighborhood—there's even one over the sotoportego. Go back, and turn right under the sotoportego, which leads onto the canalside Fondamenta Narisi. At the end, you must turn left, and suddenly, this wonderful neighborhood has vanished. You are in:

19. **Corte dell'Albero.** Walk a bit to the left, and you'll see what has swallowed up a good part of what used to be a neighborhood of narrow canals and calles:

20. the massive **Nardi Houses,** built from 1909 to 1914. This is a rare example of a 20th-century Venetian apartment building. The Veneto-Byzantine and art noveau touches help

blend it into the architectural fabric of the city. The build-ing is interesting, but it reminds us how fortunate it is that large parts of Venice were not demolished to create more such complexes.

As you face the Nardi Houses, turn right, and follow the corte as it narrows and leads to the Grand Canal. There you will find:

21. **a tiny campiello** beside the Sant'Angelo Actv stop, and to the left, a rare walkway along the Grand Canal in front of the site where the **Theater Sant'Angelo** once stood. We probably owe the existence of this mini fondamenta to the need for a landing spot to accommodate the many gondo-las that once delivered the audience. At this theater, half of Vivaldi's 40 operas were produced, beginning in 1714 with *Orlando Finto Pazzo*. Walk to your left, to the end of the fondamenta. The views from spots along the Grand Canal are always interesting. Directly across the Grand Canal, bordered by a rio, is the:

22. **Palazzo Barbarigo della Terrazza,** recognizable by its long side terrace with a white stone balustrade. Much of this palazzo's famed art collection eventually came into the possession of Czar Nicolas II. To the left of this palazzo is:

23. the large 15th-century **Palazzo Pisani-Moretta,** with elaborate gothic windows on its *piani nobili*. This house still remains in the hands of the descendants of the Pisani family, and retains much of its original furnishing and inte-rior decoration, which makes its condition very unusual. If you walk to the far right end of the fondamenta, beside the Actv stop, and look across the canal to the right, you'll notice a white three-story palazzo with triple arched win-dows in the center of its *piani nobili*. This is:

24. **Palazzo Grimani** (1520), one of the first Renaissance houses in Venice. The second gothic house to the right be-yond that, with two gothic water entrances, and two floors of six gothic central windows adorning its *piani nobili*, is:

25. the 15th-century **Palazzo Bernardo,** unusual because, if you look carefully, the two floors of central windows are out of line. Nonetheless, this is one of the most beautiful gothic facades on the Grand Canal, with fine stone tracery,

perhaps by the workshop of Giovanni and Bartolomeo Bon. The two water entrances indicate the palazzo was originally built to house two families. By the 16th century, the palazzo had become the home of the Bernardos, a citizen-class, non-patrician merchant family. Like many families during the centuries of Venice's decline, the Bernardos sold their palazzo, but managed to buy it back in 1840. The palazzo is now divided into apartments.

Retrace your steps to the Nardi Houses, turn left, and continue straight to the tiny, short calle at the far end of the corte. When you reach the canal, turn right onto the Fondamenta de l'Albero; then take a left on the first bridge you come to, which leads to Ramo Michiel. The way jogs slightly to the left as it crosses the next calle to become Calle Pesaro. As you come to the next short bridge, look to the right across the rio, and you'll see the canal facade of the Palazzo Fortuny, the next stop on our walk. Continue straight along the side of the palazzo, then turn right onto the Campo San Benedetto, and at no. 3958 is the:

26. **Palazzo Pesaro degli Orfei,** or Palazzo Fortuny, bought at the end of the 19th century by the Spanish-born couturier, fabric designer, inventor, painter, and photographer, Mariano Fortuny y Madrazo (1871–1949). The palazzo now houses a museum of Fortuny's varied works and is also a venue for temporary exhibitions. At the turn of the century, Fortuny invented and patented a method of pleating silk ("Fortuny-pleated" skirts are still produced today) from which he created diaphanous gowns popularized by Isadora Duncan, Eleanora Duse, Sara Bernhardt, and other romantic heroines of the age. Fortuny's classic "Delphos" dress, inspired by the *chiton* of ancient Greece, could be threaded through a wedding ring, and only took form as it clung to the human figure; his hanging silk lampshades, evoking a Byzantine-Islamic style, and his pleated velvet bags and capes were hallmarks of fashion and interior decoration through the early 1920s. The wide-ranging private collection of Fortuny is interesting but uneven; the studio and living quarters of this versatile genius as well as the unrestored gothic palazzo with its courtyard, ancient staircase, and wooden loggia, are all fascinating. During popular exhibits, the number of people allowed to enter the building must

be limited, because of the palazzo's fragile structure. The Museo Fortuny is open Tuesday to Sunday from 9am to 7pm; closed Sunday. Admission is approximately $3. Exit the Museum and enter the Campo San Benedetto.

The Church of San Benedetto, rebuilt in 1685, and not often open, has a painting by G. B. Tiepolo over the first altar on the left. From Campo San Benedetto, follow Calle a Fianco Ca' Pesaro to the right turn at the corner of the palazzo; at the sotoportego, turn left onto Rio Tera de la Mandola until you reach the intersecting main thoroughfare, Calle di Spezier, where you turn right. An alternative side trip is to continue straight: The way curves around to the left to become Rio Tera dei Assassini, and just at that point, you'll find:

27. **Libreria (Bookstore) Bertoni,** 3637/B Calle Mandola, packed with remaindered art books. Among these beautiful Italian editions, English readers will find many things unavailable in the English publishing world. The bookstore often stocks books about Venetian art, glass, and glass beads as well as beautiful photographic volumes about Venice.

Retrace your steps from the bookstore, and proceeding left on Calle dei Spezier, you'll enter the bright, open:

28. **Campo Sant' Angelo.** The first palazzo on the left side of the square is:

29. **Palazzo Duodo,** and directly across, on the right side of the campo is:

30. **Palazzo Gritti,** unusual for its off-center doorway. These magnificent gothic houses, because they face onto dry land, offer an unusual chance to study their carved stone ornamentation close up.

Interestingly, the campo seems devoid of a church. There was one, but it was demolished in 1837; its campanile was carted away about four hundred years earlier. According to tradition, the campanile leaned so precariously, that in the 15th century, a specialist was called in from Bologna to save it. Not only did he do so, but he also straightened the tower. The scaffolding was removed, a celebration was held in the campo, and the next day, the campanile toppled. Straight ahead, however, you have a good view of the dangerously leaning campanile of the next campo, Santo Stefano.

To the right, in the center of the campo, is the tiny 12th-century:

31. **Oratorio dell'Annunziato,** originally a confraternity for cripples, which sports an *Annunciation* by Antonio Triva. Continue straight across the campo, and cross the Ponte dei Frati (checking out the views both ways) and continue straight. On the right, on the corner just opposite the Church of Santo Stefano, is:

32. the shop of **Alberto Valese-Ebru** at no. 3470, acknowledged as one of the two or three great masters of the art of marbleized paper in Venice.

A few steps farther on your left, you'll come to:

33. the gothic doorway of the **Church of Santo Stefano,** which was built in the 14th to 15th centuries. The interior of the church is filled with rich patterning—gold and pale silver paneled squares on the ship's-keel ceiling, peach and maroon brickwork design on the upper walls, floral frescoes on the arches dividing the naves, delicately carved-and-painted beamwork crossing the central nave, and a garden of red and white marble columns leading to the gothic tracery of the apse. The space is lit by high windows recessed into the sides of the roof. On the entrance wall is the tomb of Giacomo Surian, delicately carved by Pietro Lombardo and his sons. In the sacristy, you'll find three late works by Tintoretto: *The Washing of the Feet, The Agony in the Garden,* and *The Last Supper*; behind the altar, you can see the elaborately carved 15th-century monks' choir. In the center of the nave is the tomb of Francesco Morosini, who was doge from 1688–94, and who reversed Venice's sagging fortunes by briefly reconquering the Peloponnese in Greece. One of the Republic's great leaders, to the rest of the world, Morosini is known chiefly for lobbing a shell into the Parthenon, where the Turks were unfortunately storing gunpowder. Although the Parthenon had survived relatively intact until then, the explosion turned it into the ruin we know today. The far door in the left aisle leads into the cloister, once covered with frescoes by Pordenone.

Exit the church, and turn left towards the campo; just as you enter the campo, turn right onto Calle de le Boteghe. Take the first right, and climb the steps into:

34. **Campiello Novo o dei Morti** (New Campiello or Campiello of the Dead). Today this spot is a pleasant discovery: a secluded plaza with gardens overhanging one wall, and a terraced, vine-covered locanda (or small hotel) at the right. The campiello's name, however, betrays a catastrophic history. The area was a mass grave for victims of the great plague of 1630, which accounts for its higher elevation. Until 1838, the site was closed to the public for health reasons.

Retrace your steps, and enter Campo Santo Stefano. On the left side of the Campo, just before it narrows, is the vast:

35. **Palazzo Morosini,** with its own courtyard in the corner of the campo. This was the family palace of Francesco Morosini (1619–1694), who, during the Turkish invasion of Crete in 1669, held off 17 sorties and 32 assaults before finally surrendering his besieged garrison to overwhelmingly superior forces. Morosini returned to Venice and was relieved of his command, but he refused to accept defeat. Fifteen years later, sailing into battle with his beloved cat at his side (in the true spirit of Venetian eccentricity), Morosini led the Republic in the last successful military campaign of its history, the reconquest of the Peloponnese. Like Doge Enrico Dandolo, who led the sack of Constantinople in 1204 and had sent the Four Horses of the Hippodrome back to Venice to adorn the Basilica of San Marco, Morosini envisioned sending home a spectacular trophy to mark his triumph. He chose the horses and chariot of the goddess Athena, which formed the western pediment of the Parthenon. In the attempt to dislodge the sculpture, however, it fell to the ground and was smashed beyond repair. Morosini was elected doge upon his return to Venice in 1688, and in 1694, he sailed off once more to fight the Turks. Again like Doge Enrico Dandolo, who had led an expedition in his old age 500 years earlier, Morosini died in the effort; within a few years, his conquests were recaptured by the Turks. Although Venice never made a cult of its

leaders, this last hero of the Republic was gratefully revered. To commemorate Morosini's naval triumphs, a sculptured sea horse and various marine motifs adorn the main entrance of the palazzo. In 1894, the contents of the house were sold at auction. The embalmed body of his cat is among the many Morosini possessions on display at the Museo Correr in Piazza San Marco.

One building to the left, as you face Palazzo Morosini, is Calle dei Spezier, through which we will exit the campo.

The shops on this street bespeak the neighborhood's elegance: at no. 2766, on the right, an antiques dealer often displays 19th-century glass from the workshops of Salviati and Barovier. A music shop a few steps beyond offers a delightful courtyard where you can listen to concerts of recordings. On the left, by the bridge, is one of the city's best-known patisseries. Among other things, it sells a boxed confection called "Bacci in Gondola" (Kisses in a Gondola). As you cross the small bridge, look left, and you will see that the apse of the Church of Santo Stefano has been built over the canal, and that only low canal traffic can pass beneath it. A few feet beyond, is the reserved, patrician:

36. **Campo San Maurizio,** with its neoclassical church, which was rebuilt from 1806 to 1828. We are in the antiques-gallery district of Venice, and this campo hosts occasional outdoor antiques markets; check with the Tourist Information Office if you're interested. In the corner of the campo, at no. 2666, the antiques shop called **V. Trois** sells cloth produced at a workshop on the Giudecca that uses Fortuny's patented dying and printing methods (Fortuny textiles can run $200 per square meter). At no. 2663, **Bac Art Studio** handles quality graphics and posters.

As you face the Church of San Maurizio, with the off-kilter campanile looming behind it, enter the narrow passageway to the right, which leads to another wonderful rabbit hole of twists and turns. Bear to the right, and take a right at Calle Lavezzera; at the sotoportego at the end of the calle, turn left onto the Fondamenta de la Malvasia Vecchia, which ends at an angled bridge. Proceed straight into Campiello dei Caligari, (the shoemakers' campiello) and exit through the Ramo on the far right at the opposite side of the campiello. From this srreet, turn onto the first right, the Fondamenta Cristoforo, whch becomes a bridge. At the bridge, look to the right across the canal, and you'll see the water entrance of the Fenice Theater/Opera House, with places for gondolas to tie up. If you're lucky, you'll also see barges floating in scenery and costumes on the rio. At the end of the bridge, a sotoportego takes you to the left. Turn right onto Calle de la Fenice. Turn left into the second corte you pass:

37. the delightful, vine-trellised **Campiello de la Fenice,** with the Hotel Fenice on its left side. At the left corner of the far end of the campiello, an interesting sequence of sotoportegos eventually leads back toward the Campo Sant'Angelo. The building at the end of the campiello bears a plaque dedicated to the memory of those who died in the 1848–49 insurrection against Austria.

A right turn at the end of the campiello, and then the next right turn, will lead you to:

38. **Campo San Fantin,** and on your right, the main entrance of the legendary Fenice Theater, built in 1792, during the very last days of the Republic. True to the meaning of its name (Phoenix), the Fenice rose from the ashes of a catastrophic fire in 1836. Venice was the first city to have public performances of opera, and the jewel-like 1,500 seat oval interior of the Fenice has seen the world premieres of Verdi's *Attila, Rigoletto, La Traviata*, and *Simon Boccanegro*, as well as Stravinsky's *Rake's Progress* in 1951, and Benjamin Britten's *Turn of the Screw*. During the years of the Austrian occupation (and especially during productions of works by Verdi) the Fenice was a rallying point for patriotic fervor. The best way to enjoy the the Fenice is to attend a performance here. December through May is the opera season, but the theater is in use year-round. A program of summer concerts is usually offered, culminating in a Vivaldi festival each September.

The Church of San Fantin, opposite the theater, contains a beautiful Renaissance dome by Sansovino over its apse. At the head of the campo is the Venetian Athenium, formerly the Scuola della Buona Morte, a confraternity that comforted prisoners condemned to death.

As you face the Church of San Fantin, exit the campo via the street to the left of the church, Calle dei Fruitariol, which is home to a number of the city's most stylish and personal shops and galleries. Right at the corner, is:

39. **Araba Fenice** (no. 1862), a highly rated shop which carries its own line of elegant but young-at-heart collections of custom designed clothes. Farther along, on the other side of the calle, you'll find:

40. **La Galleria Bubacco,** at no. 1845. Lucio Bubacco, born on Murano in 1957, creates contemporary glass objects that are inventive, elegant, and at the same time, zany; check out his one-of-a-kind chalices. The calle continues with interesting boutiques and galleries, including the mildly exotic **Claudia** at number 1860. As you cross the bridge, look across the rio to the right, at:

41. **the elegantly worded plaque** on the side of the building that declares that "the city of Vivaldi and Goldoni" wished to record that the young Salzburger, Wolfgang Amadeus Mozart, festively sojourned during the Carnival of 1771.

Beyond the bridge, the name of the calle changes to Frezzaria (arrowmakers). Towards the end, on the left is:

42. **Betta Scarpa** (no. 1797), mistress of the very, very little black dress and all that's needed to go with it. Across the calle, is:

43. **Paropamiso** (no. 1701), a small gem of a place that sells carefully chosen antique and ethnic art objects, beads, and jewelry from such diverse places as Turkey, the Himalayas, and Indonesia. The shop also specializes in old Venetian glass beads ranging in price from $2 to $2,000 (many 19th-century Venetian beads are $5 to $20). The owner will make your choices into earrings or necklaces. Open Monday to Saturday from 10am to 1pm, and 4pm to 8pm as well as sometimes on Sundays.

The Frezzaria makes a hard 90° turn after Paropamiso; on the left, you'll pass:

44. **M** (no. 1690), selling objets d'art, and its exclusive collection of hand printed silks and velvets, some of which have

been made into jackets, dresses, scarves, and pillow covers. M's designs are rich with dark gold, plum, rose, and blue, patterned to give the the illusion of Byzantine and Renaissance brocades with an art nouveau touch; they fit well with the heavy twilight mood of an evening in Venice.

Take a Break We're almost at the end of the walk, but if you'd like to stop for a fast, inexpensive meal, **Chat Qui Rit,** a self-service cafeteria is a few steps across from M, and a good bet for soup or a quick bite. At the 90° corner of the Frezzaria, turn right and then immediately left. It's just on that corner. There are lots of rustic dining areas to choose from, but they can be mobbed at mealtimes or when a tour group comes through.

Retrace your steps back past Paropamiso and Betta Scarpa, and take a right onto the upmarket Ramo Fusieri, home to Kenzo and a number of other international enterprises. Continue over the bridge, along the narrowing but busy calle; opposite no. 4460, turn left onto Calle de la Vida o de Locanda (Street of Life or of the Small Hotel); continue until you turn left onto Calle de Contarini dal Bovolo. On the right side of this narrow calle, you'll see the:

45. **Palazzo Contarini dal Bovolo,** with its famous spiral-staircase tower and airy arcaded loggia, built in 1499. The large Contarini family built many palaces in Venice, each with its own identifying nickname—in this case, Bovolo comes from the Venetian word for "snail shell." Outdoor staircases were the rule in older palaces, but the Bovolo is unique. During the 19th century, the palace changed hands a number of times, and even served as a hotel for a time; it now houses an educational foundation. The ivy-covered garden has become a repository for architectural fragments and carved well-heads and is home to many local cats. Interestingly, the canal facade of this palace is unremarkable.

Retrace your steps to the intersection with Calle de la Vida, but at that point turn left. Then take the first right turn, which will lead you into the bustling:

46. **Campo Manin,** named for Daniele Manin, leader of the 1848–49 Insurrection Against Austria (his house was on

this plaza; looking from the statue of Manin, it is next to the left of the two bridges at the end of the campo). The opposite end of the campo is graced by one of the city's few prominently placed modern buildings:

47. **the main bank offices of the Cassa di Risparmio** (1964), designed by the noted architects, Angelo Scattolin and Pier Luigi Nervi. When you consider that proposed buildings for other locations designed by Le Corbusier and Frank Lloyd Wright have never been granted final approval by the city's planning commission, the Cassa di Risparmio becomes all the more remarkable. The building marks the site of the Aldine Press, founded in 1495 by Aldus Manutius, who, in addition to inventing *italics*, set up an efficient assembly-line printing establishment here, with teams of diecutters, compositors, proofreaders, and an on-site research department of scholars-in-residence that at one time included Erasmus of Rotterdam (who roomed with a translator of Hebrew, Latin, Greek, and Arabic and complained of the fleas). The Aldine Press produced authoritative editions of a wide range of classical texts at affordable prices, and changed the intellectual face of Europe. The frenzied activity inside the Aldine Press can be inferred from the sign that once hung above its door:

> WHOEVER YOU ARE, ALDUS EARNESTLY BEGS YOU TO STATE YOUR BUSINESS IN THE FEWEST WORDS POSSIBLE AND BEGONE, UNLESS, LIKE HERCULES TO WEARY ATLAS, YOU WOULD LEND A HELPING HAND. THERE WILL ALWAYS BE ENOUGH WORK FOR YOU AND FOR ALL WHO PASS THIS WAY.

Exit Campo Manin by the left bridge as you face away from the statue of Manin. Continue straight on Calle de la Cortesia, a busy shopping street which changes its name to Calle de la Mandola. On this street, at **La Pantofola** (no. 3718) on the right side, you can find comfortable velvet gondoliers' slippers (in the style worn by actors in the Commedia dell' Arte); on the left, there are **shops** specializing in graceful silk and woolen paisley shawls, worn by stylish Venetian women to ward off the chill of wintery palazzo apartments. We will make a right turn onto Calle de la Verona, but a few steps beyond that on Calle de la

Daniele Manin (1804–57)

The electrifying leader of the Insurrection Against Austria in 1848–49 was a scholar conversant in German, French, English, Hebrew, and Greek, editor of a dictionary of the Venetian dialect, a devoted family man, an eloquent lawyer, and a Venetian patriot. In January 1848, he was arrested and detained in the prison behind the Doge's Palace by the Austrian authorities, who had occupied Venice since the end of the Napoleonic Wars in 1815. Vast public demonstrations followed, with Venetians demanding Manin's freedom. On the night of March 16, 1848, Manin and another Venetian leader, Nicolo Tommaseo, were released by the Austrians as the wave of protests continued to rise. Six days later, as the population of Venice gathered in the Piazza San Marco, Manin declared the Venetian Republic was reborn, and that the honor of Venice, which had been lost in 1797 when the last doge meekly surrendered the city to Napoleon without a fight, would be redeemed. The Austrian occupation authorities fled; in the months that followed, an enlightened, middle-class-oriented government led by Manin emerged. During the summer of 1849, the Austrians returned, besieged the city, and bombarded it by cannon and from aerial balloons. By August, the starving population, faced with a cholera epidemic, was forced to surrender. Sent into exile, Manin endured the death of his wife and young daughter before dying alone, nine years before the Austrians finally relinquished Venice in 1866. In later years, his body was reinterred in a place of unequaled honor—beside the Basilica of San Marco.

Mandola, at no. 3653, you might want to check out the shop of **Paolo Olbi,** acclaimed as one of the city's finest makers of marbleized paper. Continue straight on Calle de la Verona, which will lead you back to Campo San Fantin and the Fenice Theater. Continue straight across the Campo. On the right side of the campo, just beyond the Church of San Fantin, you'll notice the:

48. **Gallery of Matteo Lo Greco** (no. 1998), a Sicilian-born sculptor whose creations of joyous, overweight spirits are filled with optimism, life, and a touch of the classic tradition. The gallery is closed Sundays and Mondays.

    Exit the campo on the Calle del Cafetier, just beside the Lo Greco gallery, and keep straight until this sequence of calles ends at Calle Larga 22 Marzo, a broad pedestrian street built in the 1870s and named for the date of the establishment of Manin's new republic in 1848. Turn left onto this important shopping calle. On the left, just before the bridge, you'll pass **M.A.R.E.,** a shop carrying a good range of middle-to-upper-price contemporary glass. After crossing the bridge, on the left, at no. 1468, is **L'Isola,** among Venice's most prestigious galleries for contemporary glass. The dominant feature of this street, of course is:

49. **the Church of San Moise,** originally founded in the 8th century. The current church building dates from 1632, with its facade designed by Alessandro Tremignon in 1668, and many sculptural decorations added by Heinrich Meyring in the 1680s to create a wildly rococo presence. You either love this extravaganza or hate it. Ruskin considered the facade "one of the basest examples of the basest school of the Renaissance." Inside, Meyring created an odd sculptural altarpiece in the form of Moses receiving the Ten Commandments on Mount Sinai. Venice followed an unusual tradition of naming some of its churches for Old Testament figures. Not quite like anything else in Venice, San Moise might well be translated as "Holy Moses."

    To the left of San Moise, is Salizada San Moise, which will lead you back to the Piazza San Marco and the end of this walk.

The Other Side of the Canal: San Polo and Santa Croce

Start: Statue of Goldoni on San Marco side of the Rialto Bridge.

Finish: San Toma Actv Stop.

Vaporetto: No. 1.

Time: Two and a half hours, depending on time spent at sites.

Best Time: Weekday mornings when the market and most smaller churches along the route are open.

Worst Time: Late afternoon when markets are closed and light will not be good inside churches.

his walk begins with an exploration of the bustling vegetable and fish markets of the Rialto, and then makes its way through neighborhoods and out of the way spots that give you a feel for some of the simple pleasures of

Venetian life. Many of the small artisans' workshops, restaurants, and stores along the way are among the city's most special and least touristic. The end of the walk brings you to two of the city's important treasures: the Church of Santa Maria Gloriosa dei Frari and the Scuola Grande di San Rocco, a treasure house of Tintorettos, which Ruskin described as one of the three most precious buildings in Italy.

● ● ● ● ● ● ● ● ● ● ● ● ● ● ● ● ● ●

We start this walk at:

1. **the statue of Carlo Goldoni** (1707–93). Originally a lawyer, by 1748 Goldoni had begun to write stock comedies for the Teatro Sant'Angelo. Soon he was breaking new ground with more realistic plays, often composed in Venetian dialect, filled with the style, verve, and good humor of daily Venetian life. Goldoni loved to pick up lines for his characters from conversations overheard in the streets and markets; the bustling Campo San Bartolomeo was one of his favorite haunts for this purpose. Antonio dal Zotto's statue of Goldoni, cast in 1883 and restored in 1985, reflects the energy and boundless spirit of this much loved Venetian who wrote more than 250 plays and light operas. One of the city's main theaters is named for Goldoni, and Venetians continue to flock to productions of his plays.

   From Campo San Bartolomeo, take Salizada Pio X onto the:

2. **Rialto Bridge,** built in 1588 to replace a long line of earlier wooden bridges constructed on this site over the centuries. Until the Austrians built the first Accademia Bridge in the mid-19th century, the Rialto Bridge was the only structure to span the Grand Canal. From the time that the earliest inhabitants took refuge on the islands of Rivo Alto (Rialto or "high shore") in the center of the lagoon, this site has been the trading center and crossroads of the settlement that eventually became Venice. Designed by Antonio da Ponte (whose plan won a competition that included submissions by Palladio and Michelangelo), it was hoped that the arcade of shops would help weigh the bridge onto its support pilings in the muddy bed of the Grand Canal. From the balustraded footpath that runs along the right side of

the bridge as you cross from the direction of Campo San Bartolomeo, look ahead to the right: the first building on the right is the:

3. **Palazzo Camerlenghi** (built about 1525), a white early Renaissance structure that housed the State Treasury in the time of the Republic. The Venetian government was apparently the first in the world to come up with income taxes; the ground floor of Palazzo Camerlenghi contained prison cells for those found guilty of tax evasion.

   Before descending to the other bank of the Grand Canal, cross to the left side of the bridge, and take in the sweeping, lively view in the other direction. The fondamente on the left (or Campo San Bartolomeo) side of the canal, were once loading zones for fish and coal; the Riva dei Vin, on the right side of the canal, was the point of transfer for shipments of wine (the surrounding neighborhood would have been filled with wine shops).

   Descend the Rialto Bridge, and continue straight along the:

4. **Ruga degli Orefici** (Street of the Goldsmiths), with its beautifully arcaded structures on the left, and, a bit farther on, to the right as well. Today this is the main drag of the Rialto Bazaar, with its outdoor tourist-trinket and bargain-basement stalls (careful searching here can sometimes come up with good values). For centuries, however, this was the most dazzling marketplace in Europe, its shops filled with exotic spices, precious stones, and costly fabrics from all over the world. Most fabulous of all were the displays of artisans working in gold and silver. In 1532, one workshop was commissioned to create a jewel-encrusted helmet for the Ottoman Sultan Suleiman the Magnificent that was reported to have cost over 100 thousand ducats (it is now part of the inventory at the Topkapi Museum). Bargaining was always the name of the game. In 1574, King Henry III of France, on his lavish state visit, admired a scepter studded with gems at a workshop on this street and offered 25 thousand gold scudi, but in this case, even a king's highest bid was not enough.

   The street widens on the right to form Campo San Giacomo di Rialto, a small square usually filled with wooden

San Polo and Santa Croce

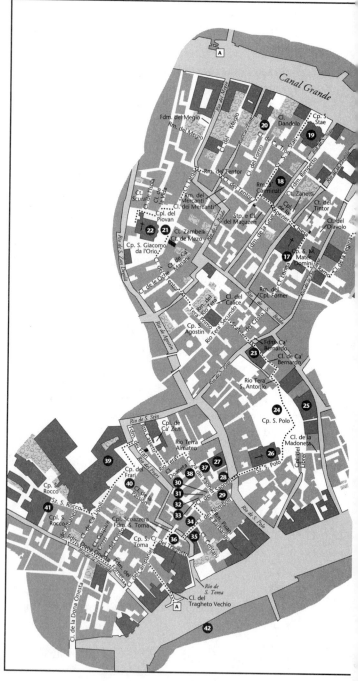

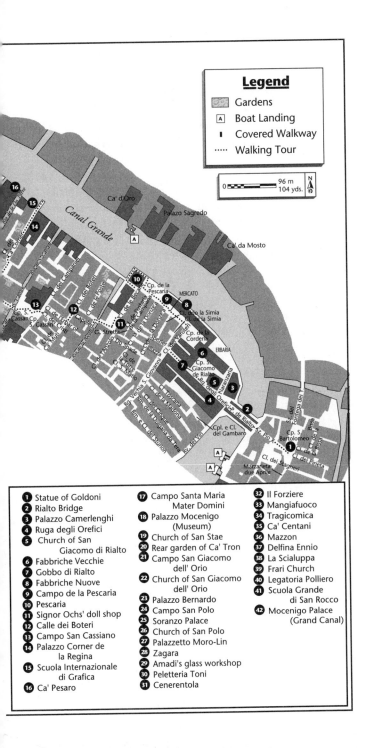

Legend

- 🟦 Gardens
- Ⓐ Boat Landing
- ▮ Covered Walkway
- ⋯⋯ Walking Tour

0 ____ 96 m
   ____ 104 yds.

N

Canal Grande

Ca' d'Oro
Palazo Sagredo
Ca' da Mosto

MERCATO
Cp. de la Pescaria
Cl. de la Simia
Cp. de la Corderia
ERBARIA
Cp. S. Giacomo de Rialto
Ruga degli Orefici/Cp. de Rialto
Cpl. e Cl. del Gambaro
Cp. S. Bartolomeo
Marzarieta dus Aprile

1 Statue of Goldoni
2 Rialto Bridge
3 Palazzo Camerlenghi
4 Ruga degli Orefici
5 Church of San Giacomo di Rialto
6 Fabbriche Vecchie
7 Gobbo di Rialto
8 Fabbriche Nuove
9 Campo de la Pescaria
10 Pescaria
11 Signor Ochs' doll shop
12 Calle dei Boteri
13 Campo San Cassiano
14 Palazzo Corner de la Regina
15 Scuola Internazionale di Grafica
16 Ca' Pesaro

17 Campo Santa Maria Mater Domini
18 Palazzo Mocenigo (Museum)
19 Church of San Stae
20 Rear garden of Ca' Tron
21 Campo San Giacomo dell' Orio
22 Church of San Giacomo dell' Orio
23 Palazzo Bernardo
24 Campo San Polo
25 Soranzo Palace
26 Church of San Polo
27 Palazzetto Moro-Lin
28 Zagara
29 Amadi's glass workshop
30 Peletteria Toni
31 Cenerentola

32 Il Forziere
33 Mangiafuoco
34 Tragicomica
35 Ca' Centani
36 Mazzon
37 Delfina Ennio
38 La Scialuppa
39 Frari Church
40 Legatoria Polliero
41 Scuola Grande di San Rocco
42 Mocenigo Palace (Grand Canal)

stalls. For centuries, this was the heart of the Rialto market area. On the right side of the campo is the:

5. **Church of San Giacomo di Rialto,** perhaps the oldest parish in Venice. According to tradition, Venice was founded in 421 A.D., and this church was consecrated in the same year. The present building goes back to the 11th century and was partially rebuilt in 1531 and 1601. The Renaissance campanile, homey lean-to front portico, and 18th-century twenty-four-hour clock (especially useful for the market neighborhood) are the most memorable features of this small landmark's facade. Unfortunately, when the clock is not broken, it is notorious for being inaccurate. Because of its many long-term breakdowns, paintings and engravings of the church can often be dated by noting the position of the clock's hands. On the apse, an old inscription warns: "Around this temple, let the merchant's law be just, his weights true, and his promises faithful."

With the church on your right, the building directly facing you behind the stalls of the campo, is:

6. **the Fabbriche Vecchie,** a unified complex of shops and offices built about 1525 after the great fire of 1514 destroyed the heart of the Rialto market area. (Only the church was spared.) The enclave of arcaded buildings around this campo housed the Banco de Giro, a transfer bank, and an early form of stock exchange. It was here that many of the mechanics and procedures of capitalism first developed. The buidings on the left side of the Ruga degli Orefici also form part of the Fabbriche Vecchie complex.

On the side of the campo opposite the church, look for:

7. **the Gobbo di Rialto,** a crouched stone figure holding up a platform from which proclamations of the Republic were read. (Check out the little flight of steps leading up to the platform.) The Gobbo, or "hunchback" (so called because of his crouching position), was also the terminus of a gamut that convicted wrongdoers were forced to run from the Piazza, stark naked, while onlookers heaped physical and verbal abuse on them.

Continue up Ruga degli Orefici to its end. Before turning right, into the market, we'll take a quick detour to the left, onto Ruga Vecchia San Giovanni. Take the second right on Ruga Vecchia, which leads under a sotoportego, continue straight, and at the first intersection, you'll come to:

☕ Take a Break   **Cantina Do Mori,** dating from 1462, and perhaps the best and most atmospheric of the city's traditional wine bars. At any hour of the day, a quick stop "in the shade" for a glass of wine is an old Venetian custom. Managed by a wine expert, Do Mori also serves the most delicious *cicchetti,* or snacks, in town, ranging from shelled crab claws served with a drop of herbed olive oil to little plates of deep fried vegetables, meatballs, and open faced, creamy *baccala* (codfish paste) sandwiches. When you pay your tab, they add up your little cicchetti plates, which are about $1.50 to $2 a throw. Everyone stands, and the crowd now includes professionals and tourists, but Do Mori still keeps hours attuned to the comings and goings of the porters and market workers who were once its main customers—8:30am to 1:30pm, and 5 to 8:30pm. It's closed Sundays and Wednesday afternoons. Another venerable wine bar, **Do Spade,** perhaps not quite as picturesque (but with tables), can be found by continuing up Calle Do Mori and jogging slightly to the left onto Calle Do Spade.

From Do Mori, retrace your steps. Turn left onto Ruga Vecchia San Giovanni, and continue the short distance until the Ruga forks into two narrower calles. There are a number of cheese shops at this intersection. Bear to the right, which leads into the Campo de la Corderia, once the important rope market of this sea-faring city, and now often filled with stalls from the busy Erberia, the fresh vegetable market. The long complex of market buildings at the far end of the campo is:

8. **the Fabbriche Nuove** (c. 1545), another market and office edifice designed by Sansovino, the architect who planned many of the public buildings around the Piazza San Marco.

At the end of the square, bear to the left into the Casaria or cheese market, and follow the flow of the vegetable market as it leads to:

9. **the Campo de la Pescaria,** or Campo of the Fish Market, one side of which is open to the Grand Canal. In the

stalls of the fish dealers, you'll see all kinds of squirming creatures of the deep, many of which are hard to imagine as edible, but this is the stuff of *real* Venetian cuisine. This campo also offers the opportunity to take in some classic views of palaces on the canal. If you're here during market hours, insinuate yourself behind the stalls and walk along the canalside quay. To the left, across the Grand Canal, you'll see the delicate white facade of the Ca' d'Oro; directly across the canal is Palazzo Sagredo, with its classic gothic facade; far to the right, the second house beyond the wide rio is Ca' da Mosto, one of the oldest houses on the canal, with narrow, Veneto-Byzantine arches.

Continuing across the campo, the red two-story building ahead, with an open, arcaded second floor loggia, is:

10. **the Pescaria,** or Fish Market. Although this building looks invitingly medieval, it was built in 1907, and replaced an iron-and-glass structure built in 1881 that just didn't seem right for Venice. The Pescaria exhibits an interesting hodge-podge of traditional Venetian motifs that purists love to hate, but it has become a major landmark on the Grand Canal. Check out the capitals above the ground-floor columns, which were fancifully designed in the form of fishermen's baskets and various sea creatures. Behind the Pescaria, the fish market continues under a truly majestic, open walled, covered structure that gets thoroughly hosed down as soon as the market closes each day, around 1pm. Alongside this rear portion of the fish market is the Calle delle Beccarie (Butchers) which leads to the Campo delle Beccarie. On the left side of the campo is:

11. **the antique doll shop of Signor Ochs** (no. 370A), its delicacy perhaps somewhat out of place at the edge of the fish market. Sig. Ochs has been restoring and selling antique dolls for over two decades; his wife designs and sews their costumes. At the far end of the campo, more in keeping with the spirit of the neighborhood, you'll see:

☕ **Take a Break** **Vino Da Pinto,** a very authentic market cantina filled with barrels of wine. You can shelter inside, or order a glass of wine and an open face *baccala* sandwich through the usually open window.

As you face Vino Da Pinto, exit the campo via the bridge immediately to the right. As soon as you cross the bridge, turn immediately left, under the sotoportego, and then right onto the narrow Calle Capeler. After another sotoportego, you'll exit this calle into a totally different environment:

12. **Calle dei Boteri** (Barrelmakers), a long, wide, courtyard-like street. The view to the left as you emerge from Calle Capeler is especially attractive, with window gardens and flower boxes on many of the buildings. The ground floor workshops on this street are medieval; some have become boutiques that sell stylish graphics or contemporary crafts. To the right, toward the Grand Canal, is one of the few Chinese restaurants in town, a good thing to know if you tire of standard Venetian fare.

From Calle dei Boteri, enter the narrow Calle dei Cristi. The calle ends at:

13. **Campo San Cassiano,** site of the world's first public opera house, which opened in 1637 (as far as Venice is concerned, Milan's La Scala is a recent upstart). The opera houses of Venice were enormously active, and the prolific Claudio Monteverdi (1567–1643), *maestro di capella* of San Marco, supplied the earliest companies with numerous works. The bleak wall of the Church of San Cassiano dominates the right side of the campo; a tiny almost Dickensian building at the far end of the campo (perched all alone at the edge of the canal) houses Ex Libris, a tightly packed shop selling interesting prints, stationery, posters, and graphics.

Exit the campo via the bridge to the left of Ex Libris, which leads to a sotoportego. At the end of the sotoportego, turn left onto the narrow Calle de la Regina. As medieval passageway widens you'll notice gardens behind many walls, and workshops for printers and graphic artists. The large building on the right at the end is:

14. **Palazzo Corner de la Regina,** now housing the archives of the Venice Biennale Exhibitions of Contemporary Art, which began in 1895. There are numerous palaces of the Corner family throughout the city; this one was built in 1725 on the site of the house of Caterina Cornaro (1454–1510), who, at the age of 14, was married to the king of

Cyprus. After his death and a series of royal plots and murders, Caterina became Queen of Cyprus, and after more intrigues, Cyprus, as the realm of a queen whose origins were Venetian, was added to Venice's empire. This represented the greatest geographical extent of Venetian power.

Across the calle, in a more modest, unrestored palazzo, is the:

15. **Scuola Internazionale di Grafica,** a school of graphic design with artists and students from all over the world; visitors are permitted to look in at its workshops. The building itself, unrenovated and often filled with activity, is interesting. At the end of the calle, a long, narrow wooden pier extends into the Grand Canal and offers an unusual chance for interesting views and photo opportunities. Steady yourself against a gondola post for balance if you decide to venture out and take pictures! As you stand on the pier and look back towards the Palazzo Corner de la Regina, the very massive palazzo three buildings to the right is:

16. **Ca' Pesaro,** Baldassare Longhena's largest and most elaborate baroque palazzo, which was begun in 1659. By 1682, when Longhena died, construction had reached the second story. From the vantage point of the pier (again, hold onto a post for balance!) you can see a row of carved grotesque masks just above the high water line on the side and front facades that you'd easily miss from a passing vaporetto. Ca' Pesaro now houses the Museum of Modern Art (heavily concentrating on Italian artists) as well as a Museum of Oriental Art that centers on a collection given to Venice by the Austrian goverment after World War I in reparation for bombing attacks against the city.

Retrace your steps up the Calle de la Regina, and pass the sotoportego on the left from which we initially turned onto this street. After passing the sotoportego, take the first right onto Ramo Santa Maria Mater Domini, leading to a small bridge (with lovely prospects each way as you cross the canal) that brings you into:

17. **Campo Santa Maria Mater Domini,** a small gem of a campo, surrounded by a mixture of interesting smaller 13th-century houses and gothic palazzettos that invites you to

take a table at the cafe/bar at the far right corner, order a coffee and a *tramezzino,* and just enjoy the ambience of this comfortable enclave. There's a fine well head at the center of the square. On the left side of the campo, you'll notice an ironsmith's shop, its doorway sunk below the level of the pavement. The renovated house at the far end of the campo (no. 2123) displays a row of gothic windows on its second floor, and arched Renaissance windows above that.

Exit the campo on the calle to the right of this house. A bit off the campo you'll pass the Renaissance facade of the Church of Santa Maria Mater Domini, freshly restored and open to the public from 9am to noon daily. The second altar on the right has a beautiful painting by Vincenzo Catena of Sta. Cristina of Bolsena (1520). In the left transept you'll find Tintoretto's *Invention of the True Cross.* At the corner of the church, turn left onto Calle de la Chiesa, which brings you to Ponte del Cristi (with picturesque views as you cross the canal). The first buiding to the right after the bridge is a narrow gabled house charmingly adorned with random pieces of Byzantine stonework. Continue straight, down the Campiello de le Spezier (Spice Merchants); as you cross the bridge at the far right corner of the campiello, notice the little bridge not far to the left, probably built so that the household on the far side of the canal could easily visit the family just across the way. Continue straight until the end of the calle, then turn right onto Salizada San Stae. On the right as you proceed down the salizada, is the large 17th-century:

18. **Palazzo Mocenigo,** which contains much of its lavish late-18th-century decor and furnishings and frescoes by Guarana. The palazzo also houses the scholarly Museum of Costumes and Textiles, with collections of Coptic textiles and European fabrics from the 14th to 19th centuries as well as 18th- and 19th-century costumes (open Tuesday and Thursday from 8:30am to 1:30pm; ring the bell for admission). The museum offers a wonderful opportunity to explore this undervisited palace. The salizada leads to the Grand Canal and the:

19. **Church of San Stae** (Eustace), with a baroque facade added in 1710. As you face the church, look to the left,

where you'll find the charming 17th-century Scuola dei Battioro and Tiraoro (Goldsmiths and Spinners of Gold Wire), which often houses small history or art exhibits. The brilliant white *marmorino* (pulverized marble) surfaces of the lavish interior of San Stae were restored in 1978 by the Swiss Pro Venezia Foundation. This was the parish church of Antonio Foscarini, and in the first chapel on the left, there's a bust of Foscarini with an inscription that notes he was wrongly executed for treason by the Council of Ten in 1621. San Stae is sometimes used for exhibitions in the

Foscarini and the Countess of Arundel

Antonio Foscarini was Venetian ambassador to England in the early 17th century, but was recalled for developing too many friendships among the English and, following his return to Venice, was imprisoned on suspicion of treason for three years. Upon his release, Foscarini became involved with the English Countess of Arundel, who had taken up residence in the Palazzo Mocenigo Nero on the Grand Canal—part of a quadruple palace (here Lord Byron would encamp two centuries later). Foscarini's visits to Lady Arundel, whose husband was a powerful member of the Court of St. James, were denounced to the Council of Ten, which quickly arrested and secretly tried him for treason. Within hours of his arrest, he was convicted and strangled to death; the next morning, his body was displayed in the Piazzetta beside the Doge's Palace. The English ambassador warned the countess, who was at her villa on the Brenta, not to return to Venice. She immediately stormed into the city, demanded an audience with the doge, and was the first woman to be granted such an interview. Her courage as well as her testimony convinced the government that Foscarini's visits had been of a romantic nature, and that he had died protecting her reputation. The Council of Ten exonerated Foscarini, gave him a state funeral, and executed his accusers. A broad pedestrian thoroughfare, built in the late 19th century alongside the Accademia (in the heart of what was then the British expatriate colony), is named for Foscarini.

summer; its opening hours at other times are often limited to 10am to 1pm.

Exit the church and begin to retrace your steps up Salizada San Stae; however, take the first right onto Calle de Ca' Tron. At the end of this calle, peek into:

20. **the rear garden of Ca' Tron,** a romantic oasis belonging to a gothic palazzo that faces the Grand Canal. The owners of this house are also fortunate to overlook another rare garden on the Grand Canal.

Returning from the end of Calle de Ca' Tron, make a right onto Calle del Forno, and follow this street to the end, which frames a tile-roofed two-story house with a marvelously off-kilter doorway and flower boxes beneath the arched second-floor windows. At this point, turn right onto Calle dei Tentor (Dyer), which is home to a number of interesting shops (at no. 1811, a young craftsperson displays humourous soft sculptures). Continue along this street, cross the bridge, with wonderful views, especially to the right, and take a left at the end of the street followed by the first left. Suddenly, tucked into the space before the next bridge, you'll find a great mini-neighborhood. Here, and at the next campo we'll be coming to are a number of inexpensive restaurant choices you should know about for your stay in Venice. On the left, just before the bridge is:

Take a Break **La Zucca** (at no. 1762), originally a vegetarian restaurant owned and run by women. The menu is somewhat broader now, but still includes inventive dishes like pasta in pumpkin sauce. The moderately priced restaurant is popular with the thirty-something-and-under crowd; closed Mondays. Just across the bridge and to the left on Calle Larga is **Trattoria al Ponte,** at no. 1666, a family-run restaurant specializing in traditional Venetian cooking where a bowl of pasta fazoli or sopa de tripe costs under $7.

Continue on Calle Larga, which leads to the large, irregularly-shaped, tree-shaded:

21. **Campo San Giacomo dell' Orio,** a family-oriented campo with a number of pleasant surprises. The ancient Church of San Giacomo dell' Orio is just to the right (the

name of the church may be derived from a laurel tree that stood here in remote times). The triple apse of the church faces the campo; to get to the front of the church turn right onto Campiello del Piovan, which flanks the church (notice the roof-garden grapevine trellis on the first building on the right). Farther along, on the right, you'll come to a street-side portego in front of some shops that have the air of a provincial town in the l920s. On the right, just before the porticoed shops, there is a covered alleyway that leads to the Corte Scura (Dark Courtyard), which exits through another sotoportego to a canal. Retrace your steps to Campiello del Piovan, and follow it around to the front of the church, which faces a charming, shelterd canalside campiello. (In good weather, the trattoria/pizzeria by the canal sets out tables here.)

At last you'll be facing the rather undramatic entrance to the:

22. **Church of San Giacomo dell' Orio,** founded in the 9th century. The present building and its campiello were rebuilt in 1225. The interior of the church displays many restorations and new elements added over the centuries; it is an intricate Chinese box of differing styles, ornaments, and use of space. The beautifully carved ship's-keel ceiling is from the 14th century and may have been designed to help distribute the weight of the church over its marshy foundations. There is an altarpiece by Lorenzo Lotto of *The Madonna and Four Saints* (1546). On either side of the Veronese at the altar of the left transept, are Palma Giovane's *Scenes From the Life of St. Lawrence.* The great column of rare *verde antico* in the right transept was probably among the loot brought to Venice after the sack of Constantinople in 1204.

Exit the church, and retrace your steps back around to the main campo. A number of the houses facing the campo contain sotoportegos that lead down passageways to the canal at the rear of these buildings. You might want to follow one of these sotoportegos, just to see how the neighborhood is structured.

Exit Campo San Giacomo dell' Orio on Calle del Tintor, which is in a straight line opposite the calle from which we entered the campo. As you proceed down Calle del Tintor, on the right side, at 1552, you will pass:

☕ Take a Break **Al Ocche,** a pizzeria that serves over fifty varieties, and acknowledged by many as the best in Venice. Open Tuesday through Sunday from noon to 3pm and from 7 to 11pm, it's popular with students and often mobbed by 8pm. It's closed on Mondays.

The next part of this walk, well away from the tourist zone around San Marco, is designed to pass many artisans' workshops and unusual little stores. The final part of the walk will bring you to the imposing Frari Church, and the Scuola Grande de San Rocco, both major sites that deserve a lengthy visit. With this in mind, you'll have to decide how best to allot your time.

Cross the Ponte del Parucheta and continue straight down the narrow Rio Terra Primo. We've now left the Sestiere of Santa Croce and entered the Sestiere of San Polo. As you look ahead, you'll see that the view at the end of the street frames two very fine second-story gothic windows. Venetians tended to align large windows with the end of a street, not only for the view but for the wind-tunnel ventilation that narrow calles sometimes create in summer.

At the end of Rio Terra Primo, turn left onto Rio Terra Segundo. Take the second right onto Calle de Scaleter. At 2204, you'll pass **Dalla Venezia,** a workshop that restores and sells antique furniture. Examples of turned wood, wooden tops, and wooden eggs are also sold here. Just over the bridge at the end of this narrow calle, is:

23. Palazzo Bernardo (c. 1442), an interesting example of an intricately ornamented palace on an interior waterway. The four stories of gothic windows, including the top floor, are unusual.

Take the narrow calle just to the left of Palazzo Bernardo. At the end, bear to the right and then to the left onto Rio Terra San Antonio. Suddenly, you'll find yourself at the entrance to:

24. Campo San Polo, one of the most spacious campos in the city. After the sequence of narrow streets we've trod, San

Polo almost seems like a ballroom, and indeed, for almost three hundred years, from the 16th to the 19th centuries, this campo was used for balls and banquets during Carnival as well as outdoor theatrical performances and bull running. In earlier centuries, Campo San Polo hosted a market; its open space was also used for cross-bow practice. At times, the lively nature of San Polo turned more serious. The campo was also used for religious revival events that periodically took place in the city; in the late 1400s, San Bernadino of Sienna staged a bonfire of vanities here during one of his evangelizing crusades into Venice. With the recent revival of Carnival, Campo San Polo has again become a center for festivities at that time of year; in summer, it is used as an outdoor locale for screening films during the annual Venice Film Festival.

Until the mid 1700s, the palaces that line the left side of the campo faced Rio San Antonio, a narrow canal that has since been filled in. Each palazzo's entrance would have had its own bridge over the canal to the campo. The most eye-catching palace on the campo is:

25. **the double Soranzo Palace** (c. 1500), a red building with its second and third floors faced with delicate white Byzantine-gothic windows (on the left side as we entered the campo, at nos. 2169 and 2170). According to tradition, the exterior walls of this palace were once decorated with frescoes by Giorgione, but no trace of this artwork survives, and many believe that the tradition stems from exaggerated tales of the Soranzo family's great wealth. A more bonafide tradition attached to the palazzo concerns Casanova, who, as a young man first came here as a hired violinist; the owner of the house, a senator, was so impressed with him that he adopted Casanova as his son. With this stroke of luck, Casanova gained access to the world of Venice's patrician class; from there, he went on to seduce and outrage the decadent and dying world of 18th-century aristocracy throughout Europe.

At the far end of the campo, notice the pharmacy, with its elaborate 19th-century interior. To the right is the:

26. **Church of San Polo,** founded in the 9th century and renovated many times. The apse of the church faces the campo. To get to the entrance (which is on the side of

the church), turn right after the apse. Inside, to the left of the entrance, there's a passionate *Last Supper* by Tintoretto in which Jesus seems almost frenzied; in the Oratory of the Crucifix, entered under the organ, there is a cycle of paintings of the *Stations of the Cross*, by Giandomenico Tiepolo.

Turn right after exiting the church. At the base of the free-standing 12th-century campanile, note the carved lions playfully devouring a monstrous snake and a human head. Continue down the Salizada San Polo; just as you cross the bridge, look across the canal to the second house on the right:

27. **Palazzetto Moro-Lin,** with its delicately carved second-floor balcony on the side that protrudes slightly into the canal. The assortment of gothic windows and the balconied windows of the *piano nobile*, all contribute to an elegant 15th-century facade.

At the far side of the bridge is the busy Calle dei Saoneri (Soap Dealers), with lots of interesting shops. Before window shopping, look back across the bridge to the right, where you'll notice an unusual house with a second-floor glass conservatory, and beyond, a walled garden. Just over the Ponte Saoneri, on the right, is:

28. **Zagara,** at no. 2740, which often carries an interesting selection of jewelry and contemporary glass. Farther down, on the left side of the street, is:

29. the tiny glass workshop of **Amadi,** at no. 2747. Here you'll find an extraordinary craftsman creating his glass menagerie of sardines, dragonflies, spiders, and other delights, each with a wit and delicacy unrivaled anywhere else in Venice. On the right side of the calle, look for:

30. **Peletteria Toni,** at 2722, a highly regarded little leather workshop where Antonio Passudetti does custom calfskin bags. The leather, from tanneries in the Brenta, is beautiful, and the prices are very fair. Some items may be in stock, but generally orders can take three or more weeks; Toni, of course, will ship your order. Next door is:

31. **Cenerentola** (Cinderella), at 2721, a tiny shop that was the dream of its owner, who worked as a switchboard operator for twenty years before finally making it a reality.

The place is packed with antique lace clothing and table-cloths as well as pieces of lace that have been reinvented into decorative objects or incorporated into contemporary clothing. One door down is:

32. **Il Forziere** at 2720, selling custom-designed sequinned evening wear and accessories, sometimes totally brash and new, sometimes created from older pieces of sequin-sewn fabrics. On the same side of the street, on the corner, you'll enjoy looking into:

33. **Mangiafuoco,** at 2718, where two young craftspeople make marionettes of all sizes and complexities, as well as finger puppets, and traditional jacks-in-the-box.

     At the end of Calle dei Saoneri, turn left, and then take the first right onto Calle dei Nomboli. On the right, you'll come to:

34. **Tragicomica,** at 2800, one of the most inventive mask shops in town. Among this shop's most interesting creations is a mask in the form of the *Boca de Leon*, the lion's head mail slot into which secret denunciations to the Council of Ten were dropped back in the days of the Republic. The shop also specializes in excellent traditional masks.

     Just across the street is the entrance to:

35. the 15th-century **Ca' Centani,** home of Carlo Goldoni, Venice's beloved playwright, whose statue we saw at the beginning of this walk. Goldoni was born here in 1707, and lived in this house most of his life. Now a museum of Venetian theater, the house is a beautiful example of a small gothic palazzo. The courtyard contains a fine well-head ornamented with lions' heads and a traditional outdoor staircase with a lion's-head banister. Before climbing the staircase, check the large ground floor *androne*, or water-entrance lobby, which served as a warehouse and loading dock for cargo that arrived by canal. Like the great palaces on the Grand Canal, this building was designed to house both the family business and family home. In the ceiling of the *androne* there is a trap door and a rope for communicating with the main reception room in the living quarters just above. Upstairs, you can get a sense of what the home of a comfortable merchant-class family was like. The views

from the windows offer a new perspective on these labyrinthine neighborhoods we've been exploring. Ca' Centani is open Monday to Saturday from 8:30am to 1:30pm.

Exit the Goldoni house and turn left onto Calle dei Nomboli. Once you've crossed the little bridge at the end of this calle, turn back for a view across the canal (to the right) of the gothic canalside facade of Goldoni's home. A few steps farther and you'll enter Campiello San Toma, dominated by the Church of San Toma, currently under reconstruction. On the left, as you enter the campiello, is:

36. **Mazzon,** at 2807, where you can see a master leatherworker and his assistants creating designer handbags. Delivery time on an order here can be as long as two or three months, but both Venetians and tourists in-the-know have come to value the high quality of Mazzon's workmanship. Prices are not cheap, but they are bargains.

Retrace your steps the short distance back into Calle Saoneri; take the first left, halfway down the calle, onto Calle 2a dei Saoneri (the Second Calle dei Saoneri). On the right side of this little street, you'll come to:

37. **Delfina Ennio,** at 2672, a woodcarving and furniture workshop where you can find or order an ornate hand carved mirror frame, a small, beautifully detailed console shelf for an entryway (you may just manage to carry one onto your flight), or a magnificent hand-carved lion's head, sea shell, or mask in the $160 range that would make a striking architectural detail. Although this work is traditionally painted or gilded, when left unpainted, these pieces fit in nicely with contemporary decor. On the other side of the street, you'll see the shop of another traditional Venetian craftsman:

38. **La Scialuppa,** at 2681, where Gilberto Penzo makes collector models of Venetian vessels and sells kits from which simpler models can be built.

At the end of this calle, turn left onto the wider Rio Terra Almateo; just after no. 2585, take a right onto the narrow Calle Tagiapiera, which leads to the hidden Campiello de Ca' Zen. Exit this campiello via the sotoportego on the left side. You will emerge from this passageway facing the massive gothic brick facade of the:

39. **Church of Santa Maria Gloriosa dei Frari** (completed in 1469), better known as the Frari. Built by the Franciscans, the Frari is the largest place of worship in Venice, slightly outsizing its Dominican rival on the opposite side of the city, the Church of SS. Giovanni e Paolo. The stark, powerful mass of the facade is ornamented by brickwork patterning on the cornice, and a graceful curved crowning touched by three gothic pinnacles. Entrance to the church is normally from its side door. Inside, the Frari is a masterpiece of gothic architecture. The center of the interior is dominated by the astounding monks' choir, its three-tiered wooden stalls carved by Marco Cozzi; the choir screen (c. 1475), with marble figures of saints and prophets in relief, was made by Pietro Lombardo in the workshop of Bartolomeo Bon. (Lombardo's tomb, carved by his son, Tullio, is also in the Frari.) This is the only choir in Venice that still occupies its original site in the nave.

In the central apse, framed by the arch of the high altar, is the Frari's most famous treasure, Titian's *Assumption*, in which the Virgin seems to ascend toward the heights of the apse, surrounded by soaring gothic tracery windows that flood the space with light. Painted in 1516–1518, this revolutionary altarpiece, filled with movement and drama, was Titian's first major public commission in Venice; it sent his reputation soaring. Another Titian masterpiece, *The Madonna of the Ca' Pesaro*, is midway down the left side of the interior of the church, as you face the central apse, and was completed eight years after his *Assumption*.

To the far right of the main altar, at the end of the right transept, is the sacristy; above the Pesaro altar in the sacristy is a radiant triptych by Giovanni Bellini, *The Madonna and Child with SS. Nicholas of Bari, Peter, Mark, and Benedict* (1488), all the more wondrous in its original site and frame. The first chapel to the right of the main altar contains a painted wooden sculpture of St. John the Baptist by the Florentine sculptor, Donatello. In the third chapel of the left transept is a rich, traditional altarpiece by Alvise Vivarini. A plaque in the floor marks the burial place of Monteverdi.

In addition to the tombs and monuments to numerous doges and patricians, partway down the left side of the church is the Mausoleum of Antonio Canova, the sculptor, who died in 1822, and whose heart is buried here. Across the church from Canova's monument, is the Mausoleum of Titian, erected 300 years after the artist's death, according to a design by Canova. (Titian had planned his masterwork *Pieta*, now in the Accademia, to hang above his tomb.) It is not certain that Titian is actually buried here—he died past the age of 90 during an outbreak of plague, and plague victims would not normally have been buried inside the Frari. It is believed an exception was made for Titian.

A variety of guidebooks to the Frari are available on the premises. Alongside the church, the vast Franciscan monastery is now the State Archives of the Republic, with records going back to the 9th century. The Frari is open Monday to Saturday from 9:30 to noon, and 2:30 to 5pm; Sundays from 2 to 5pm. There is an admission fee of 1,000 lire (about 70¢).

Titian

Tiziano Vecellio, known as Titian, was born about 1485 in the town of Preve di Cadere, and came to Venice while still an adolescent to study in the workshop of Giovanni Bellini. With his fellow apprentice, Giorgione, Titian went on to be commissioned to fresco the exterior of the Fondaco dei Tedeschi (only fragments of this work remain); after Giorgione's death in 1510, Titian became the foremost painter of the Venetian Renaissance. A cosmopolitan man of the world who socialized with leading academics, writers, and aristocrats, Titian included not only Venetian churches and patricians among his patrons but also kings, popes, and emperors. His portraits were prized for their technical mastery and psychological perception; among his subjects were Pope Paul III, Philip II of Spain, and Francis I of France. Much of his work is in museums and collections outside Italy, especially in Vienna and at the Prado in Madrid. Titian worked until the very end of his life; he was at least 90 years old or more when he died in 1576.

Exit the Frari and turn right, into the campo that runs along the side of the church. In a row of shops facing the gothic apses of the Frari's chapels is:

40. **Legatoria Polliero,** at 2995, a venerable bookbindery and Venetian institution famous for its marbleized paper. This is the place to come for blank notebooks and sketchbooks; the quality of Polliero's paper is especially good for artwork.

At the end of the campo, turn right onto Salizada San Rocco, which runs behind the Frari, and leads to Campo San Rocco. At the beginning of the campo, on the left, at No. 3047, is **Baldan,** famous for fine quality shoes made in factories in the Brenta. At the end of the campo is the Church of San Rocco, and on the left:

41. **the Scuola Grande di San Rocco,** completed in 1560 as the headquarters of a confraternity committed to helping victims of plague.

The Scuola Grande di San Rocco houses a visionary cycle of more than fifty paintings by Tintoretto, created over a 23-year period, that has been ranked with Michelangelo's Sistine Chapel as one of the most precious buildings in Europe. In 1564, this important confraternity held a competition among four artists to decide who would paint the inaugural picture, *The Glorification of St. Roch* (San Rocco), for the as-yet-undecorated interior of its new building. Instead of submitting a sketch, Tintoretto completed the painting and secretly had it installed behind a curtain in the spot where the proposed painting was to hang. When asked by the judges to show his sketches, he unveiled the painting and offered it as a gift to the confraternity. To the outrage of the other artists, the judges accepted Tintoretto's dramatic gesture; over the years they commissioned another 54 paintings to fill almost every square inch of wall space in the building. The Scuola Grande di San Rocco is so spectacular that it demands a lengthy return visit. After getting an initial feel for the sweep of what Tintoretto has achieved inside this building, center your attention on five paintings in the Sala dell' Albergo, a small room on the upper floor dominated by the monumental *Crucifixion* (1565), a tumultuous, all encompassing image of the event (the masterpiece of the entire cycle), which Ruskin described as "beyond all analysis and above all praise." In the center of the ceiling of the Sala dell' Albergo is the first painting Tintoretto completed for the Scuola, the prize-winning *Glorification of St. Roch;* the Sala dell' Albergo also contains the serenely powerful *Christ Before Pilate,* as well as *The Way to Calvary* and *Christ Crowned With Thorns.* In the Great Hall that adjoins the Sala dell' Albergo, the ceiling paintings depict scenes from the Old Testament, while those on the walls show scenes from the New Testament. Again, a supplementary guidebook or pamphlet to the Scuola Grande di San Rocco is highly recommended. The Scuola is open Monday to Saturday from 10am to 5pm and on Sundays from 2 to 5pm. Off-season weekday hours may be limited to 10am to 1pm; hours are sometimes slightly longer in summer.

Tintoretto

Jacopo Robusti (1518–1594) known as Tintoretto, came from an humble background (his father was a dyer); unlike Titian, Tintoretto was an unworldly man, who traveled beyond Venice only once, in the company of his wife and family, to deliver a painting. Devout, totally absorbed in the painting of religious subjects, Tintoretto rebelled against traditional representations of religious scenes and recreated them from new perspectives, working at a furious pace with fluid brushstrokes. His canvasses are filled with phantasmagoric light and intense, mystical spirituality. Tintoretto's principal assistants and companions were his two sons and his daughter, Marietta Robusti, a skilled portraitist whose work can possibly be detected in a few of her father's paintings. Only sparsely represented in museums and collections outside of Venice, Tintoretto's paintings are seen in churches and scuole throughout his home city. In addition to the Scuola Grande di San Rocco, Tintoretto filled the walls of his parish church, the Madonna dell' Orto, with his dynamic, visionary canvasses.

Exit from the Scuola Grande di San Rocco and turn right onto the Campo San Rocco. Turn right onto the narrow Calle dei Albanesi (the third right after exiting the scuola). The calle ends with a sotoportego; turn left onto the Fondamenta de la Donna Onesta (Quay of the Honest Woman), a delightful canalside walkway that changes its name to Fondamenta dei Forner as it slightly widens. Continue straight to the end of the Fondamenta, then turn left onto Calle del Campaniel. From this street, take the second right onto Calle de Tragetto Vecchio, which ends on the Grand Canal at the San Toma Actv stop. From here, you can pick up a vaporetto in either direction. While you are waiting at the Actv stop, look directly across the canal to:

42. the quadruple **Mocenigo Palace,** with its central double palace, and slightly taller palaces on either side. The leftmost section, with the white stone facade, was the residence of the English Countess of Arundel, lover of Antonio Foscarini (see box on page 110). Two centuries later, the central part of this palace was rented by Lord Byron, whose tumultuous stay there is described at Stop 16 of Walk 4.

THE ACCADEMIA

Start: The Accademia.

Finish: The Accademia.

Time: Variable, depending on your interests.

Best Time: Summer afternoons are generally less crowded.

Worst Time: Summer mornings when there are often lines waiting to get in.

The Accademia Galleries display works almost exclusively by Venetian artists. That limitation does not consign it to second-class status—the city that produced Bellini, Titian, Tintoretto, and Tiepolo doesn't need to look elsewhere. The Accademia is one of the world's great art galleries. Venice was built by commerce and cunning, but it was also built of art and illusion, and a tour of the Accademia is a unique walk through the history of Venetian civilization.

Note: The Accademia Galleries are generally open Monday through Saturday from 9am to 2pm, and on Sunday from 9am to 1pm. From July through September, visiting hours are usually extended to 6pm Monday through Saturday. Because of fire regulations, only 180 visitors are allowed inside the building at any given time. In the summer, if the hours are extended, you rarely have to wait in the afternoon. In the winter getting in is less of a problem, but it's a good idea to be there around 9am or a little before, and do dress warmly; it's hard to enjoy art when you're shivering. Photography is not allowed inside the gallery.

The rooms of the museum form a rough circle: at the end of the tour, you'll end up more or less where you began. The rooms are theoretically numbered, but they are not well labeled. Where the number exists, it is usually above the door, behind you as you enter the room. The number of each room ("Sala") is included, since at least the guards should know which is which. Some of the most wonderful things are in the last rooms on this tour. Plan your visit to allow plenty of time for them.

Cleaning, restorations, and simple lack of personnel seem to keep the Accademia in flux. You may need to adapt this tour creatively.

• • • • • • • • • • • • • • • •

Begin your tour in the small square, or campo, in front of the Accademia the:

1. **Campo della Carità**. Its name comes from the former church, monastery, and confraternity (or scuola) into which the Accademia was moved in the early 19th century. The large brick structure at the end of the Accademia Bridge used to be the church. The bell tower was more or less where the steps to the bridge are now. In the tradition of Venetian bell towers (like the Campanile of the Basilica of San Marco, which collapsed in 1902), it fell down of its own accord, in 1741.

The door just to the right of the church (labelled ACCADEMIA DI BELLE ARTI) leads to the art school. It was the original entrance to the confraternity, the Scuola Grande della Carità. Above the doorway is a statue of the Madonna and Child surmounted by the symbol of the confraternity, two concentric circles intertwining a cross. A bit lower down are the two patron saints of the Scuola, St. Christopher (on the right) and St. Leonard (on the left, dated 1377). St. Leonard is adored by two diminutive brothers of the Scuola with a whip dangling from each wrist; another whip decorates the inscription. The whip motif is tied to the confraternity's medieval origins, when members periodically

The Accademia

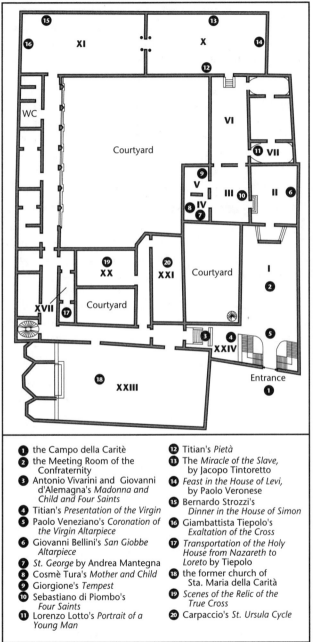

1. the Campo della Carità
2. the Meeting Room of the Confraternity
3. Antonio Vivarini and Giovanni d'Alemagna's *Madonna and Child and Four Saints*
4. Titian's *Presentation of the Virgin*
5. Paolo Veneziano's *Coronation of the Virgin Altarpiece*
6. Giovanni Bellini's *San Giobbe Altarpiece*
7. *St. George* by Andrea Mantegna
8. Cosmè Tura's *Mother and Child*
9. Giorgione's *Tempest*
10. Sebastiano di Piombo's *Four Saints*
11. Lorenzo Lotto's *Portrait of a Young Man*
12. Titian's *Pietà*
13. The *Miracle of the Slave,* by Jacopo Tintoretto
14. *Feast in the House of Levi,* by Paolo Veronese
15. Bernardo Strozzi's *Dinner in the House of Simon*
16. Giambattista Tiepolo's *Exaltation of the Cross*
17. *Transportation of the Holy House from Nazareth to Loreto* by Tiepolo
18. the former church of Sta. Maria della Carità
19. *Scenes of the Relic of the True Cross*
20. Carpaccio's *St. Ursula Cycle*

engaged in self-flagellation during public processions. In later centuries most of the members concentrated on less painful kinds of religious and charitable services.

Pass through the entrance to the museum (labeled "Gallerie") which is framed by giant columns, added in the 18th century. After you've bought your ticket and left your backpack or umbrella in the vestibule, go up the curving stairs. On your way up notice the statue of Charity, or Love, (1765, by Giovanni Morleiter), who lifts up a child with her left hand as she presses a flaming heart with the plump fingers of her right.

At the top of the stairs you will find the:

2. **Meeting Room of the Confraternity** (SALA I), which is splendid in a way very different from the stairs. It was built three centuries earlier, from 1461 to 1484, with a lavishly intricate late gothic ceiling alive with 515 angels. Unusually, the angels have eight wings apiece, perhaps because the head of the Scuola when the room was built was named Ulisse Aliotti—"eight wings" in Italian. On the walls you can see fragments of the painted frieze that once surrounded the room, bearing the Scuola's symbol, the encircled cross.

On your left as you emerge from the entrance turnstile, close to the stone balustrade of the stairway, is a door leading to the room built for the governing body of the Scuola. (The stairs were inserted later, so that now the second door to the room opens surrealistically in mid-air above the "down" staircase.) Go through the door into the boardroom (or "Albergo," SALA XXIV). It is now essentially a passageway; originally it was an enclosed room, with benches and an impressive altarpiece opposite the entrance. The altarpiece hasn't gone far. Go up to the stairs, and you'll see it on the wall facing the window.

3. **Antonio Vivarini and Giovanni d'Alemagna's** **Madonna and Child with Four Saints,** dated 1446, a wonderful devotional image, filled with solid and serious saints and such a quantity of objects that it seems almost airless (presumably the saints in heaven don't need to breathe). Its large size, extensive use of gold, and vast amount of detail speaks as much of the wealth as of the piety of the organization.

Behind you, above the entrance to the room, is one of the loveliest and most famous paintings in the Accademia:

4. **Titian's *Presentation of the Virgin*** (1534–38). The radiant girl in light blue is the Virgin Mary, who as a child was supposed to have been presented to the Temple in Jerusalem to be a handmaiden of the Lord until she married.

The painting was made for this very spot—the figures seem lit by the actual window and Titian even incorporated the door on the right into the composition by framing it with painted stones.

The lighting and color of the painting are as beautiful as they are natural. Most important is the believable humanity of every figure, from the seated old woman selling eggs to the child holding out a donut-like treat toward a playful white dog. Some of the faces are clearly intended as portraits, probably of members of the confraternity who sat in this very room. In the shadows above the door, one of the men dressed in the red robes of the Scuola's governing body gives charity to a woman holding an infant, thereby illustrating the confraternity's name.

Return to the large room with the angelic ceiling (SALA I), and stand in front of the painting that faces the turnstile and the stairs:

5. **Paolo Veneziano's *Coronation of the Virgin Altarpiece*** (around 1340), the first painting that greets visitors to the gallery, and rightly so, for it represents the beginning of a truly Venetian school of painting. Paolo Veneziano has brilliantly succeeded in creating something as splendid as the best of the Byzantine religious works that had previously dominated Venetian art. You'll rarely see anything more gorgeous in color and patterning than the robes of Jesus and Mary in the center, and the cloth behind them, held up by angels. You can also see a very Italian love of active humanity in such details as the two angels below, each playing a small organ and singing with open mouth. The frame, which is spectacular in its own right, is original.

The lower two tiers of scenes on either side illustrate the life of Christ and the upper register that of St. Francis. On the top right closest to the center, St. Francis receives the stigmata (Christ's wounds) in his hands, feet, and side.

Lateral figures and scenes almost always had a special relevance to the original location of the painting. In this case the altarpiece was made for a nunnery of the Franciscan order, the Little Sisters of the Poor (or Poor Clares) founded by St. Francis. In the middle scene on the top left, Francis gives to St. Chiara (or Clare) a striped habit, which she then wears as she enters a tiny church.

Most of the rest of the paintings in the first room are by artists of the later 14th and early 15th centuries. The figures they painted may be more believable than Paolo Veneziano's, but they still remain somewhat unreal in their late gothic style, and the saints are still surrounded by gold.

Go around the large painting by Lorenzo Veneziano at the end of the room and up the stairs to SALA II. Here the paintings are from the early Renaissance and clearly represent a revolution in painting.

The central painting on the right wall is:

6. **Giovanni Bellini's *San Giobbe Altarpiece*** of around 1487. Thanks to a recent cleaning (1994), we can see it in much of its original splendor. Bellini loves colors as much as Paolo Veneziano, but his are the real tints of three-dimensional bodies, lit by an apparently real light that glows off the mosaics in the vault overhead, and the pink-and-blue loincloth of the man on the left. Where Paolo Veneziano's altarpiece was like a jewel richly glowing and designed to be studied close up, Bellini's is like a real room with real people. Everything is so precisely and lovingly depicted that it's almost impossible to think of this scene as just paint. Each figure is individualized, dignified, and serene. Immediately to the left of the enthroned Madonna and Child is the patron saint of the church, Job (*Giobbe* in Italian), of the Old Testament. It was believed that Job's sufferings prefigured the sufferings of Christ, but Venice was unusual among Roman Catholic cities in invoking the righteous of the Old Testament as Christian saints. Near Job is St. Francis, displaying the stigmata that we saw him receiving in Paolo Veneziano's painting, for San Giobbe was also a Franciscan church. The most prominent figure on the other side of the altarpiece is St. Sebastian, who was martyred by being shot full of arrows and who, in later centuries, was invoked for relief from the plague (his arrow

wounds were associated with plague sores). As long as plague was common, Sebastian was a popular saint.

The painting's original frame is still in the church of San Giobbe, and it's a pity that the altarpiece and its frame are separated since Bellini's painted architecture was designed as an inward extension of that stone frame.

Pass through the next room (SALA III) and enter the door on the left (SALA IV). Here and on the other side of the partition are several smaller paintings by Giovanni Bellini, mainly half-lengths of the Madonna and Child, each one serenely beautiful.

SALA IV also has works by some of Bellini's contemporaries from the mainland who had a very different sense of beauty. The first painting on the left-hand wall is:

7. *St. George,* **by Andrea Mantegna,** Bellini's slightly older brother-in-law. It has a strength uncompromised by its small size and unsoftened by Bellini's gentle light.

Immediately opposite the door is:

8. **Cosmè Tura's *Mother and Child,*** of around 1455. The exaggerated contrasts of light and dark and bulges of flesh and bone give a quirky intensity to the painting. The naked, sleeping child, incidentally, alludes to the death of the adult Jesus Christ.

Go to the next room, really the other side of the partition, for works by Giorgione, the most revolutionary artist of the early 16th century:

9. **Giorgione's *Tempest*** (ca. 1504–10), in the corner, is set at an angle to the rest of the room. It is a hauntingly inexplicable juxtaposition of a man with a staff and a nude woman nursing an infant, in the foreground, with a stormy view of Castelfranco, the artist's hometown, in the distance. This may be the first painting with no other significance than what is shown. Giorgione's colors are simpler and richer, and emerge from darker and more mysterious shadows— just compare his *Tempest* with the five odd but captivating little allegories by Giovanni Bellini, just to its left. *The Tempest* is a poetic reverie, however many have been tempted to analyze it for a symbolic or allegorical message.

You can see just how naturalistic Giorgione could be in the painting to the right of *The Tempest*, a picture of an old woman labeled *Col Tempo* ("with time"), a warning to the young and beautiful. Giorgione's own time passed all too quickly. He died of the plague in 1510, while still in his thirties.

As you enter the next room (SALA III, the room you crossed to get to Bellini's *Mother and Child*), you'll see:

10. **Sebastiano del Piombo's *Four Saints*,** of 1507–09, painted on four separate canvasses that originally served as hinged organ shutters, with the lateral paintings on the back of the two in the middle.

    Sebastiano's niched figures are "Giorgionesque" in their calm dignity, heightened by the deep shadows from which they emerge and by their deliberately limited range of colors. They have a more formidable, convincing presence than do the people in a painting by Bellini and have fewer distracting details.

    To see how Sebastiano achieved his effects, go to within a foot or two of the drapery of St. Sebastian—the white of the cloth is made of broad strokes of heavy paint resting almost in blobs on the heavily textured canvas. Rembrandt, who was born almost a century later, would have loved it; but few people would have ever been able to see the texture of the paint, since the organ and its shutters were high on a church wall. It was not until the later 16th century that artists would paint so freely on work designed to be seen close to.

    Enter the next room (SALA VI) by the door to the left of Sebastiano's *Four Saints*, and immediately take a hard right into the small room next to it (SALA VII). The first painting on your left is:

11. **Lorenzo Lotto's *Portrait of a Young Man*,** painted around 1524. Lotto (c.1480–1556) may have taken some of Giorgione's naturalism and power of suggestion, but little of his tranquility. Lotto manages to make even an apparently straight-forward portrait slightly nervous and unsettling. The studious gentleman seems all the more captivating for the odd lizard on his desk.

    Retrace your steps. After passing Lotto's portrait, turn right into the room with the odd zigzag walls (SALA VI), and enter the next room, a large and well-lit gallery

(SALA X) that contains some of the greatest masterpieces of 16th-century Venice.

The large painting in the middle of the wall just to your left as you enter the next room, is:

12. **Titian's Pietà** (1576), the artist's last painting, intended for his tomb in the church of I Frari. St. Jerome, who kneels by the dead Christ, bears the features of the 90-year-old artist. Mary Magdalene runs away in anguish on the left. On either side are the stony figures of Moses and a Sibyl, representing the Hebrew and pagan worlds that (from the Christian point of view) predicted Jesus Christ and, at his death, became obsolete.

As Titian (c.1485–1576) grew older his style of painting became increasingly broad and complex. According to Palma Giovane, who completed the unfinished canvas after Titian's death, the old man painted more with his fingers than with the brush. Titian also seems to have thought and felt ever more deeply about the forms he painted. If ever a painting can be said to be profound, it is this one.

Venice produced two other brilliant artists in the 16th century: Tintoretto and Veronese. SALA VI, the lofty room you passed through to enter this one, has several fine paintings by them, and this room and the next have even more.

On the wall opposite Titian's *Pietà* is a large horizontal canvas:

13. **The Miracle of the Slave** (1548), by Jacopo Robusti, better known as **Tintoretto** (1518–94). It was painted for the Scuola di San Marco (today the city hospital, near the church of SS Giovanni and Paolo) to illustrate a legend of Venice's patron saint. It was the artist's first big success.

According to the story, a slave, who had left his master in southern France in order to worship at the shrine of St. Mark in Venice was, on his return, to be punished violently; but thanks to the miraculous intervention of the saint, flying overhead, every attempt to hurt the slave came to nothing. The master was so convinced of St. Mark's power that he too made a pilgrimage to Venice.

Tintoretto combined the coloring (and free paint) of Titian with the drawing (and dramatic postures) of Michelangelo. He also probably liked the sort of elongated figures that Paolo Veneziano had used 200 years before. He rarely concentrated on individual faces. It is the complex groupings, twisting postures, strong light, and free paint that give his scenes such a striking sense of drama.

The two other works from the series are even more audacious. The painting to the right of the *Miracle of the Slave* is the **Transportation of the Body of St. Mark,** painted 14 years later, in 1562. Here Tintoretto's exaggerated perspective became virtually hallucinogenic, and his painting as free as a sketch. This is artistry that wants to be seen and admired.

The enormous painting on the end wall that dominates the entire room, is:

14. **Feast in the House of Levi** (1573), by Paolo Calieri, better known as **Veronese** (1528–88). Originally it was a *Last Supper,* and like Leonardo da Vinci's *Last Supper,* it was painted for the dining hall of a monastery; in this case, that of SS. Giovanni and Paolo. With its elegant people, wandering dogs, and atmosphere of luxury and pleasure, the painting posed a problem for some ecclesiastical authorities. The local Inquisitor was unhappy with Veronese's explanation (namely, artistic license) for the dwarf, the man with a nosebleed in the left foreground, and, worst of all, the soldiers on the right, who, from the Inquisitor's point of view, were at least German and probably Protestant heretics. Veronese was ordered to alter the painting. However—and it says a great deal about Venetian practicality and tolerance—he got away with just changing the name from *The Last Supper* to *Feast in the House of Levi.* Whatever it's called, it's a splendid painting.

The next room (SALA XI) has a number of excellent works by Tintoretto. At the far end of the room are paintings, from the 17th and 18th centuries. The last painting on the long wall to your right as you enter is:

15. **Bernardo Strozzi's Dinner in the House of Simon** (around 1630). Strozzi treats the same general theme that Veronese had done half a century earlier, but in the more down-to-earth and concentrated idiom of the early 17th century (the "early baroque"). There are wonderfully realistic touches, such as the rumpled clothing, the man

beating the cat off the sideboard, and the fact that more people are interested in their food than Christ. All such details, however, are subordinate to the conversation between Jesus and Simon the Pharisee (the man opposite him, apparently wearing a pious Jew's side-locks) and Simon's surprise on hearing Jesus say that his own formal hospitality is inferior to the devotion of the sinful woman, who has washed Jesus's feet with her tears, dried them with her hair, and anointed them with ointment.

Strozzi, like several of the other outstanding artists in Venice at that time, was born and trained elsewhere, specifically in Genoa. The "Golden Age" of Venetian painting—stretching from Bellini to Tintoretto—may have passed, but a "Silver Age" was still to come, and its greatest master was Tiepolo.

The large circular painting on the end wall of SALA XI is:

16. **Giambattista Tiepolo's** *Exaltation of the Cross,* (1745). It was intended to grace a ceiling; but if we no longer see it as it was intended to be seen at least we don't have to strain our necks. The subject is St. Helena's discovery, in the early 4th century, of the cross on which Jesus died. A shoveler in the foreground shadows has just excavated the True Cross along with a couple of "false crosses," one of which lies rejected in the lower right.

Tiepolo has returned to the sort of pageantry that Veronese painted almost two centuries earlier, but everything Tiepolo paints becomes color and light, all the more vibrant for the inky shadows that thread through the robes or fill the foreground. How ponderous the earlier artists seem by comparison! The 18th century was a true "Silver Age" for Venetian painting.

The exit to SALA XI takes you to a corridor filled with landscapes. The first door on the right leads to the WC. The other rooms along this corridor have smaller paintings of the 16th, 17th, and 18th centuries. Perhaps the most interesting is in the last of the small rooms that make up SALA XVII, entered through the first door on your left, about half-way down the corridor.

17. **Tiepolo's** *Transportation of the Holy House from Nazareth to Loreto* (1743), a study for a large ceiling

fresco is the best work here. Tiepolo's precise and vivacious style makes the peculiar legend—that Mary's house was carried by angels from Galilee to Italy—perfectly acceptable, even glorious. Unfortunately we can no longer compare this study with the finished work, for the original was destroyed in 1915 by an Austrian bomb.

You will also find small works by some of the greatest Venetian painters of the 18th century, including landscapes by Francesco Guardi and Canaletto, genre scenes by Pietro Longhi, and portraits by Rosalba Carriera.

After you leave this room, follow the corridor around the corner (this continuation of the corridor is SALA XVIII). On your left is the former:

18. **Church of Sta. Maria della Carità,** or at least the top half of it (SALA XXIII), and with it we come back into the 15th century. On the right as you enter the first of the two doors is the front of the "church," which displays various altarpieces of the 15th century. The rear of the "church" (the part to your left as you enter) is used for temporary exhibitions.

Return to the corridor that runs parallel to the church, and go in the first open doorway on your left, opposite the church. (SALA XIX; if you came out of the church near the bookstall you'll have to backtrack a bit.) Halfway down this short hallway, on the left, is the entrance to a room (SALA XX) with one of the real treasures of the Accademia:

19. *Scenes of the Relic of the True Cross,* painted between 1494 and 1505 for the Confraternity of St. John the Evangelist. The paintings are as richly decorative as tapestries and are especially fascinating for the view they give us of life in Venice 500 years ago.

The painting just to your right as you enter is **Carpaccio's** *Miracle of the Possessed Boy* (the curing of the boy takes place on the balcony in the upper left) with the Grand Canal as it was around the year 1500. Gondoliers maneuver their boats around the old wooden Rialto Bridge. The elegant houses have laundry drying on poles, while, higher up, are the funnel-shaped chimneys and an occasional roof platform (*altana*) where upper class women would bleach their hair in the sun. (In the central painting on the right wall, **Gentile Bellini's** *Retrieval of the Cross;* you'll notice that far more of the women than the men are blond (which is still the case in Venice.)

The large painting on the end wall is the most famous, the *Piazza San Marco,* by **Gentile Bellini** (Giovanni Bellini's brother). The actual subject is the miraculous cure of a boy in Bergamo, which occurred precisely as his father (the kneeling man in red, to the right of center) adored the scuola's relic in Venice. For us the miracle is the recreation of the brick piazza with its surrounding buildings and freshly gilded church. Gentile's painting also gives us some idea of splendor of the confraternities' processions.

Once you've finished this room you have one more dazzling treat. As you leave the room with the *Scenes of the True Cross*, turn left and round the corner, and you'll be in SALA XXI, surrounded by:

20. **Carpaccio's *St. Ursula Cycle*** (1490–1500), made for another confraternity, the Scuola di Sant' Orsola, which once existed near SS. Giovanni and Paolo. The odd medieval legend of St. Ursula and her 11,000 virgins is ennobled by Carpaccio's great narrative skill. The story begins with the first painting on the left on the wall opposite you, and continues around the room clockwise. Despite the distant locations in which the story takes place, the scenery Carpaccio creates is largely a Venetian-oriented fantasy.

One. We are in Brittany, in France, in the middle of the 5th century. Ambassadors from England kneel before the Breton king to propose marriage between the English prince and the Breton princess Ursula. On the right, in an upper room, we again see the long-suffering Breton king, listening to his pious daughter Ursula lay down her conditions for the marriage: that the prince become a Christian and that their marriage be chaste for three years, during which time 10 select virgins will attend her, each (including Ursula) accompanied by another 1,000 virgins. The old woman on the steps is Ursula's maid, patiently awaiting the end of the conference.

Two. The English ambassadors take their leave from the Breton court to convey Ursula's conditions to their king.

Three. The ambassadors return to England. On the left is one of the low, oared galleys that formed the mainstay of the Venetian navy. This painting has survived in the best condition; once all of the scenes were at least this fresh.

Four (on rear wall). On the left the English prince leaves his father. On the other side of the flagpole and, in the conventions of Carpaccio's narrative syle, on the other side of the English channel, the prince greets Ursula. Together they say farewell and, with their accompanying virgins, prepare to board the great round merchant ships in the distance for a pilgrimage to Rome.

Five. While passing through Cologne, Ursula dreams of her martyrdom. This scene is the most famous of the series for the actuality of the bedroom and the delicacy of communication between angel and saint.

Six. Together with her husband and the 11 thousand virgins, Ursula is blessed by the pope before the Castel Sant' Angelo in Rome.

Seven. The entourage arrives back in Cologne to find it besieged by the Huns. This scene was the first one painted (1490) and is the least elegant.

Eight. On the left the Huns kill all of them; Ursula is about to be shot with an arrow because she has refused marriage with the prince of the Huns. On the right Ursula is buried.

Nine (the other end-wall). The altarpiece, with Ursula in glory, surrounded by her virginal companions, whose palms of martyrdom provide a platform for her.

As you leave you'll once again see Titian's *Presentation of the Virgin.* His grander, more unified, and more deeply shadowed artistic vision may have made Carpaccio's seem old-fashioned and even fussy to Titian's contemporaries; but Titian learned from the older master how to decorate a confraternity. The ancient woman sitting by the steps was certainly inspired by Ursula's nurse, in the first scene of Carpaccio's cycle.

With these highlights under your belt, feel free to explore the Accademia at your leisure. You will see works by the artists you've been introduced to as you wander in and out of buildings throughout the city.

THE OTHER SIDE OF THE CANAL: DORSODURO

Start: Church of Santa Maria della Salute.

Finish: Church of Santa Maria della Salute.

Vaporetto: No. 1.

Time: Three to five hours, depending on time spent at sites.

Best Time: Mornings or late afternoon, when churches are open.

Worst Time: Midday, when churches are closed, or Tuesdays, when the Peggy Guggenheim Collection is closed.

Dorsoduro is a fascinating mix of elegance, art, charm, and students and everyday Venetian neighborhoods which gives the district something of the spirit of the old Greenwich Village or the Left Bank. At the center of Dorsoduro as well as at its heart is the Accademia; its presence has attracted artists, students, and long-term foreign residents to this district since the 19th century. East of the Accademia, you'll find the fabulous Church of Santa Maria della Salute, the Peggy Guggenheim Collection of modern art, the dramatic, open vistas of the Punta Dogana and the Zattere. To the northwest lies the lively university district. In between, you'll find the galleries, artisans' shops, and neighborhood markets that make walking here a constant delight. You'll also have a chance to visit Ca' Rezzonico, the quintessential 18th century Venetian palace, as well as the more modest but interesting gothic palazzo in which the playwright, Carlo Goldoni lived.

● ● ● ● ● ● ● ● ● ● ● ● ● ● ● ● ●

The No. 1 vaporetto will take you to the Santa Maria della Salute stop.

1. **The Church of Santa Maria della Salute** (Maria of the Health), one of the most extraordinary baroque structures in the world, designed by the 32-year-old Baldassare Longhena as a votive church in thanksgiving for the deliverance of Venice from the great plague of 1630–31, when a third of the popuation perished. The Salute rests on a foundation of more than a million piles, and was begun even while the plague still raged: It was completed in 1681, just one year before Longhena's death. The Salute was designed to be approached from the water, and its domes were meant to create an affinity with the Basilica of San Marco (the great circular volutes surrounding the dome, known locally as *orecchioni*, or "big ears," serve as buttresses, and are not merely flights of rococo whimsey). Each year on the Feast of the Presentation of the Virgin (November 21), the doge led a great procession from San Marco across a special pontoon bridge spanning the Grand Canal to the Salute. The tradition (the pontoon bridge is set up each year for approximately forty-eight hours) continues to this day and offers a wonderful chance to see the Salute as Longhena envisioned it, with an uninterrupted view through the open doors to the high altar framed by the chancel arch. There are six side chapels around the octagonal periphery of the interior; Longhena may have decided on the building's circular shape in order to keep the central area beneath the brilliantly lit dome free for the arrival of the annual procession. Above the raised sanctuary, a great arch, supported by four ancient Roman columns, spans the high altar. Here you'll find a sculptural ensemble, *The Queen of Heaven*

Expelling the Plague, designed by Longhena, and executed by Juste Le Court. There is also a Byzantine *Madonna and Child,* sent to Venice from Crete by Francesco Morosini in 1672; it may seem a bit out of place amid all this baroque opulence. To the left of the altar look for a door to the sacristy; to enter, you must usually pay a fee to the sacristan. Here you'll find Tintoretto's recently restored *Marriage at Cana* (1561) as well as three ceiling canvasses of *Cain and Abel, The Sacrifice of Isaac,* and *David and Goliath,* all painted by Titian from 1542 to 1544. Above the sacristy altar is an early work by Titian: *St. Mark Enthroned Between Saints Cosmas, Damian, Roch, and Sebastian* (1512). The Salute is open daily from 8am to noon and 3 to 5pm.

Exit the church and walk back to the Actv stop. From here, looking almost directly across the Grand Canal, tucked in between two large Gothic palaces, is the narrow 15th century:

2. **Palazzo Contarini-Fasan,** nicknamed "The House of Desdemona" (to the left of this tiny one-room-wide palazzo, you'll see an extra gothic window tucked above a connecting arch to the next palazzo). The palazzo's richly carved window frames and colonettes as well as its lacy stone balconies and delicate size may have have moved some Renaissance-era tour guide to palm the building off as the home of Othello's Desdemona; the association caught the public fancy, and has been popular ever since. A patrician lady named Desdemona really was murdered by her jealous husband—Shakespeare knew the basic outline of the story from a collection of stories by Giovanni Battista Giraldi published in 1565. Venetians, of course, love Shakespeare's *Othello,* but are mystified by the transformation of the husband, a member of the illustrious Moro family, into a Moorish general, a situation that would have been historically and politically impossible.

Farther to the left, look for the:

3. **Gritti Palace Hotel,** a 15th-century palazzo once covered with frescos by Giorgione. A favorite of Ernest Hemingway, the Gritti Palace's restaurant terrace on the Grand Canal is one of the most romantic dining spots in Venice.

Facing the canal, turn right, proceed across the Campo della Salute, and continue along the narrow Fondamenta della Dogana (Customs House), with its wonderful views of the Basin of San Marco. The long building on your right is the:

4. **Customs warehouse,** built in the 17th century. Beginning in 1414, all goods arriving by sea were unloaded here for customs inspection.

Continue straight to:

5. **the Punta della Dogana** (the Customs Point), with its truly fabulous views in all directions. A fortified tower guarding the mouth of the Grand Canal was replaced with the present structure in the 17th century; atop the tower, two bronze Atlases hold a gilded globe above which a weathervane of the Goddess of Fortune blows in the wind.

Across the mouth of the Grand Canal, you'll see the Hotel Bauer Grunwald, with a small terrace to its side. The first building to the right of the Bauer Grunwald is the:

6. **Palazzo Giustinian,** now headquarters for the Venice Biennale. In the 19th century, this was the Hotel de l'Europe; its guests included Verdi, who made it his Venetian headquarters, Theophile Gautier, and Marcel Proust. The British novelist George Eliot (*Middlemarch; Silas Marner*) honeymooned here. Soon after their arrival, her husband, J. W. Cross, threw himself from his bedroom window into the Grand Canal. He was fished out by gondoliers, sedated, and sent to Verona for rest—his doctors felt the intense beauty of Venice had overtaxed his nervous system.

On the ground floor of the next building to the right, with three floors of balconied gothic windows on its facade, was the:

7. **Ridotto,** the famed gambling casino of 18th-century Venice, open every night during the long Carnival season. As Venetians no longer had the opportunity to gamble their fortunes at sea, they turned to cards, which many claim were invented in Venice. In order to enter the Ridotto, you had to be a patrician, but if you wore a mask (Carnival was the great equalizer) who could tell? Fortunes were squandered in a night; the flow of money was so clearly away

Dorsoduro Stops 1–8

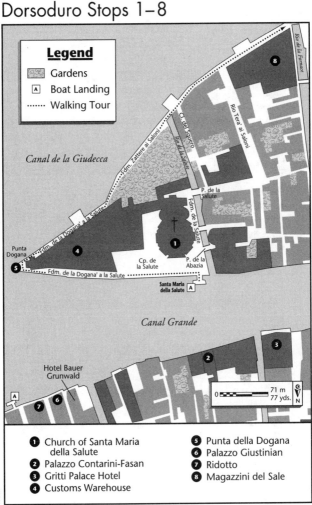

Legend

🟫 Gardens

Ⓐ Boat Landing

······ Walking Tour

Canal de la Giudecca

Fdm. Zattere ai Saloni

Ci del Squero

Rio de la Salute

Rio Tera ai Saloni

Rio de la Fornace

P. de la Salute

Fdm. de la Salute

Punta Dogana

Fdm. de la Dogana' a la Salute

Cp. de la Salute

P. de la Abazia

Santa Maria della Salute Ⓐ

Fdm. de la Dogana' a la Salute

Canal Grande

Hotel Bauer Grunwald

0   71 m
     77 yds.

N

❶ Church of Santa Maria della Salute
❷ Palazzo Contarini-Fasan
❸ Gritti Palace Hotel
❹ Customs Warehouse
❺ Punta della Dogana
❻ Palazzo Giustinian
❼ Ridotto
❽ Magazzini del Sale

9758A

from the patrician families that in 1774, the Senate ordered the Ridotto closed, even though it was a great money-making enterprise for the state. Gambling then moved to the private "casinos" ("little houses," or love nests) that had already sprung up all over the city, and the meaning of the word "casino," as we know it today, was born.

Ahead of you, the panorama takes in the island of San Giorgio Maggiore, with its white Palladian church. Continue around the point. You will now be walking on the long series of fondamentas known as *zattere* (rafts), from

Dorsoduro 9-30

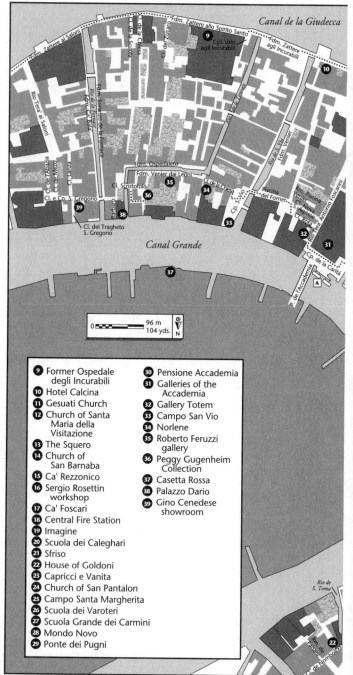

Canal de la Giudecca

Canal Grande

0 — 96 m / 104 yds.

9 Former Ospedale degli Incurabili
10 Hotel Calcina
11 Gesuati Church
12 Church of Santa Maria della Visitazione
13 The Squero
14 Church of San Barnaba
15 Ca' Rezzonico
16 Sergio Rosettin workshop
17 Ca' Foscari
18 Central Fire Station
19 Imagine
20 Scuola dei Caleghari
21 Sfriso
22 House of Goldoni
23 Capricci e Vanita
24 Church of San Pantalon
25 Campo Santa Margherita
26 Scuola dei Varoteri
27 Scuola Grande dei Carmini
28 Mondo Novo
29 Ponte dei Pugni

30 Pensione Accademia
31 Galleries of the Accademia
32 Gallery Totem
33 Campo San Vio
34 Norlene
35 Roberto Feruzzi gallery
36 Peggy Gugenheim Collection
37 Casetta Rossa
38 Palazzo Dario
39 Gino Cenedese showroom

97588

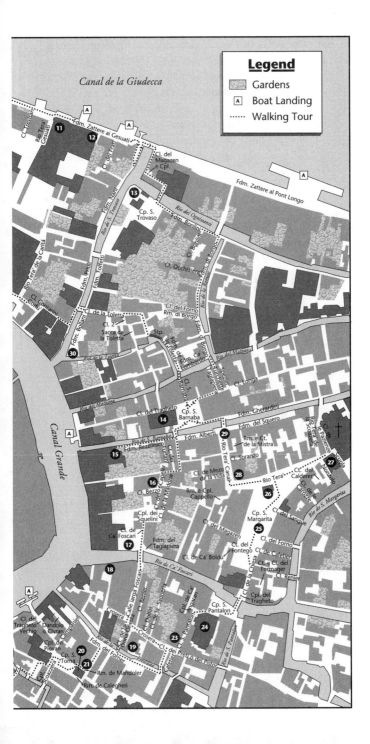

Canal de la Giudecca

Legend
Gardens
A Boat Landing
..... Walking Tour

Fdm. Zattere ai Gesuati

11
A
12

Cl. del
Magazen
e Cpl.

Fdm. Zattere al Pont Longo
A

13
Cp. S.
Trovaso

Fdm. Bonlini
Rio del Ognissanti

Cl. Bonlini

Cl. Occhialera

Cl. del Forno
Rm. di Borgo

Cl. de la Toletta

Cl. 2.
Sacca de
la Toletta

Stp.

30

Rio del Malcanton

Cl. Longo

Cl. del Traghetto

14
Cp. S.
Barnaba

Fdm. Gherardini

Fdm. del Squero

Fdm. Alberti
29
Rm. e Ct.
de la Mistra

A
15
Fdm. Rezzonico

Cl. Soranzo

28
Cl. de Mezo
de la Vida

27
Ct. del
Calderer

16
Cl. Bezzo

Rm. e Cpl.
Cappello

Rio Tera'
26

Cpl. dei
Squelini

Cp. S.
Margarita

Cl. del Sangue

25
Cl. del Forno

17
Cl. de
Ca Foscari

Fdm. del
Tagiapiera

Cl. del Magazen

Cl. del
Fontego

Cl. de Cafetier

Cl. de Ca' Boldu'

Cl. e Ct. del
Formager

18

Cl. Renier

Rio de Ca' Foscari

A
Cl. del
Tragheto
Vechio

Dandolo
o Civran

Crosera

Calle larga Foscari

Cpl. del
Tragheto

Cpl. del
Plovan

Cp. S.
Pantalon

24

20
Cp. S.
Toma

Fdm. del Forner
19

Cl. dei Pietro o del Pistor
23

21
Rm. de Mandoler

Rm. de Calegheri

the time when this entire shoreline consisted of floating wooden docks which were used for the unloading of bulky cargoes. Across the broad Giudecca Canal lies the island of Giudecca. Immediately across, you'll see the white complex of Palladio's early Le Zitelle; farther along is his masterpiece, Redentore Church.

Continue along the fondamenta. You'll soon come to the floating wooden terrace of Linea d'Ombra, an excellent restaurant/cafe with a piano bar in the evenings, a good place for future reference (the wonderful panorama is better for a leisurely meal than a quick walking-tour break). Continue onward, and you'll pass the vast:

8. **Magazzini del Sale** (Salt Warehouses), which held 45,000 tons of salt in the days when the Republic maintained a state-run monopoly on salt production. Like the customs buildings around the corner, these warehouses are now eerily empty (except for a section used as an indoor boatyard by the Bucintoro Rowing Club).

Pass the Renaissance facade of the Spirito Santo Church. At no. 423, you'll be at the center of the facade of the enormous:

9. former **Ospedale degli Incurabili** (Hospital of the Incurables), designed by Antonio da Ponte, who was also the architect of the Rialto Bridge. After the discovery of the New World, many of the "incurables" were victims of syphilis. A girls' orphanage was added to the complex in the late 16th century; like the Pietà and other Venetian orphanages, its conservatory trained an internationally famous choir. At the end of the building, above the blocked doorway at no. 424, notice the face of the serenely beautiful young girl.

Continue on across two bridges. At the corner of a little campiello is :

10. **Hotel Calcina,** at no. 780, long a favorite of British travelers, despite the ugly 1950s renovations that are only now being undone. John Ruskin, author of the landmark *Stones of Venice* rented rooms here; they were his favorite Venetian digs.

Continuing along, at no. 792, notice the baked-clay rope motif around the door, a cheaper way of decorating than carving stone or wood. The gothic window design indicates this buiding's medieval origins. A bit beyond, you arrive at the powerful classical facade of the:

11. **Gesuati Church** (or Santa Maria del Rosario), designed by Giorgio Massari and built between 1726 and 1743. The white classical facade seems in some ways to echo Palladio's Church of the Redentore across the Giudecca Canal. Giambattista Tiepolo painted the Gesuati's ceiling panels of scenes from the life of St. Dominic (1737–1739) as well as the first altarpiece on the right, *The Virgin in Glory*, in which the Madonna is upstaged by the three saints in the foreground.

A few steps beyond this church is the smaller:

12. **Church of Santa Maria della Visitazione,** with a Renaissance facade; note the lion's mouth letter box on the right of the facade, used during the time of the Republic for civic complaints (and occasionally for political denunciations—anonymity was assured). Inside the church (enter through the vocational school on the right), you'll find a beautiful coffered wooden ceiling with panels painted by Umbrian or Tuscan artists.

At number 917B, notice the doorway, eroded by centuries of winds blowing off the lagoon. Here the rope motif frame has been carved by hand.

Take a Break   A few steps more along the Zattere, and you'll come upon **Gelateria Nico,** at 922, one of the best ice cream places in town, with a large sunny terrace by the water for sampling the many flavors offered. It also serves coffee and light snacks. The *gianduiotto* is Nico's unique hazelnut concoction. You can, of course, ask for your order to take away. Virtually next door is another waterfront place where you can sit down to pizza, a simple plate of pasta, or a salad. If you're up for a major meal, there will be a good restaurant choice a bit farther on in this walk.

Take a right turn from the zattere onto the Fondamenta Nani, which runs along the Rio de San Trovaso. Soon, across the Rio de San Trovaso, you'll notice:

13. **the Squero,** a small boatyard for building and repairing gondolas. Timber for shipbuilding was sent to Venice from

the mountains of the Cadore, and with the wood, came artisans skilled in woodworking, who built the rustic, chalet-like houses of their native region that surround the boatyard. In the 16th century, when 10,000 gondolas cruised the lagoon, there were many such places in Venice, but today only four still function; this one is surely the most picturesque. Beyond the squero, you can see parts of the two white facades and the campanile of the **Church of San Trovaso** (SS. Gervasio and Protasio). The building contains two fine Tintorettos, a *Last Supper* and a *Temptation of St. Anthony.*

Retrace your steps back to the zattere, turn right, cross the Ponte Longo and turn immediately right into the soto-portego. Follow the way around to the left, then to the right and over the next bridge, which leads to the Campo San Trovaso. At the foot of the bridge, turn left onto the Fondamenta Bontini. Just past the Ponte Trevesan, turn right onto the Fondamenta di Borgo.

Take a Break At number 1147 is the **Locanda Montin,** a good but reasonably priced restaurant with a pensione upstairs, and a history of guests that includes Hemingway and Ezra Pound in the 1920s, and continues with art luminaries like Jackson Pollock, Mark Rothko, and Peggy Guggenheim, and even Jimmy Carter. The owners have covered the walls with paintings donated by, or purchased from, their many friends and clients; in the back, there's a beautiful trellised garden for summer dining. It's open for lunch Thursday through Tuesday from 12:30pm to 2:30pm and for dinner Thursday through Monday from 7:30pm to 9:30 pm.

Proceed up the Fondamenta di Borgo, cross the bridge, and continue straight onto the narrow Calle de le Turchette (Street of the Little Turkish Women). At the end of this calle is the shop-filled Calle Longa. At this intersection, look for **Annelie** at no. 2748, a shop specializing in carefully chosen, delicate blouses and dresses from 30 to 40 years ago as well as old lace and hand-embroidered linens and tablecloths (closed Monday mornings). Turn right onto Calle Longa and follow it to Campo San Barnaba. At the far side of the campo is the:

14. **Church of San Barnaba,** with its heavy, massive 18th-century classical facade. If it looks familiar, perhaps you remember it from an Indiana Jones film, where the crawl space under the stone floor was filled with snakes. The campo was first immortalized in the Katharine Hepburn film, *Summertime* in 1955. Just to the left of the church is the small shop in which Hepburn found the single 17th-century red Murano goblet of her dreams as well as a romance with Rossano Brazzi (now a furniture restorer's workshop). On the left side of the campo is the canal into which Ms. Hepburn's character fell while backing up to capture the shop with her camera. The shot had to be redone a number of times, and Katharine Hepburn developed a chronic eye infection that plagued her for decades.

In the 18th-century, the San Barnaba neighborhood was home to many impoverished patricians, who were legally forbidden to take up petty trade, and although indigent, were still required by law to maintain patrician standards and to dress in silk (visiting foreigners reported amazement at the elegance of the city's paupers). These disaffected *barnabotti* were a source of worry to the Republic, especially as the spirit of the French Revolution began to sweep Europe. Today the neighborhood has a middle-class feel.

Pick up a Snack A bread bakery at the beginning of the calle to the right of the church sells freshly made rolls and bread. On the side of the campo, opposite the church, there's an excellent fresh pasta shop with mountains of different colored and shaped pastas in its window (a great option if you have simple cooking facilities). A few doors down you'll find a delicatessen where you can pick up sliced cheese or cold meat for your bread. Turn left at the end of this side of the campo, and you'll see San Barnaba's famous vegetable barge, which sells tomatoes and cucumbers, tied up to the fondamenta; a shop facing the barge sells quality fresh fruit. We'll pass this campo again in the walk, if you want to stock up later.

As you face the Church of San Barnaba, take the little bridge just to the left of Katharine Hepburn's fateful souvenir shop. A right turn onto the Fondamenta Rezzonico will lead you to the land entrance of:

15. **Ca' Rezzonico,** one of the great palaces on the Grand Canal, now a remarkable museum of 18th-century Venice. You'll find a description of Ca' Rezzonico in Walk 4, at Stop 12. The museum is open Monday to Thursday and on Saturday from 10am to 5pm; Sunday from 9am to 12:30pm, closed Friday.

    From Ca' Rezzonico, retrace your steps to the foot of the little bridge from Campo San Barnaba and turn right onto Calle de le Boteghe, where you'll pass more wood and furniture workshops. The calle makes a right angle to the right: take the first left after the right angle (Calle Capeler). You'll pass antiques shops, a kilim rug gallery; and at 3215, a shop makes theatrical papier-mâché and ceramic objects. At no. 3220 is:

16. **the metal workshop of Sergio Rosettin,** its walls covered with examples of old and antique cast bronze lion's-head door knockers, door knobs, and drawer pulls as well as gothic icon frames and hundreds of other architectural and decorator items, in stock or available for reproduction. You can even order copies of exotic objects, such as a medieval candle holder or a 17th-century Renaissance Hanukkah menorah. The shop is open Monday to Friday in normal business hours.

    Continue into the brick paved, tree shaded Campiello dei Squelini (if it's a hot day, you can refill your canteen at the campiello's fountain). Take the diagonal path across the campiello to the far right corner and onto Calle de Ca' Foscari, the center of the university district. A short distance down the calle on the right, enter the gate and go into the often busy courtyard of:

17. **Ca' Foscari,** the largest and one of the most impressive gothic palaces on the Grand Canal; it now houses the university's economics, statistics, and Anglo-German language departments. The magnificence of the palace was such that it was chosen to lodge King Henry III of France on his state visit to Venice in 1574. (See the introduction.) Although the Grand Canal facade remains a dazzle, the interior of Ca' Foscari has been largely stripped away and adapted to the needs of the university. If you pass from the main courtyard into the courtyard to the right, you'll see the

imposing outdoor staircase (older palaces usually did not contain indoor stairways), a vestige of the palazzo's former greatness.

Exit the courtyard, turn right onto Calle de Ca' Foscari, and continue to the top of the bridge, from which you can see across the canal to the right the:

18. **Central Fire Station,** built in 1932, in a style that helps to blend it into its surroundings. If you're lucky, you'll be able to see the red fire brigade vessels, just inside the water level arches.

After the bridge, continue straight until you come to the Crosera; continue straight onto Calle de la Dona Onesta. In passing through this eclectic neighborhood, you might want to look into:

19. **Imagine,** an antiques shop on the right at no. 3921. It specializes in English jewelry from the Victorian period to 1930, including pre-1920 Scottish silver and agate jewelry, which has become increasingly fashionable in Europe. There are also interesting pieces of Sheffield plate and silver hollow ware. The shop is open Tuesday to Saturday and Monday afternoons.

Cross the short bridge, turn right onto Fondamenta del Forner; at the end of this calle, turn left onto Calle del Campaniel, which leads into Campo San Toma. On your left as you enter this campo, is the charming brick:

20. **Scuola dei Caleghari** (Confraternity of the Shoemakers), with its doorway dated 1478. The scuole were continually in competition, modernizing and glorifying their headquarters; this is an example of an important but less imposing confraternity building than the Scuola Grande di San Marco or San Rocco. The central portal with its gothic arch is decorated with reliefs of shoes, and the lunette relief, believed to have been made in the workshop of Pietro Lombardo, shows St. Mark healing the cobbler, Ananias. A number of excellent leather workshops and stores are still clustered in this neighborhood, among them, Baldan, San Polo 3047 on Salizada San Rocco; Mazzon, 2807 on Campiello San Toma, just off Campo San Toma; and Toni Passudetto, San Polo 2722 on Calle Saoneri.

On the opposite side of the campo from the Scuola, is the Church of San Toma, currently being restored. At the corner of the campo to the left of the Scuola, you'll find:

21. **Sfriso,** at no. 2849, one of the city's most famous silver shops, with its unique line of hollow ware especially designed by the Sfriso family over the past sixty years.

    Exit Campo San Toma into Campiello San Toma, just to the left of the church, make a right turn at the end of the campiello, and follow the way around to the bridge, from which, if you look to the right across the canal, you'll see the gothic waterfront facade of Palazzo Centani, the family home of the playwright, Carlo Goldoni. Cross the bridge, and you'll find the land entrance to the house on the right side of the calle at no. 2793.

22. **The House of Goldoni** will give you an idea of a comfortable, but not palatial upper-class Venetian home (those interested in Venetian theater will want to see the small museum). The building is open Monday through Saturday from 8:30am to 1:30pm; admission is free. For a full description, see Walk 5, Stop 35.

    Retrace your steps to Calle Crosera, and turn right onto this busy street of local shops groceries, and student restaurants: a right turn farther up Crosera onto Calle dei Scaletier (under a sotoportego), leads to a cafeteria with a cheap but good student luncheon special. Continue straight on the Croseria, and turn left, onto Calle San Pantalon. As you walk down this street, you might want to note on the left:

23. **Capricci e Vanita,** at number 3744, an antique-lace shop that specializes in tablecloths, but also carries old blouses and other pieces of old or antique clothing.

    Calle San Pantalon bears around to the right to the front of the:

24. **Church of San Pantalon** with its unfinished facade. Inside, you'll find what must be the most incredible as well as the largest trompe l'oeil ceiling in Venice, *The Miracles and Apotheosis of St. Pantalon,* rising up to the heavens on sixty canvas panels painted by Gian Antonio Fumiani, who died in 1704 as the result of a fall from the painting's

scaffolding. He had been working on the project since 1680. In the Chapel of the Holy Nail, to the left of the chancel, there is a *Coronation of the Virgin* (1444) by Antonio Vivarini and Giovanni d'Alemagna.

Exit the church, and exit Campo San Pantalon on Ponte Santa Margherita, and continue straight into the lively:

25. **Campo Santa Margherita,** with many interesting smaller 14th-century gothic houses along its right flank, and an almost daily vegetable-and-fish market in the center. This is one of those campos worth enjoying for its everyday streetlife.

Take a Break   Campo Santa Margherita offers a variety of useful choices. For ice cream, **Causin,** at 2996, on the right side as you entered the campo offers many rich flavors ranging from mullberry to hazelnut. It's been regarded as one of the best gelateria-pasticcerias in the city for over half a century. **Il Caffe,** on the same side at 2963, is an excellent little atmospheric coffee house, with mirrored walls and marble tables. A natural foods shop, **El Quetzal,** at 2932, sells healthy fiber-filled snacks to carry along as you explore; a supermarket with an inconspicuous entrance at 2998 RioTera Canal (the left exit of the far side of the campo) has an excellent delicatessen department in the back where you can pick up sliced cold cuts for a sandwich, or a freshly roasted chicken (pollo) for approximately $5. If you're ready for a main meal, try the ever popular and inexpensive **Antico Capon,** in the center of the left side of the campo as you entered; it offers many kinds of pizzas, as well as reasonably priced lunch and dinner specials (closed Wednesday and on other days from 3pm to 6pm).

The Church of Santa Margherita was deconsecrated 200 years ago, and its campanile (to the left as you entered the campo) was truncated in the early 19th century. The visual focal point of the campo is now:

26. the free-standing **Scuola dei Varoteri** (Tanners and Furriers Guild), off center toward the far end of the campo. Built in 1725, its exterior is decorated with a Madonna della Misericordia sheltering the tanners with her mantle. These days, a plaque on the side of the building shows the

minimum permitted sizes of the fish sold at the nearby market.

The real prize of the campo is hidden off in the far right corner, where it seems to narrow into a calle. Here you'll encounter:

27. the 17th-century **Scuola Grande dei Carmini,** one of the six scuole designated as "grande" in Venice. Longhena is credited with the design of the building; the interior is richly decorated (note the stuccoed staircase to the upper hall). The building is a showcase for the work of Giambattista Tiepolo, who covered the ceiling of the upper hall with nine masterpiece paintings completed in 1744. The central panel represents St. Simon Stock receiving the scapular from the Madonna (a scapular consists of two small squares of cloth with religious images, connected by strings, and worn across the shoulders; it is especially associated with the traditions of the Carmelite Order).

Exit the Scuola Grande, and cross the campo, passing the Scuola dei Varoteri, and exit the campo on the Rio Tera Canal, which turns sharply to the right. After the turn, on your right, you'll pass:

28. **Mondo Novo,** no. 3063, which wins our award as the most original of all mask shops in Venice. Here you'll find masks of such composers as Verdi, Rossini, and Wagner; you can also disguise yourself as a passionate self-portrait by Van Gogh, or one of the pre-Cubist faces from Picasso's 1907 *Les Demoiselles d'Avignon,* or perhaps as a character from a Minoan wall painting from the Greek island of Santorini. Even if you have little interest in masks, this shop is worth a visit.

At the end of Rio Tera Canal, cross the:

29. **Ponte dei Pugni** (Bridge of the Fists), which for centuries was the battleground of the Castellani and the Nicolotti, opposing groups of toughs from two different regions of the city. You can see white footprints marked on the bridge; these were the starting positions for confrontations that involved throwing as many foes as possible off the bridge. These were not friendly encounters; they often involved sharpened poles and serious injury and death. So violent was the bloodletting in a demonstration presented for King

Henry III of France on his state visit in 1574 that the king demanded that the spectacle cease. In 1705, the Republic prohibited these traditional neighborhood free-for-alls.

After crossing the Ponte dei Pugni, turn left and then right into Campo San Barnaba. Cross the campo, and exit at the center of the far side through the sotoportego that leads to Calle San Barnaba, which becomes Calle de la Toletta. Follow this sequence of streets around until you reach the Rio San Trovaso. Before crossing the bridge here, turn left onto the Fondamenta Bollani. The fondamenta ends at:

30. **the Pensione Accademia** (once the Russian Embassy), no. 1058, located in a 17th-century villa at the junction of two canals that run into the Grand Canal a few feet beyond. As nearly as most people can reckon, this pensione, with its vine-covered gardens, was the model and setting for Katharine Hepburn's romantically sited hotel in *Summertime*, although the views that take in almost all of Venice from the windows of her room seem to have been the creation of the film's director, David Lean. There should be no problem entering the garden for a quick look; although this beautifully located hotel is usually booked months in advance, the management is happy to have more people know about it. After seeing the Pensione Accademia, you may want to make a reservation for your next stay in Venice.

Retrace your steps to the Ponte delle Marvegie at the end of Calle della Toletta, and cross the Rio San Trovaso Canal. At the foot of the bridge, take a left onto the fondamenta, and from there take the first right onto Calle Contarini Corfu. Follow this sequence of calles around and you will come to the Campo de la Carita, at the foot of the Accademia Bridge. The enormous buildings that face the bridge compose:

31. **the Galleries of the Accademia,** the great repository of Venetian art. The Accademia is covered in Walk 6.

At the far corner of the Accademia, turn right onto Rio Tera Antonio Foscarini, named for the Venetian diplomat unjustly executed for treason in 1621 (for his story, see the box and stop 18, Walk 5). At the beginning of this street, look for:

32. **Gallery Totem Il Canale,** at 878B which features an interesting collection of tribal and primitive art. The gallery
also sells earrings and necklaces made from old Murano
glass beads.

     Turn left onto Calle Nova S. Agnese, and follow this
sequence of streets to:

33. **Campo San Vio,** with its benches and pleasant view of the
Grand Canal. On the far side of the campo is the Anglican
St. George's Church. Exit Campo San Vio on Calle de la
Chiesa, which runs in front of St. George's. On the left side
of this calle, at no. 727, is:

34. **Norlene,** the collaboration of Helene and Nora Feruzzi,
who create hand-painted and printed designs on silk, velvet, and cotton. Norlene's exclusive textiles are filled with
the soft, rich colors of Venice; the designs play with patterns of reflected light on water or echo the subtleties of
Byzantine mosaics as they glisten in the sun. The shop's
ready-to-wear-clothing and fabrics have been exhibited in
galleries and museums throughout Europe and capture the
poetry and exoticism of Venice with contemporary flair.

     Continue straight onto Fondamenta Venier dei Leoni,
which runs along an especially charming canal. Here you'll
pass:

35. **the gallery of Roberto Feruzzi,** heir to a tradition as
well as a family of Venetian artists. Feruzzi's landscape paintings are filled with powerful blocks of Venetian color and
light; his interiors are enchanting and personal.

     At the end of the fondamenta, you must turn left. Here
you'll find a sculptured metal gate embedded with chunks
of once molten glass that leads to the:

36. **Peggy Guggenheim Collection,** which is housed in the
Palazzo Venier dei Leoni (or the Palazzo Non Finito—it
was begun in 1749, but never finished beyond its first floor).
Peggy Guggenheim bought the palazzo in the years after
World War II and filled it with her exuberance as well
as with her exceptional collection of modern art. In keeping with the wish of Peggy Guggenheim, who died in
1979, the building remains as welcoming and open as possible. As you enjoy the overgrown sculpture garden with its

excellent cafeteria, and visit the terrace overlooking the Grand Canal, you may almost feel like an invited guest at Peggy Guggenheim's palazzo. Only part of the collection can be exhibited at one time, but you'll find an entire room of paintings by Jackson Pollock as well as early Picassos and Chagalls, a wonderful sculpture by Alexander Calder that Peggy Guggenheim used in lieu of a headboard over her bed, and important works by Braque, de Chirico, Brancusi, Dali, Kandinsky, Mondrian, Giacometti, Magritte, Robert Motherwell, and Max Ernst, who was Peggy Guggenheim's husband. The foundation also sponsors special events and exhibitions.

Be sure to take in the terrace on the Grand Canal, and compare the joyous energy of Marino Marini's equestrian statue, *Angel of the Citadel,* with the famous 15th-century statue of Bartolomeo Colleoni on horseback in macho splendor at the side of the Church of SS. Giovanni e Paolo. As you look to the left across the Grand Canal from the terrace, you'll see the:

37. **Casetta Rossa,** a small private house painted a deep red and named for its large rose garden fronting on the water. This romantic landmark, with its pergola of vines at the water's edge, housed the studio of Antonio Canova (1757–1822), the last of the great Venetian sculptors. During World War I, the dashing and nationalistic poet, novelist, and war hero, Gabriele d'Annunzio, lived here while he recovered from his wounds.

Take a Break The new **cafe/restaurant at the Guggenheim Collection** offers a stylish, top quality menu. Located at the far end of a garden filled with ivy, oleander, and a canopy of loquat, you couldn't find a more enchanting place for a coffee, a light meal, and time to rest before moving on to the end of this walk.

Exit the museum and cross the next bridge to the Campiello Barbaro, which hosts two antique shops. To the left is the rear garden of:

38. **Palazzo Dario,** with flowers and vines overflowing its walls. Look up, and you'll see the gothic windows, porches, chimneypots, and rooftop terrace of this small palazzo. In

1487, the waterfront facade of this house was faced with lavish polychrome marbles by the Lombardo family, who also built the beautiful marble Miracoli Church. (See Walk 2, Stop 13.) Look for the palazzo's exotically rich asymmetrical facade of arched porticos and marble as you pass by on the Grand Canal; it's an eccentric masterpiece.

Cross the next bridge and continue straight. On the right, at no. 175, you will come to:

39. the showroom and landmark glass factory of **Gino Cenedese.** You couldn't find a more wonderful place to see glass production. The showroom is open from 9am to about 6pm except on Saturday; the hours when master artisans will be blowing glass are never certain, but you might check at the Cendese showroom at 153A on Piazza San Marco for current information.

Exit the Cenedese showrooms and turn left, continuing along the calle to the gothic brick facade of the Church of San Gregorio. The buildings on the left as you pass down this narrow calle are the former abbey of San Gregorio, now a center for restoring works of art. You will see the great Salute looming at the end of the calle. Across the bridge, you'll be back at the Campo de la Salute. Before boarding a vaporetto, you may want to walk out to the Punta Dogana again for one last look at the ever-changing panorama before ending this tour.

To Cannaregio and the Ghetto

Start: Rialto Bridge.

Finish: San Marcuola Actv Stop.

Time: Two to four hours, depending on time spent at museums and markets.

Vaporetto: Nos. 1 and 2.

Best Time: Afternoons, when many stops along other walks are closed. The Ca' d'Oro is open afternoons; the one-hour synagogue tours in the Ghetto are given until 3pm.

Worst Time: Saturdays, when no synagogue tours are given.

his walk takes us from the bustling Rialto Bridge through the northern sestiere of Cannaregio.

For Venetians, each sestiere is like another province of their homeland; some residents of the city claim they can identify the sestiere a fellow Venetian comes from merely by listening to clues in his or her accent. Others say the light in each sestiere is different—that in Cannaregio, which faces north, it has a certain melancholy, especially in winter. The spirit of Cannaregio is filled with paradoxes. It seems less touristed and spectacular than other parts of town, though it contains many of Venice's most impressive sites, including the wondrous Ca' d'Oro. The Strada Nova, Cannaregio's main pedestrian thoroughfare is lined with busy shops that fill the everyday needs of the city, and the canals here are straighter and more workaday than the gondola-filled, mysterious labyrinths of San Marco and Castello, yet the area seems more private and inward looking. The fantastical palaces all face outward across the Grand Canal; all are the outer surface of this diverse, pensive, complex part of Venice.

At the heart of Cannaregio lies the Ghetto, originally set on a walled island whose gates and bridges to the rest of the city would be closed and locked every night. Architecturally austere and hauntingly quiet today, almost 500 years after its founding, the Ghetto was once the most densely populated place in Venice, its street markets teeming with visitors from all parts of the city and, indeed, from all parts of the world. Though separate from the rest of the city, and though its inhabitants were restricted in many ways, and often hounded into poverty and bankruptcy by the demands of the Republic, the Ghetto was also intimately tied to Venetian culture. During the 16th and 17th centuries, the Ghetto of Venice evolved into the most elegant, worldly, and vivacious Jewish community ever to arise in Europe.

• • • • • • • • • • • • • • • •

The walk begins at:

1. **the Rialto Bridge,** constructed during the years 1588–1592 to replace an earlier wooden drawbridge, and designed by Antonio da Ponte, whose proposal for the bridge was chosen in a competition over submissions from Michelangelo and Andrea Palladio. The name "Rialto" is derived from *Riva Alto*, the high shore, and it was here on the highest of the muddy islets in this part of the lagoon that fishermen came to trade for centuries before a permanent settlement developed in what is now Venice. Marco Polo, Titian, and Tintoretto lived in Cannaregio, but it was Shylock, Shakespeare's imaginary inhabitant of the

Venetian Ghetto who provided the world with the most famous quotation uttered by any Cannaregian, "What news on the Rialto?" The very greeting centers on the crossroads of a city that was a world unto itself and reflects the hustle and steady devotion to commerce that made Venice great. For a thousand years, the city's fish, meat, and produce markets have crowded around every incarnation of the Rialto Bridge at this site. Here the Banco de Giro, the world's first stock exchange evolved, dealing in transfers and credits on its outdoor tables with a curiously hushed decorum that contrasted with the bedlam of the surrounding markets.

Coming from San Marco, stand at the right side of the top of the Rialto Bridge and look out over the Grand Canal, which is the direction our walk will take. To the right is the massive, white Fondaco dei Tedeschi, the Fondouk of the German Traders, with its crenelated roof cornice, or *merlatura,* an architectural term that carries the connotation of "lace" in Italian. Trade that came down the rivers of Europe from the German-speaking regions of the north was of crucial importance to the Venetian Republic's economy, and the extraordinary location of the German trading enclave just beside the Rialto Bridge attests to this fact. Completed in 1508 with a magnificence unimaginable for what was essentially a commercial structure, the canalside facade was once covered with frescos by the young and brilliant Giorgione (a few surviving fragments have been preserved in the Ca d'Oro). The facades facing the calles were frescoed by his slightly junior (and, at the time, slightly less promising) contemporary, Titian. Giorgione died at the age of 32; Titian lived and painted until he was 90. Since 1939, the Fondaco dei Tedeschi has been the city's central post office. Because of the curve of the Grand Canal, the view in this direction does not carry very far beyond the Fondaco— the view, like Cannaregio itself, seems to recede quickly away from the center of the city.

Descend the bridge in the direction of the Fondaco and turn immediately to the left at the foot of the bridge. Continue straight until you reach the side of the Fondaco, then turn right and proceed down the narrow passageway that runs alongside the building (this route helps you to get a feel for the Fondaco's enormous dimensions). At the end

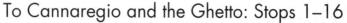

To Cannaregio and the Ghetto: Stops 1–16

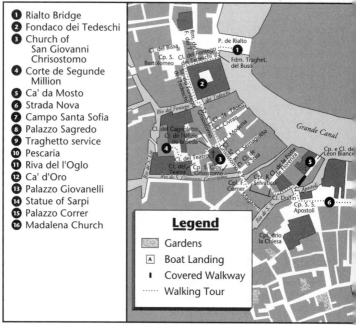

1. Rialto Bridge
2. Fondaco dei Tedeschi
3. Church of San Giovanni Chrisostomo
4. Corte de Segunde Million
5. Ca' da Mosto
6. Strada Nova
7. Campo Santa Sofia
8. Palazzo Sagredo
9. Traghetto service
10. Pescaria
11. Riva del l'Oglo
12. Ca' d'Oro
13. Palazzo Giovanelli
14. Statue of Sarpi
15. Palazzo Correr
16. Madalena Church

Legend

🗺 Gardens

Ⓐ Boat Landing

❙ Covered Walkway

...... Walking Tour

9759A

of the passageway, turn left onto the busy Salizada Fondaco dei Tedeschi and enter the:

2. **Fondaco dei Tedeschi,** which was most recently restored in 1937. The courtyard and lower floors were once filled with merchandise and warehouses; the upper floors with offices and apartments for the merchants. Despite their prestige and privileges, the German traders were subject to constant surveillance and inspection by the state. The courtyard is surrounded by the arches of porticos and loggias that diminish in height the higher they rise, creating a feeling of carefully ordered mystery, like a cityscape by the 20th-century painter, de Chirico. It would be hard to find a more wonderful place to buy a postage stamp.

Turn left onto the Salizada as you exit the Fondaco, and continue straight past the Coin Department Store. Not far beyond, on your right amid the bustle of the narrow shopping street, you'll come to the:

3. **Church of San Giovanni Crisostomo** (St. John of the Golden Mouth), named after an especially eloquent

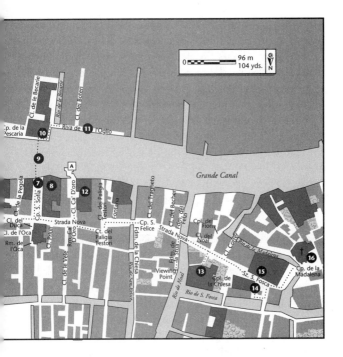

archbishop of Constantinople. Completed in 1504, this was the last work of Mauro Coducci, who designed the Torre dell' Orologico (Clock Tower) in Piazza San Marco. He also designed the facade of the Church of San Zaccaria and the Church of San Michele in Isola. Most of Coducci's facades were dressed with Istrian stone; here the facade is humble plaster (colored reddish gold by the addition of brick dust), ornamented only by delicate pilasters and the curved crowning that so often marks Coducci's churches. Inside, you'll find an intimate Greek cross plan with altarpieces painted by Giovanni Bellini and Sebastian del Piombo as well as a delicately carved marble altar on the left by Tullio Lombardo.

Exit San Giovanni Crisostomo and take Calle de Ufizio de la Seda, the narrow alley running along the right side of the church, which jogs slightly to the left to become Calle de Teatro. This quickly leads to the 19th-century Teatro Malibran, overlooking a small *corte*. Bear to the right of the theater. At the end of this passageway, on the right, you'll come to a double sottoportego, very medieval, leading into the:

4. **Corte de Segunda Million,** site of the family home of Marco Polo (1254–1324). The houses that stood here during Marco Polo's lifetime have been gone for many centuries. Even so, the courtyard is old and historic in its own right. The carved Byzantine archway, ornamented with astrological signs (often claimed to have been part of the Polo house), and various reused architectural details in the present buildings clearly come from medieval times. Go through the sottoportego at the far end of the courtyard, and look out onto the canal. According to local wisdom, the water entrance of the Polo house would have opened onto this canal, a bit to the left of the sottoportego. If this is

Marco Polo

Born into a prosperous family of Venetian traders in 1254, Marco Polo was a child when his father and uncle set off for the Volga and an unprecedented journey to the glittering capital of Kublai Khan's Mongol Empire. They returned to Venice as the Khan's ambassadors to the pope, and in 1271, young Marco joined them on their return jouney along the Silk Road to China. A favorite of the Khan's, Marco was made an administrator, and traveled extensively throughout China and the East. When the three Polos returned to Venice in 1295, after a quarter century's absence, they were at first not recognized by their family and friends. But memories were quickly jogged when the travelers ripped open their tattered bags and clothes to reveal unimaginable treasures. The story of the Polos' travels might have been lost had Marco not become a prisoner of war in 1298, in a battle against the Genoese. While in prison, he dictated his experiences, *A Description of the World,* to a fellow captive who was a professional writer. So incredible was the empire Polo described, that the book was dubbed *Il Millione* by readers unwilling to believe the vast numbers constantly reported. On his deathbed in 1324, Polo was asked to admit that he had made exaggerations. His answer was that he had not told one half of what he had really seen.

so, then the large Teatro Malibran now covers most of the site.

Retrace your steps back to the church, and turn right onto Salizada San Giovanni Crisostomo. The way jogs constantly to the left, and soon arrives at an atmospheric 12th-century arched sotoportego that runs alongside the S.S. Apostoli canal (and gives you an impression of the architecture of Marco Polo's time). Most pedestrians going in our direction will turn right at the end of the sottoportego and continue across the canal, but before following them, continue in a straight line and you'll quickly come to a small, rather neglected courtyard dominated by a broad outdoor staircase. This is the back of the:

5. **Ca' da Mosto,** one of the oldest great houses on the Grand Canal. Built in the 13th century, Ca' da Mosto is noted for its Veneto-Byzantine facade, among the best preserved in Venice. Alvise da Mosto, one of Venice's most famous explorers and the first European to discover the Cape Verde Islands, was born here in 1432. Like Marco Polo, Alvise da Mosto sojourned in exotic places for long periods of time, including a seven-year stay in Lagos, on the Nigerian coast of Africa. In later centuries, Ca' da Mosto became the Albergo del Leon Bianco, a fashionable hotel that even counted Emperor Joseph II of Austria (who traveled semi-incognito) among its guests. The building's long history as the Leon Bianco was so overpowering that researchers did not discover its original identity as the Ca' da Mosto until the 19th century. Later in this walk, we'll take a traghetto across the canal for a view of the Ca' da Mosto's facade.

Exit the courtyard, cross the S.S. Apostoli Bridge to Campo S.S. Apostoli and bear left onto the straight, relatively broad:

6. **Strada Nova,** or "New Street," built in the 1870s as a shop-lined pedestrian thoroughfare to connect the Rialto area with the Railroad Station. Tourists who base themselves in San Marco or Dorsoduro are often amazed to find that such a part of Venice even exists. An extensive amount of demolition and new building had to occur in order to create this 10-meter wide thoroughfare, the first radical piece of urban planning to be undertaken in Venice in modern

times. Perhaps because the Strada Nova proceeds in segments, it has a homey, almost small-town feel. In the shop windows you'll see moderately priced, well designed clothing, home furnishings, and other items that have little to do with the tourist trade. There are also a number of places that are good for a quick snack or coffee. As you proceed down the Strada Nova, the first wide street you come to on the left is actually not a street at all, but rather:

7. **Campo Santa Sofia,** leading to a view of the Grand Canal. The Church of Santa Sofia, on the right side of the Strada Nova, opposite the campo, is almost entirely hidden by houses built to conform to the axis of the new street. As you walk through the campo toward the canal, on the left note the iron work resembling illuminated manuscript design above the gothic doorway to number 4204. On the right you'll pass the land facade of the 14th century:

8. **Palazzo Sagredo.** Because we are not gliding swiftly past this palazzo on a vaporetto, there is time to mention a bit about the Sagredos, a story typical of the histories behind so many of the great houses on the Grand Canal. The Sagredo family traces its origins to imperial Rome (as do many of Venice's patrician clans), and its name to a tradition of being entrusted with Roman state secrets. Sagredos in the Roman period were governors of Dalmatia, and from there they migrated to Venice in the 9th century. An 11th-century Sagredo was a Benedictine monk and missionary to Hungary, where he became a bishop and died a martyr outside Buda in 1067. In addition to this saint, the family gave the Republic one doge and one patriarch of Venice. A 17th-century scion of the family, Giovanni Sagredo, is perhaps the most illustrious Sagredo associated with the Campo Santa Sofia house. At the age of 27, Giovanni became Venice's ambassador to the court of Louis XIV, and was knighted by the Sun King; later, appointed ambassador to Oliver Cromwell, he sailed up the Thames with a Venetian flotilla displaying over a hundred pieces of artillery and manned by more than a thousand mariners. In the 19th century, Agostino Sagredo, last of the line, a passionate anti-Austrian, refused numerous offers to serve in the government of the empire that occupied his homeland. The

palace was restored in 1974, and is now largely rented out as office space.

At the end of the campo, directly across the canal, you have a perfect view of the Pescaria, or Fish Market, with its hip roof and open second-floor loggia. (Despite the fact that it incorporates many traditional Venetian architectural motifs, it was built in 1907 in a style that might be called neo-Veneto–Byzantine.)

9. **A traghetto service** runs across the canal from the foot of Campo Santa to the Pescaria and the busy vegetable markets. Traghettos run directly across the Grand Canal at fixed locations and hours and are great shortcuts from one side of the city to the other. If you've arrived at this point of the walk before 1:30pm, Monday through Saturday, when the traghetto is in service, this is one of the best opportunities you'll find to join the grandmothers, businessmen, housewives, students, and toddlers who pile into the center of these gondola-like vessels and nonchalantly remain standing for the one-minute voyage across the canal while waves lap at their ankles. The ride costs about 500 lire (about 35¢ each way). All you need is a normal Venetian's sea legs and death defying gumption. After surviving the traghetto ride, you'll land at the:

10. **Pescaria,** from which you get a wonderful view of the gothic Palazzo Sagredo, directly across the canal. Across the canal to the far right, the second house after the wide rio is the Ca' da Mosto, which we approached from its land entrance earlier in this walk. From here, you can see its facade, marked by narrow arched Byzantine-Veneto windows and ornamented with decorative stone roundels and panels. The two top floors were added in the 17th century. To the left, across the canal and beyond the Actv stop, you'll see the fabulous facade of the Ca' d'Oro (our next stop), completed around 1440. As you face the Pescaria, if you walk around to the right side of the structure and under the sotoportego to cross the Ponte de Pescaria, you can walk along the:

11. **Riva del l'Oglo,** where you'll have a more direct view of the Ca' d'Oro, and time to enjoy the ornate, almost snowflake lightness and harmony of the facade. When the

tide floods the Ca' d'Oro's water entrance, the entire building seems to float. It is difficult to believe that the Ca' d'Oro's
facade could have been more wonderful in its original state,
when the stone tracery was outlined with costly gold leaf,
ultramarine, and vermilion. If you are not planning to take
Walk 5, which includes the Pescaria and the vegetable markets, you might want to explore a bit of these lively markets
(open daily except Sunday from early morning until about
1pm) before taking the traghetto back across the canal to
Campo Santa Sofia. From the Campo Santa Sofia, turn left
onto the Strada Nova. Signs at the next left, the Calle de
Ca' d'Oro, will direct you to the land entrance of the:

12. **Ca' d'Oro,** open Tuesday to Friday from 9am to 5pm;
    Monday, Saturday, and Sunday from 9am to 2pm; admis-
    sion fee. Built according to the design and supervision of
    Matteo Raverti, a Milanese sculptor, in collaboration with
    the Venetian stonecutters Giovanni and Bartolomeo Bon,
    this is probably the most famous example of Venetian gothic
    architecture in the city. Unfortunately, the interior has suf-
    fered over the centuries, especially after the Russian Prince
    Alexander Trubetskoy bought the house in 1847 and pre-
    sented it to his mistress, the ballerina Marie Taglioni, who
    promptly embarked on a savage remodeling program.
    Ruskin, who was working on *The Stones of Venice* at the
    time, was appalled as Taglioni and her architect, G. B.
    Meduna, tore out the "glorious" interior staircase and sold
    the marble for scrap, demolished the fine exterior staircase,
    and destroyed the magnificent original portal that opened
    to the calle. In 1894, the Ca' d'Oro was bought by the Baron
    Georgio Franchetti, who restored the interior to something
    of its original style, and presented the building, along with
    his extensive art collection, to the city in 1916. As you
    explore the building, it is a special treat to stand at the lacy
    portego windows of the *piano nobile* and look out onto the
    Grande Canal. Two of the most interesting architectural
    features are the interior courtyard, with its well-head
    designed by Bartolomeo Bon, and the 15th-century carved
    wooden staircase (brought from another house by
    Franchetti).

    The Franchetti collection forms the core of the art work
    on display. Look for Mantegna's painting of St. Sebastian

in an alcove on the second floor, Tullio Lombardi's double portrait bust, *The Young Couple*, and the few surviving fragments of the frescoes by Giorgione and Titian that once adorned the exterior of the Fondaco dei Tedeschi.

Exit the Ca' d'Oro, and turn left onto the Strada Nova. After passing the Church of Santa Felice on the right, you will come to the Rio de Noale. Just before crossing the bridge, turn right onto the short Fondamenta de la Stua. From the Fondamenta, you have a good view to the right across the rio of the:

13. **Palazzo Giovanelli,** a 15th-century building with carved quadrilobate openwork above the gothic arches of its *piano nobile*, and lovely corner windows on its top two floors. Famous for its art collection, which once included Giorgione's *The Tempest* (now a star attraction at the Accademia), the Palazzo Giovanelli was the scene of legendary entertainment and celebrations from the 16th to the 18th centuries. Interior renovations in 1847, the same fateful year that Marie Taglioni got her hands on the Ca' d'Oro, resulted in the construction of an elegant neo-gothic spiral staircase, designed by G. B. Meduna that is an early herald of 19th-century art nouveau. This immense palazzo is currently owned by a major art dealer and is filled with European and Oriental antiques. The building is not open to the public as a museum, but because it serves as Venice's auction house, you can explore parts of the interesting interior during the pre-auction exhibitions, which are listed in major Italian newspapers. You can also ask your hotel to check the exhibition schedule by calling Semenzato (tel. 721-811). The entrance to Semenzato is at 2292 Strada Nova, just after the Ponte Pasqualigo. This may be an offbeat way to visit a palazzo, but you also can have the fascinating experience of seeing what treasures from old Venetian houses (and from all over the world) are in the process of changing hands.

Continue up the Strada Nova. You'll pass the side of the Church of Santa Fosca on your right, at which point the name of the street becomes Salizada Santa Fosca. The campanile of Santa Fosca is one of the most interesting in the city, built after the original bell tower collapsed in 1410. It has a double arched gothic belfry and four delicate gothic corner pinnacles that surround an oddly shaped Byzantine-style dome. The church faces a small campo graced by:

14. the rather ordinary 19th-century **statue of Fra Paolo Sarpi** (1552–1623), one of Venice's great national heroes and perhaps the most brilliant scholar produced by Venetian society. The statue is one of the few public monuments honoring a native Venetian that was erected in the city.

Fra Paolo Sarpi was a scientist, mathematician, discoverer of the mechanics of the contraction of the iris of the eye, friend of Galileo, and diplomatic historian. He was also a Servite priest and adviser to the Republic on religious affairs. Always a believer in the separation of church and state, Sarpi helped guide Venice through the diplomatic and theological twists of its landmark confrontation with the Vatican in 1606. Traditionally, secular courts had no jurisdiction over members of the clergy accused of crimes; all such cases were tried in ecclesiastical courts. When the Republic refused to relinquish its long tradition of trying members of the clergy accused of secular crimes in secular courts, Pope Paul V, already exasperated with Venice's lackluster interest in the Inquisition, its toleration of Jewish, Greek, Muslim, and Armenian enclaves, and the limits it had set on the amounts of money Venetian church establishments could send to Rome, placed the entire Republic under a Papal Interdict. All religious services were forbidden, effectively excommunicating every Catholic in Venice. The Republic found this a delightful excuse to exile the always troublesome Jesuits, and decreed that throughout its empire, the interdict would be ignored. When a lone priest in Padua announced that the Holy Spirit had moved him to obey the interdict, the Council of Ten replied that the Holy Spirit had moved them to hang any priest who refused to say mass. Sir Henry Wotten, the English ambassador to Venice, gleefully reported that Venice was on the verge of becoming Protestant. All of Europe held its breath. French mediation finally helped end the crisis, with the Republic allowed to continue its traditional practices.

Six months after the interdict was lifted, while crossing the narrow bridge to the Campo Santa Fosca late at night, Sarpi was stabbed and left for dead by three assassins, supposedly dispatched from Rome. He survived, however, and while recovering was able to make the pun that he recognized the stylum (meaning both style and pen or sharp instrument) of the Roman Curia in the attack. Sarpi continued to counsel the Republic in a policy of religious tolerance at a time when Rome was obsessed with the Counter-Reformation and the Inquisition. As always in its history, the ways of Venice were entirely its own.

On the Strada Nova, opposite the campo, is the:

15. **Palazzo Correr,** that includes the Veneto-gothic brick building with elaborate second-story gothic windows at number 2217, and the contiguous house with a white Renaissance stone facade at 2214. Interestingly, what at first appears to be two separate buildings is really a double palace with two separate facades. The Renaissance facelift on the right provides a textbook illustration of how Venice's endless fixation on facade has transformed so many of the city's buildings. The two halves of the building have diverged in many ways, as evidenced by the ground floor shops on the newer facade and the tall, imposing ground floor windows on the gothic side, nevertheless, both sections have been visually tied together by the row of white second-story stone balconies.

Continue straight. On the left, just after crossing the Ponte San Antonio, you'll see:

16. the round, neoclassical **Maddalena Church,** designed by the architectural historian and theoretician, Tommaso Temanza, and begun in 1760. A product of the Age of Enlightenment, the Maddalena, with its strong, unadorned lines and intellectual proportions, is amazingly devoid of any traditional religious imagery and symbols. In the center of the tympanum above the entrance portal, a circle superimposed over a triangle symbolizes the Trinity, and the dedicatory inscription simply states that "Wisdom has built itself a home" (Proverbs 9:1) in this place. Fra Paolo Sarpi, had he lived a century and a half later, might well have felt at home. Although the Maddalena is rarely open except for weddings and special services, if you do get inside, you'll find a series of chapels placed around a hexagonal interior, and an oval presbytery; the monumental style and the almost tiny dimensions of the interior play

against each other. This was the last church to be built in Venice during the time of the Republic.

Continue straight on the Rio Terra de la Maddalena.

Take a Break This neighborhood contains inexpensive cafeterias and bars where you can pick up a snack or quick meal without spending a lot of time. **Leon d'Oro,** 2345 Rio Terra della Maddalena, serves assorted *cicchetti,* such as shelled crab or lobster claws, and an assortment of sandwiches that usually includes *porchetta* freshly carved from a roast suckling pig. Open Monday to Saturday from 7:30am to midnight. **Alla Maddalena,** 2348 Rio Terra della Maddalena, is a busy, counter restaurant where you can have a good plate of pasta or a sandwich, and watch the local street scene through the window. Open Monday to Saturday for lunch from 12:30pm to 2pm.

Across the next rio, and straight on, the way widens as you pass through the Campiello de la Anconetta. On your right, take note of the:

17. **Teatro Italia,** at no. 1943, an ornate example of neogothic revival built early in this century. No longer used for the theater or cinema, the building is now part of the university system.

At the upcoming major street on your right, Rio Terra Farsetti, turn right; then take the first left onto Calle Selle. Continue straight on this line of calles until you reach the ugly wooden bridge crossing the Rio del Ghetto. The unadorned buildings at the far side of the canal offer a high, fortress-like prospect. At the other side of the bridge you will enter one of the most miserable, prison-like gateways in the city. You have reached:

18. **the sotoportego of the Ghetto Novo,** the entrance to the New Ghetto, that, despite its name, is actually the oldest of the three parts of the Ghetto. As you enter the sotoportego, check the portal frames—you can still see where the hinges and bolts to the gates of the Ghetto were once fastened. From sunset to sunrise for almost 300 years, the inhabitants of the Ghetto were locked behind those gates.

You will emerge from the sotoportego in the:

19. **Campo de Ghetto Novo.** This part of the ghetto, originally consisting of a disused foundry on a small, easily isolated island, was set aside for Jewish merchants and their families in 1516. Jews had lived and traded in Venice and the Veneto for hundreds of years before the founding of the Ghetto. Usually they resided under special short term permits that could be revoked at a moment's notice. There is evidence that Jewish traders and their families were allowed to live in Mestre, on the mainland, and on the Giudecca in the 12th century (many believe the name Giudecca refers to these Jewish settlers, but it's probably not so). In 1386,

Leon de Modena

According to legend, Leon de Modena (1571–1648), Venice's most famous and flamboyant rabbi, was able to lead synagogue services and translate the Pentateuch from Hebrew into Italian by the age of three. He received both a religious and a Renaissance education and at the age of 18, began work in the humble post of children's religious teacher and preacher. So brilliant and elegant were his monologues and sermons that they were often attended by church leaders, patricians, and visitors to the city. In 1629, the Duc d'Orleans, brother of the King of France, attended one of de Modena's sermons in the company of his entire retinue; in 1637, de Modena's *History of Jewish Ceremonies* was written at the request of the English ambassador to Venice for presentation at the court of King James I. De Modena acted as secretary and *maestro di cappella* of a music academy established in the Ghetto in 1632; he also wrote and produced at least one theatrical comedy in Italian. An adventurer and incorrigible gambler, in his autobiography, de Modena lists 26 occupations he pursued in order to support himself, including musician, actor, stockbroker, alchemist, translator, classical scholar, ghostwriter of political speeches, and matchmaker. His rabbinical opinions and critiques of Jewish mysticism and Christian dogma are models of lucidity.

Jews were given the right to found a cemetery at San Nicolo on the Lido; but it was not until the early 16th century, with thousands of Jews fleeing the great expulsions from Spain in 1492, and from Portugal in 1497, that the Republic finally agreed to allow a permanent settlement of Jews.

The word "ghetto" comes from the Venetian verb "to cast," from which the word for "foundry" also is derived. It has been said that with the coining of the word "ghetto" the Republic of Venice made the most long-lasting contribution to the vocabulary of persecution. However all foreign communities in Venice were segregated to some degree. Overcrowded though the Ghetto was, with its buildings rising seven and eight stories, and with low-ceiling extra floors squeezed in wherever possible, it was one of the few safe havens in Western Europe available to Jews during the tumultuous centuries of the Reformation and the Counter-Reformation.

Turn around and look back at the sotoportego through which you entered the Ghetto. Just to the left is:

20. **the Banco Rosso** (Red Bank), with its arcaded brick portico. Upon payment of a hefty tax, Jews were permitted to live in Venice in exchange for performing the very necessary functions of money lending and pawnbrokerage, which were not regarded as completely ethical professions for Christians. They were also permitted to buy and sell used clothes and to practice medicine, and were encouraged to develop trading relationships with Jewish communities in northern Europe and the Middle East. In exchange, the Republic forbade arbitrary violence against Jewish persons or property, a guarantee virtually unthinkable at that time in the rest of Europe.

The Banco Rosso, the Ghetto's most important pawn-shop, derived its name from the color of its pawn tickets and promissory notes. For centuries, the treasures of Venetian houses, both great and modest, were brought here as collateral. During the Ghetto's height, the Campo de Ghetto Novo was filled with outdoor stalls selling "used clothes" a term which could be loosely extended to include draperies and carpets. Especially during times of economic hardship or after a plague, the campo would be packed with Venetians and foreigners rummaging through mountains of rare

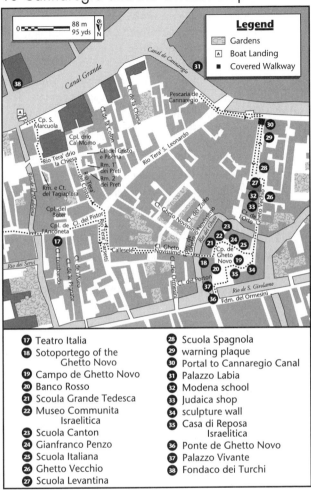

17 Teatro Italia
18 Sotoportego of the Ghetto Novo
19 Campo de Ghetto Novo
20 Banco Rosso
21 Scoula Grande Tedesca
22 Museo Communita Israelitica
23 Scuola Canton
24 Gianfranco Penzo
25 Scuola Italiana
26 Ghetto Vecchio
27 Scuola Levantina
28 Scuola Spagnola
29 warning plaque
30 Portal to Cannaregio Canal
31 Palazzo Labia
32 Modena school
33 Judaica shop
34 sculpture wall
35 Casa di Reposa Israelitica
36 Ponte de Ghetto Novo
37 Palazzo Vivante
38 Fondaco dei Turchi

brocades from the Near East, silk embroidered gowns, and velvet mantles that had survived both their original owners and their owners' heirs. The women of the Ghetto resewed and reworked these textiles. According to contemporary reports, visitors to the Ghetto came specifically to admire the Jewish women, many of whom were richly adorned in costumes designed to show how beautifully the used materials could be refashioned. Bargains could be found at every turn and were carried away to every corner of Europe. Sir Henry Wotten, the English ambassador to

Venice in the early 17th century, decorated his palazzo on the Grand Canal with fine furniture, carpets, paintings, and tableware, all bought or rented from merchants in the Ghetto.

At night, the open space of the campo was sometimes used for theatrical performances and musical events. The Jewish festival of Purim, with its costumes and merry-making, coincides with the season of Carnivale, and thousands of Venetians would flock to the Ghetto after dark to join in the festivities.

Less visible than the market was the Ghetto's vibrant intellectual life. As the newly invented printing industry developed, Venice became the preeminent center for Hebrew publications; the Ghetto's literary and intellectual salons, as well as its synagogues, were frequented by Venetians and foreigners alike.

Today, the once bustling Campo de Ghetto Novo is often eerily quiet. The campo's three wells attest to the dense

Sara Coppio Sullam

A Renaissance poet, Sara Coppio Sullam (1592–1641), was born in the Ghetto and became famous through the sonnets and letters she exchanged with Ansaldo Ceba, a Genoese nobleman and monk. Married to a prominent member of the Venetian Jewish community, she presided over the city's most luminous salon, which served as a meeting place for Jewish and Christian scholars. In 1621, the powerful Baldassar Bonifaccio, who later became Cardinal of Capo d'Istria, attacked Sara Coppio Sullam in a pamphlet, claiming that she had denied the immortality of the soul. Walking a tightrope between courtly intellectual discourse and the Inquisition, she replied with two adroit and caustic sonnets in which she declared pride in both her faith and in her own beliefs. The religious liberty which Venetian Jews enjoyed also enabled her to publish a witty manifesto refuting the accusations. After her death, a volume of her collected poems was edited by her former teacher, the ubiquitous Leon de Modena.

population once concentrated here. A tree of liberty was planted in the center of the Campo in 1797, when the Republic fell, and Napoleon, in the spirit of the French Revolution, ordered the gates of the Ghetto torn down. By then, the Venetian Jewish community, which had been declared bankrupt by the Council of Inquisitors in 1735, had undergone over a century of progressive ruin and decline and the Ghetto's population had shrunk from over 5,000 to fewer than 1,600 inhabitants. In the decades after the fall of the Republic, the intense commitment of Venetian Jews to their city was amply demonstrated. Daniele Manin, leader of the 1848–49 Insurrection against Austria, was the descendant of a Jewish family, and two of the ministers of his republic, as well as many of the insurrection's most ardent supporters were Jews. The Jewish community of Venice now numbers approximately 1,000. Only a small number of Jews continue to reside in this neighborhood, although the Ghetto remains the center for Jewish institutions and houses of worship.

As you look back at the sotoportego through which you entered the Ghetto, the third house to the right contains a row of five tall, arched windows (two of them now bricked up) on its fourth floor. This is the:

21. **Scuola Grande Tedesca,** or German Synagogue, established in 1528, and the oldest of the Ghetto's five remarkably beautiful houses of prayer. The five contiguous arched windows symbolize the five books of the Torah, and conveyed the location of the synagogue to Jewish travelers arriving in the Ghetto for the first time. Synagogues in the Ghetto were located on the upper floors of buildings, partly as protection against flooding, and partly because synagogues have traditionally been located on the highest ground of the community. An additional factor in placing synagogues on the upper floors of buildings behind unremarkable facades may have been fear of attack, but as the Jewish community became more established in Venice, this became less of a consideration. Just to the right of the German Synagogue is the entrance to the:

22. **Museo Communita Israelitica,** or Jewish Museum, a small treasure house of Italian Judaica, open June 1 to Sep-

tember 30, Sunday to Friday from 10am to 7pm; from October 1 to May 31, Sunday to Friday from 10am to 4pm; closed on Saturdays and Jewish holidays. The Museo Communita Israelitica also provides entrance to the German Synagogue. Admission to the museum only is approximately $2.50; the museum offers a synagogue tour, which includes admission to the museum, for $6. We highly recommend the informative tour, which includes three of the Ghetto's five synagogues (the three available for viewing vary according to season) led by members of the Venetian Jewish community. As the synagogues are not open to the public except through these tours, this is the only way you'll be able to visit them. Tours generally begin at half past each hour. It's a good idea to let the ticket vendors know ahead of time if you want to reserve a place on a tour. There is a unique mixing of Venetian and Jewish traditions in the synagogues you'll visit. The German Synagogue, with its irregular interior space shaped into a graceful oval by means of the trompe l'oeil techniques employed on its upper gallery, is an especially delicate Venetian creation. The twisted vine columns of the Scuola Canton's *bimah*, or reader's platform, and the ornate, spiraling carved floral columns of the Scuola Levantina are uniquely Venetian interpretations of the great columns that once stood in front of Jerusalem's long-lost Temple of Solomon.

Before joining the synagogue tour, we'll continue with a quick walk through all three parts of the Ghetto. As you face the entrance to the Jewish Museum and look to the far right, you'll notice that the Campo tapers into a narrow alleyway. The building at the end of the alleyway is crowned with a small, off-kilter octagonal cupola reminiscent of the distorted, almost cubist buildings of Chagall's early Russian paintings. This is the cupola of the:

23. **Scuola Canton,** built in 1531. The word *canton* means "corner" in Venetian dialect, but it is not certain whether the synagogue derives its name from this meaning, or whether it was originally the private prayer hall of the Canton family, which originated in France. The cupola, which covers the *bimah,* on which the Torah is studied, provides readers with good natural light, and is another telltale sign of a synagogue's presence. The white stone inscription

beside the entrance to the synagogue reads: "Many are the wrongdoers, but whomsoever trusts in the Lord shall be surrounded by mercy" (Psalms, 32).

From this corner, turn to the right, and walk along the south side of the campo. The first shop, no. 2895, belongs to:

24. **Gianfranco Penzo** (tel. 716-313), who has developed a worldwide reputation as a traditional painter and decorator of Venetian glass. You'll see a sampling of Sig. Penzo's hand-painted plates and goblets in the window; a good part of his creations are designs in Judaica derived from illuminated manuscripts. You can order all kinds of decorative motifs from the large collection of medieval and Renaissance art books and catalogs on hand in the workshop. Sig. Penzo also does his own classic and art deco designs, using diamond-point engraving on clear crystal. Prices are not cheap, but quite reasonable when you realize that anything created here is an instant heirloom. A Renaissance man in many ways, Gianfranco Penzo is also a musician and performs with a local jazz group. If the shop is closed, try knocking loudly on the metal door (no. 2898) to Sig. Penzo's workshop, which is around the corner, next to the Canton Synagogue.

A bit farther along this side of the campo is the:

25. **Scuola Italiana,** or Italian Synagogue, a three-story building with a ground-floor entrance portico resting on four white columns that suggest a classical temple. Again, you will notice the five arched windows on the top floor, and if you stand back from the building, you'll also see the synagogue's silver cupola above the wrought-iron balcony to the right of the windows. On the second floor, a row of five smaller round-arched windows, some of them now walled up, may indicate the location of an earlier synagogue, from a time before the upper stories of the building were added. This congregation developed in the 1570s among families originally from southern Italy (especially from the ancient Jewish community of Rome) who moved northward, intermingling with Jews of the Veneto. A fire severely damaged the interior of the synagogue in 1987, but it has been carefully restored.

Turn left at the corner and cross the small Ponte di Ghetto Vecchio, which takes you off the island originally allotted to the Jews, and into a newer area that was added to the Ghetto in 1541 to alleviate overcrowding. Paradoxically, this is called the:

26. **Ghetto Vecchio,** or Old Ghetto. This narrow neighborhood, with a few side passageways, contains no large campo and was less frequented by outsiders than the Ghetto Novo. At first it was home to prosperous and worldly Jews from the Middle East and from the Iberian peninsula. As you proceed down the one main street, the Calle de Ghetto Vecchio, you come to the Campiello de le Scuole. On your left, as you enter the campiello, is the:

27. **Scuola Levantina,** or Synagogue of the Levantine Jews, founded in 1538, and elegantly redesigned in 1635, probably by Baldassare Longhena, the baroque master who created the Church of Santa Maria della Salute. By the time this synagogue was reconstructed, the community felt no need to camouflage its exterior. Built during the Ghetto's golden age, the carved doors to this synagogue are sensually opulent. The ground floor, with an additional entrance on the calle, housed the 17th-century Luzzato religious school. Rabbi Simon Luzatto, spiritual leader of the Ghetto during its golden age, reportedly issued an opinion permitting gondola travel on the Sabbath (Orthodox Judaism does not normally allow the use of vessels or other means of transportation on the Sabbath). The Scuola's ornate pulpit, carved by the master woodworker, Andrea Brustolon, was restored in 1973 by Save Venice.

On the opposite side of the campiello is the:

28. **Scuola Spagnola,** or Spanish Synagogue (c. 1635), also attributed to Longhena. A plaque beneath the synagogue windows of this facade memorializes Venetian victims of the Holocaust. It was at the Spanish congregation that, in 1629, the Duc d'Orleans and his retinue made his majestic appearance to hear Rabbi Leon de Modena preach. In addition to their own special traditions, the Spanish Jews shared an unusual legal and theological situation. Expelled from Spain in 1492, many sought refuge in Portugal, where they were faced with a second expulsion order in 1497. At

the harbor of Lisbon, as they waited for passage out of Portugal, thousands of Jews were forcibly baptized before being allowed to leave. Although this forced baptism was soon annulled, at times it was reinvoked by certain church authorities. Other Ponentine (Iberian) Jews had remained in Spain and Portugal, living outwardly as Christians while they waited for better times or a chance to escape. All Jews of Spanish origin in Italy were under suspicion of having once been converted to Catholicism, or descended from converts to Catholicism, which made them subject to the Inquisition (the Inquisition normally had no power to investigate non-Christians). Jews from Iberia, hoping to resume their Jewish identities, continued to appear in Venice for more than 200 years after the expulsion from Spain.

Continue down the Calle di Ghetto Vecchio. On your right, on the wall of the red house near no. 1126, look up and you'll see:

29. **a white stone plaque** dated September 20, 1704, forbidding any Jew or Jewess converted to Christianity from approaching the Ghetto under penalty of "the lash, the galley, or the gallows."

Proceed through the sotoportego, which opens to the busy Cannaregio Canal. At the:

30. portal leading to the airy **Fondamenta di Cannaregio,** look to the left: In the Istrian stone frame you will again see where the gates to the Ghetto were once fixed. From here, before retreating back into the closed world of the Ghetto, we'll take a quick walk to the left down the fondamenta and straight past the Ponte de le Guglie to the narrow Pescaria, from which you can view across the canal:

31. the richly ornamented **Palazzo Labia,** built from 1720 to 1750, and famous for its ballroom which is framed by dazzling trompe l'oeil architectural details, and decorated with Tiepolo's frescoes depicting the life of Cleopatra. The immensely wealthy and slightly deranged Labia family was famous for extravagant entertainment. After one banquet, one of the more legendary Labias tossed the entire gold dinner service into the canal, while declaiming the most melodramatic pun ever created in Venetian dialect: "L'abia, o non l'abia, saro sempre Labia" ("whether I have it or don't

have it, I will always be Labia"). According to legend, nets previously placed in the canal insured that whether the Labias had it or didn't have it, somehow they would manage to retrieve it.

In 1951, the Palazzo Labia was bought for a half million dollars by Don Carlos de Beistegui, a Mexican millionaire who spent an additional $750,000 on renovations. In true Labia tradition, for a palazzo-warming celebration, de Beistegui held a masked ball and banquet with entertainment that included the presentation of 18 fully costumed baroque period tableaux, acrobats, a ballet, and a simultaneous public ball for the people of Venice in the adjacent Campo de San Geremia. Guests ranged from Europe's postwar nobility to film and stage celebrities. The host changed costumes six times, one guest arrived by gondola in the guise of a 13th-century Chinese potentate that reportedly cost $55,000, and the Aga Khan reported he had never seen anything like de Beistegui's masquerade in his entire life.

The Palazzo Labia is now the Venetian headquarters of RAI, the state radio and television network. Appointments to see the ballroom are given weekdays from 3 to 4pm; telephone 781-111 in advance. You can also inquire about the free twice-weekly recording concerts that are held in the ballroom.

Return to the entrance to the Ghetto Vecchio and retrace your steps back up the Calle di Ghetto Vecchio, passing the Campiello de le Scuole. On the right is:

32. **the school of Rabbi Leon de Modena,** no. 1222, with an arched door flanked by two arched windows. Interestingly, this configuration is typical of the facades of old houses in Jerusalem and the Galilee. A few steps beyond on the right is:

33. **a shop run by the Fusetti and Mariani families,** who have lived in the Ghetto for centuries and continue to live there today. It sells moderately priced Venetian Judaica, including painted wine goblets and bronze reproductions of baroque 17th-century Italian wall menorahs designed to burn oil at Hanukkah.

Continuing back across the Ponte di Ghetto Vecchio into the Campo de Ghetto Novo, the wall to the left contains:

34. **a series of seven sculptural reliefs** by the Lithuanian artist, Arbit Blatas, together with a poem by Andre Tranc in memory of those who perished in the Holocaust.

Directly ahead, at the far side of the campo (once lined with high tenement buildings, torn down in 1836), is:

35. **the Casa di Reposa Israelitica,** the Jewish Rest Home, founded in the 19th century. A number of community offices are housed in this building. Travelers who are kosher can arrange to have meals here by telephoning 716-002. To the right of the Casa di Reposa is a garden wall with the names and ages of the members of the community who were captured during the Nazi manhunts of World War II and sent to their deaths. Among those listed are a two-month-old infant and the revered Rabbi Adolfo Ottolenghi, spiritual leader of the Venetian Jewish community from 1919 to 1943. Many of those who escaped owe their survival to the help of their non-Jewish friends and neighbors.

To the right of the Memorial Wall is:

36. the graceful iron **Ponte de Ghetto Novo,** built in 1865. As if in compensation for the demeaning entrances that were imposed on the Ghetto in the past, this is the most beautiful (as well as the last) of the many iron spans erected by the Austrians, who ended their fifty-year occupation of Venice in 1866. From the summit of the bridge, look back to your left at the:

37. **Palazzo Vivante** and, beyond the next rio, the more impressive **Palazzo Treves,** with its many balconies and double water entrances on the canal, which give direct contact to the outside world. This is the Ghetto Novissimo, or Newest Ghetto, the third and last area, added to the Jewish community in 1633 to house the families of prosperous Sephardic bankers and traders. Gates that were closed every night sealed off these privileged families from the rest of Venice, just as they imprisoned less prosperous families. Again, from this bridge, you can get a feel for the insular nature of the original Ghetto. To this day, when a member of the Jewish community dies, the body is carried in a funeral launch that slowly circumnavigates the Ghetto Novo before sailing out to the lagoon and the Jewish cemetery on the Lido.

If you plan to take the synagogue tour, return to the Museo Communita Israelitica at this point. After the synagogue tour, if you want to reach the nearest No. 1 Actv stop, retrace the route to the Ghetto taken earlier. Where Rio Terra Farsetti meets Calle dei Plater, instead of turning left, continue relatively straight onto Rio Terra dei Criato. Turn left at Rio Terra dei la Chiesa, which runs along the back of the Church of San Marcuola. Turn right at the end of the church, and the San Marcuola Actv stop will be at the end of the calle. While standing at the Actv stop, you have a perfect view just across the Grand Canal of the:

38. **Fondaco dei Turchi** (Turkish Fonduk), which dates from the early 13th century, and is one of the most unusual landmarks on the Grand Canal. Just as the German and Jewish merchants were allowed to establish their own communities in Venice, so were businessmen from Islamic lands. The Fondaco's name (from the Arabic *fonduk*, or caravan hostel) refers to its use, from 1621 to 1838, as an inn and trading center for merchants from the Ottoman empire. Originally the Fondaco was an important palazzo that at one time belonged to the Duke of Ferrara, but during its two centuries as the center for traders from the Middle East, the Fondaco was outfitted with two mosques and a Turkish bath, and, in deference to Muslim sensibilities, entrance was forbidden to immodestly dressed Western women. By the time of the Turks departure, both Venice and the Ottoman Empire had fallen into steep decline, and the building was a virtual ruin. In 1859, a massive restoration effort began. The building you see today is a textbook example of some elements of 13th-century Veneto-Byzantine style, including the long rows of tall, narrow arched windows, but the end towers and the roof crenelation are pure 19th-century interpretations. The Fondaco dei Turchi now houses Venice's Museum of Natural History.

THE ISLAND OF SAN MICHELE

Start: San Michele vaporetto stop.

Finish: San Michele vaporetto stop.

Time: Approximately one hour.

Vaporetto: No. 52.

Best Time: From 8:15am to 4pm when the cemetery is open.

If you have any taste for cemeteries, you'll find San Michele an absolute delight. You may also want to visit the graves of such luminaries as Ezra Pound and Stravinsky.

But even if you don't much care for cemeteries you'll still find this island worth a visit for its gorgeous early Renaissance church, one of the most beautiful buildings in Venice.

Note: Although visitors are welcome, they are expected to be dressed and to behave in a manner "appropriate" to a cemetery.

● ● ● ● ● ● ● ● ● ● ● ● ● ●

After disembarking from the vaporetto, go through the gate just to the right of the church and you'll find yourself in a lovely:

1. **cloister,** of 1436–53, the covered passageway built around a courtyard and well. It connected the various buildings of the monastic compound. Its style is late gothic with swirling capitals on the columns. It was built shortly before the church, whose entrance is halfway down the cloister on your left.

2. **The Church of San Michele** was the first church in Venice to be built in the Renaissance style, in 1469–79, by Mauro Coducci, and it is a real gem. Its lovely white classical facade of Istrian stone is one of the most handsome of the 15th century.

   The nave and aisles culminate in a domed sanctuary and chapels. Balancing this stonework on the other end of the church is a raised monk's choir supported by arches intersecting the church.

   Everywhere you look you'll find rich decoration in an inexhaustible variety, whether the rosettes in the coffers of the ceiling or the capitals of the columns or the relief panels that decorate the raised choir.

   Pass under the raised choir and into the rear section of the church. Just inside the main portal you will find the simple stone gravemarker of Fra Paolo Sarpi, one of the most brilliant intellectuals of Venetian history (see Walk 8, Stop 14).

   In the far corner is a door leading to a tiny pentagonal room, covered all over in delicate reliefs. This serves as a vestibule for:

3. **the Emiliani Chapel** (or, Chapel of the Annunciation). It is a little hexagonal temple, built slightly later than the church (1527–43), with three carved altarpieces and with a door opposite each one. It and its vestibule are if anything even richer in sculpture and spatial effects than the church itself. Curiously, Margherita Vitturi, the woman who had it built in memory of herself and her husband, never knew what it would look like since it was paid for by a legacy.

   Retrace your steps to the cloister, and as you emerge from the church, turn left and follow the cloister in a clockwise direction. At the second corner you'll find the entrance to the Large Cloisters of the monastery—actually a U-shaped structure—and:

4. **the Cemetery.** This is the only cemetery in Venice, and it's relatively new. Up until the early 19th century Venetians were buried in or near their parish church. The French conquerors of Venice thought that burial in a city was unseemly and unsanitary; so two small islands that formerly had nothing but a monastery apiece were appropriated, the canal between them was filled in, and San Michele was born as an island of the dead.

   In the past funeral corteges of large black gondolas decorated with golden angels processed to the cemetery; today they have generally been replaced by flower-laden black motor launches. The island is fair-sized, but still too small for its purpose, and most of the residents can afford only a twelve-year's lease before they are exhumed and moved elsewhere. The richer, the more notable, and the non-Catholics have a better chance of staying put.

   Follow the signs that direct you to the graves of STRAWINSKJI and EZRA LOOMIS POUND. You will turn left after you get past the monastic buildings and go through the arched passageway.

   Continue straight ahead, but on your way notice the children's graves to your left. The last stone, depicting a Miss Nadia Eliana Lucchesi standing at the bottom of stairs leading to heaven is a sort of sentimental masterpiece.

   Leaving the children behind, pass through the next arch and veer ever so slightly to your left and you will come to:

5. **the Protestant Section** (Rep. Evangelico). It looks something like a 19th-century American cemetery, but with a remarkable number of languages represented in the inscriptions, for this is the final resting place of many of the foreigners who have lived in Venice and loved it enough to be buried here. The foreigners' graves far outnumber those of Venetian Protestants. On your left, beneath a rounded bush and probably decked with flowers, is the tomb of **Ezra Pound**. This expatriate from Idaho was one of the most influential poets of the 20th century, and, in the opinion of many, one of its greatest. He was also an outspoken fascist

and supporter of Mussolini who remained in Italy throughout World War II. He was confined for some time to psychiatric hospitals in Pisa and Washington, D.C., after the war ended, in lieu of being sent to prison for treason. He lived the rest of his life in Italy. His gravemarker is a simple stone carved by his friend, the American sculptor Joan Fitzgerald. It lacks the epitaph he playfully created for himself:

> Ezra Pound
> Got around
> He was born in Hailey
> But he was buried in San Michele
> not the *terzo cielo*
> but socially *meglio.*

Just to the right of Pound is the grave of **Sir Ashley Clark.** He served as British ambassador to Italy in Rome, but his real love was Venice. He founded the Venice in Peril fund, whose first major project was the church of the Madonna dell'Orto; and when he donated a stained-glass window to the Anglican Church in Venice, he had a small picture of the Madonna dell'Orto included within it. He was much admired by the Venetians, who made him an honorary citizen of their city.

Go to your left as you leave the Protestant graveyard and enter the first major gate on your left. It takes you to:

6. **the Orthodox Section** (Rep. Greco), which is immediately next to the Protestant one. Opposite the entrance is a chapel. To the right of the chapel and against the rear wall, are the simple and beautiful tombs of **Vera and Igor Stravinsky,** which were designed by the Italian sculptor Giacomo Manzù. Stravinsky (1882–1971) was possibly the greatest composer of this century. Stravinsky died in New York, but it was his wish to be buried in San Michele. Venice honored him with a memorial service among the tombs of the doges in the great church of SS. Giovanni e Paolo.

His neighbor on the other side of the chapel, also against the rear wall and under a kind of stone canopy is **Serge Diaghilev** (1872–1929), the art critic and impresario who

San Michele

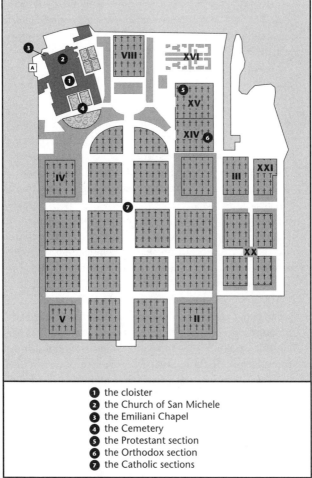

1. the cloister
2. the Church of San Michele
3. the Emiliani Chapel
4. the Cemetery
5. the Protestant section
6. the Orthodox section
7. the Catholic sections

revolutionized the dance world when he formed his Ballets Russes and brought together in a seamless whole, music, dance, and scenic design. Stravinsky's compositions, *Petrushka, Firebird,* and *Rite of Spring* were first performed by Diaghilev's company.

Diaghilev's unexpected death rocked the European cultural world. When he was laid to rest, if that expression can be used, his burial included scenes that were downright theatrical—an overwrought companion supposedly threw himself into the grave.

If you continue counter-clockwise around the Ortho-dox Section, you'll find the marvelously art-nouveau bronze-and-stone tomb of "Sonia," about halfway down the the wall running back toward the entrance.

From here, if you have time and inclination, you can turn to your left on leaving the Orthodox section and wander around:

7. **the Catholic sections** of the cemetery which naturally occupy most of the island. The tombs range from complete temples to humble graves that get recycled periodically. Sculpture of every kind and quality abounds. The cemetery has the additional advantage of being the largest expanse of greenery in Venice.

Buried in this section is **Frederick Rolfe,** the eccentric and mysterious English writer and Catholic convert known as Baron Corvo. He is notable for his scathing satires on foreigners living in Venice, and for his beautiful descriptions of the city.

To leave the cemetery from the Rep. Greco, cross the stone path and go through the pointed arch, and you will be on the inside curve of an enormous tomb-lined semi-circular structure. Turn to your right and continue around the semicircle. In the middle of it is the 19th-century chapel of St. Christopher (the other island-monastery, leveled to make the cemetery, was dedicated to him). Continue past that chapel until you come to the triple gate on your right. Go through it and you will find yourself once again in the Large Cloister, from which you can return to the smaller cloister and the vaporetto stop.

If you wish, you can take a boat heading toward your right to the next stop, on Murano and Walk 10.

MURANO

Start: Colonna Actv Stop, Murano. *Note:* To continue on to Burano and Torcello, you must depart Murano from the Faro Actv Stop at the foot of Via Garibaldi.

Finish: Colonna Actv Stop, Murano.

Time: 1¹/₂ to 2 hours (not including shopping).

Vaporetto: Nos. 5 or 52.

Best Time: Weekdays.

Worst Time: Saturdays and Sundays, when few furnaces are functioning or open to visitors.

In a city that floats amid interplays of light and delicate reflections on the surface of its canals and lagoon, it seems only natural that its inhabitants would turn to the creation of glass, their one major export industry. The very process of glassblowing—the capture of air, light, and liquid into fleeting shapes of translucence—is an alchemy akin to the process that created Venice itself out of unlikely mud banks and tidal flatlands.

History and economics also contributed to the rise of Venice as a center extraordinaire for the production of glass. The ancient art of making glass first developed in Egypt and along the coasts of Phoenicia and Israel. It was picked up by

Rome, Byzantium, and the Islamic Middle East, each of which evolved a style of its own. In medieval Europe, only Venice, with its trading ties to the Middle East, had access to the raw materials necessary for glass production. It also probably had a unique access to the craftspeople who guarded the secrets of glassmaking.

By the year 1291, the glass industry had become so large and so important to the Republic that all glass furnaces were transferred to the island of Murano, ostensibly to prevent the possibility of mass conflagration but also to make foreign industrial espionage more difficult.

In 1376, the Republic decreed that male offspring of a Venetian patrician and a glassblower's daughter could be listed in the Libro d' Oro and have the right to sit in the Great Council, an honor not offered to any other group of artisans. On the other hand, laws restricted the rights of glassblowers to travel beyond the Republic, to move away from Murano, or to reveal their secrets to foreigners. Families of defecting glassblowers were subject to severe punishment, and the Council of Ten could order assassins to hunt down renegade glassmakers (who, according to legend, would be dispatched by razor thin daggers of Murano glass). Despite such threats and surveillance, over the centuries many Muranese glassmakers lived openly and practiced their art in cities throughout Europe. So highly prized were the products of Murano that in 17th-century Paris, a Murano mirror, 26 x 42 inches, belonging to a minister of the French Court was assessed at three times the value of a painting by Raphael.

By the 15th and 16th centuries, in addition to housing the glass industry, Murano had become a Venetian summer retreat, dotted with villas, minor palaces, gardens, and orchards. Here Renaissance humanists and Venetian literati gathered in what was extolled as one of the most delightful places in the world. The gardens and orchards of Murano were filled with rare botanical specimens. Fields running down to the lagoon were covered with violets and narcissi, musk and damask roses; the air was scented with mint, rosemary, and lavender. By the 18th century, however, the gardens were long forgotten. As the Republic glided through its final century of decadence, glass production on Murano did a swan song of rococo kitsch, and had virtually ceased by the time of Napoleon's conquest in 1797.

In the mid-19th century the glass industry began to revive, and the island took on the look of an industrial town. Today, Murano gives the impression of a small scale, somewhat homey version of Venice. Like Venice, it is bisected by a broad, S-shaped Grand Canal; unlike Venice, you will have to use your imagination to get a sense of the island's elysian past. The 12th-century Basilica of SS. Maria e Donato and the Museo de Vetrario (Glass Museum) are the historical highlights of this walk, but you'll also find an incredibly vast concentration of glass on sale here, ranging from multicolored crystal interpretations of the Mona Lisa to delicate recreations of traditional Murano glass designs and sleek examples of contemporary art.

This walk includes establishments where you can find the best in Murano glass, but keep in mind that production lines and the contents of showrooms are constantly changing. It is also difficult to know exactly when glassblowers will be working. Prices on Murano can be as high as those in Venice during busy season, but on a cold winter day you may come up with a real bargain (bargaining is a watchword here). As you explore the showrooms of the island, make a note of shops in which you find interesting pieces, but buy only when you have a good idea of the range of designs, quality, and prices. The Glass Museum, midway through this walk, is a good place to see the originals of designs and styles still produced throughout the island.

If you have taken Walk 9 on the cemetery island of San Michele, Murano can be reached by taking the No. 52 vaporetto (which makes left and right directional circles around the Venetian periphery) from the Fondamente Nove. The ride is approximately 15 or 20 minutes, and gives you a wonderful view of the beautiful Renaissance Church of San Michele. You can also pick up the No. 52 vaporetto in the direction of the Arsenale at the San Zaccaria Actv stop, near the Piazza San Marco. You'll get to cruise through the monumental gates and eerie, forlorn dockyards of the once great Arsenale. A third option is to board the No. 52 at the Railroad Station in the direction of the Fondamente Nove. But if you're interested in a fascinating but much longer (one hour) scenic ride, choose the opposite direction, which passes along the shores of the Giudecca, with its Palladian churches, stops at San Giorgio Maggiore (visit the church and the dazzling view of Venice from the campanile), and continues past San Marco, the Arsenale, San Michele, and on to Murano. Obviously, a 72- or 48-hour Actv pass gives you the most flexibility for the best price, especially if you plan to continue on to Burano and Torcello.

● ● ● ● ● ● ● ● ● ● ● ● ● ● ● ● ●

After disembarking at the first Actv stop (Colonna) on the island of Murano, bear to the right and you'll find yourself on the now densely commercial Fondamenta dei Vetrai, running alongside the Rio dei Vetrai, or the Glass Canal. At no. 4 to 6, housing glass showrooms, you'll see a commercial building that, like many on Murano, was once more elegant. Look up at the second and third stories, and notice elements of the facade of:

1. **Palazzo Contarini,** a once fine 16th-century villa with five rounded Renaissance windows in the center of the second story *piano nobile*. In style, this building looks much like a small urban palazzo, but in Murano's heyday as a summer retreat, it would have been an especially delightful place, with views across the lagoon to San Michele and Venice.

Continuing past the the shop windows of the Fondamenta dei Vetrai, at no. 28 you'll find:

2. **Barovier and Toso,** one of the oldest and most prestigious firms on Murano. The Barovier family has been involved in glassmaking since at least the early 14th century and their workshops created the famous late-15th-century Barovier Wedding Cup, a masterpiece of Renaissance elegance on display at the Museo Vetrario. (You'll also see all kinds of reproductions of this dark blue ceremonial goblet at glass shops throughout Venice and Murano.) It is not always easy to walk into this august establishment, which now deals in a large range of vases, cups, lamps, and lighting fixtures. If you are able to enter, inquire about visiting the firm's museum-like collection of artistic glassware in both traditional and contemporary styles.

Just beyond the first bridge that crosses the rio (Ponte S. Chiara) note:

3. **no. 37,** a late-15th-century house, with a square carved entrance portal and triple gothic windows on the *piano nobile*. Also note:

4. **nos. 39–42,** where, if you look up above the two rounded entrance portals, you'll see the structure of a small Renaissance palazzo, with two floors of *piani nobili*, a sight unusual on Murano.

   Take a Break   Murano is not a great island for restaurants, but the **Fondamenta dei Vetrai** is home to a number of bars and shops which sell *tremezzini* (small sandwiches), as well as coffee, tea, and cold beverages. There are also establishments farther up the Rio dei Vetrai, closer to the Church of San Pietro Martire.

   As you pass no. 57, look directly across the Rio dei Vetrai to the Fondamenta Manin on the opposite side, and you'll have a perfect view of:

5 & 6. the two-story medieval **Sodeci and Obizzi houses,** with their second floors projecting over a canalside colonnade or sotoportego, handy for loading goods in transit to or from the ground floor workshops. The smaller Sodeci house contains a single apartment on the second floor and the facade reveals the shape of its fireplace. The second floor of the Obizzi house is ornamented with an interesting variety of gothic widows. These buildings, restored in 1986, are rare surviving examples of an almost rustic house/workshop type of structure, once traditional on Murano and probably seen in Venice as well in the 13th and 14th centuries.

   Window shopping and exploring showrooms are the main attractions along this canal, so take your time. Just past the Ponte Ballarin, you'll see:

7. **Campiello de la Pescaria** (at one time the fish market), with trees and a usually flowing fountain where you can fill your canteen or cool your face on a hot day. A number of broad, two-story 18th-century houses face the campiello. Back on the Fondamenta, note:

8. **no. 87,** a charming two-story cottage with an elaborate attic dormer typical of modest lagoon houses outside of Venice. The stone panel between the two second-floor windows bears the date 1769, when both the glass industry and the island of Murano were in decline.

   In the vicinity of no. 110, you have a good view directly across the Rio dei Vetrai to:

Murano

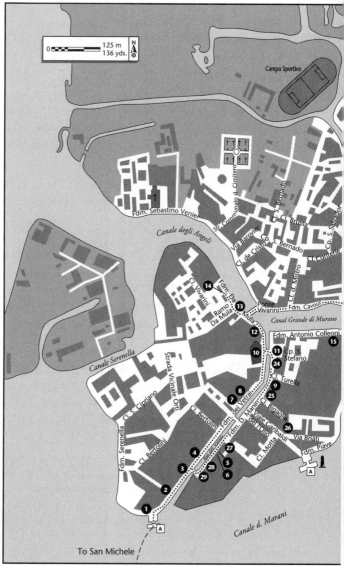

9. the 14th-century **Palazzatto Corner** (71 Fondamenta Manin) with its canalside sotoportego, similar to but more beautiful than the Sodeci and Obizzi houses we passed farther back on the rio. Palazzatto Corner's gentle curve as it

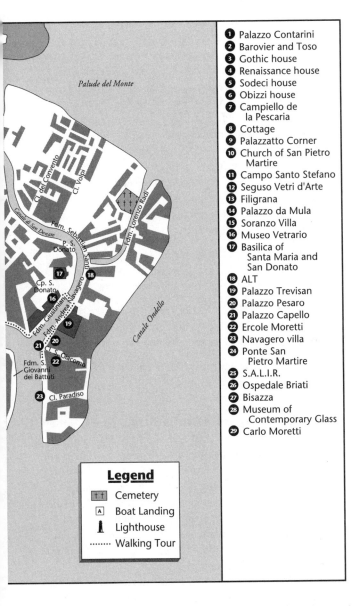

1. Palazzo Contarini
2. Barovier and Toso
3. Gothic house
4. Renaissance house
5. Sodeci house
6. Obizzi house
7. Campiello de la Pescaria
8. Cottage
9. Palazzatto Corner
10. Church of San Pietro Martire
11. Campo Santo Stefano
12. Seguso Vetri d'Arte
13. Filigrana
14. Palazzo da Mula
15. Soranzo Villa
16. Museo Vetrario
17. Basilica of Santa Maria and San Donato
18. ALT
19. Palazzo Trevisan
20. Palazzo Pesaro
21. Palazzo Capello
22. Ercole Moretti
23. Navagero villa
24. Ponte San Pietro Martire
25. S.A.L.I.R.
26. Ospedale Briati
27. Bisazza
28. Museum of Contemporary Glass
29. Carlo Moretti

Legend

††† Cemetery

Ⓐ Boat Landing

⚓ Lighthouse

.... Walking Tour

adheres to the shore of the rio, and its asymmetrical second floor facade, filled with an assortment of gothic windows, add to the building's medieval, almost rural charm.

Straight ahead on the Fondamenta dei Vetrai is:

10. the gothic **Church of San Pietro Martire,** one of the island's two still functioning churches (compared to 17 before the fall of the Republic in 1797). San Pietro's greatest treasures are a *Madonna and Child with St. Mark, St. Augustine, and Doge Barbarigo* (1488) by Giovanni Bellini on the right wall, and Veronese's *St. Jerome* (1566) over the door to the sacristy. The sacristy is lined with carved panels depicting an array of classical characters that includes Socrates, Pythagoras, Nero, Caesar, Herod, and Castor and Pollux, as well as scenes from the life of John the Baptist. Local touches, like the glass Madonna and Child and the Murano chandeliers are especially interesting.

Directly across the rio, at the other side of the Ponte San Pietro Martire, you'll see the:

11. **Campo Santo Stefano,** with its leaning medieval campanile. The actual Church of Santo Stefano was demolished during the Napoleonic suppression of churches.

Take a Break   On the campo you'll see, in good weather, the outdoor tables of the **Trattoria Busa alla Torre.** This is a good local option for a sit-down meal.

For now, we'll stay on the Fondamenta dei Vetrai as it curves around to meet Murano's Grand Canal. At number 139 is:

12. **the site of Seguso Vetrai d'Arte,** founded during the 19th-century revival of the Muranese glass industry. In 1934, Flavio Poli became chief designer for the Seguso factory, producing contemporary glass derived from his credo: "Simplicity of form, but variety of color and material." Seguso Vetrai d'Arte helped pioneer a technique that finishes glass in a sandy, opaque surface reminiscent of the soft-hued patina found on glass from ancient archaeological excavations. This kind of finish, called *scavo* (from the word for "excavation") is now a favorite of many Muranese artisans, and can be seen on both contemporary designs, and in reproductions of ancient glassware sold throughout Venice. Paolo Rossi, who has a showroom in Venice (see box below), is an outstanding and affordable creator of Scavo glassware in ancient styles that could easily be taken for museum reproductions.

Now under the ownership of Abarello and Nielsen, Seguso Vetrai d'Arte includes a wonderful display of glass produced in the 1930s and 1940s.

It's tempting to cross the sweeping Grand Canal on the Ponte Vivarini, but first continue a few steps down the Fondamenta da Mula to check out:

13. **Filigrana,** at no. 148, with its varied production line directed by the well-known Paolo Crepex.

A few steps beyond Filigrana, is the:

14. **Palazzo da Mula,** the finest medieval house on the island, with origins in the 12th or 13th centuries. The facade, with gothic second-story windows, is most likely late 15th century. Note the inlaid carved stones decorating the walls and the differing tracery designs on the delicate round windows, on the second floor. This palazzo was built not as a summer house, but as a family seat and head-quarters for trade.

Retrace your steps to the Ponte Vivarini and cross, stopping to enjoy the views from the bridge's summit. Our tour turns right at the foot of the bridge onto the Fondamenta Cavour, but you might want to take a lengthy optional stroll to the left first. This walk along the canal eventually leads to the the now closed Church of Santa Maria degli Angeli, whose convent provided Casanova with a number of pleasant memories.

From the foot of the Ponte Vivarini, the Fondamenta Cavour is dotted with more shops selling glass. Just before passing through the sotoportego, look across the Grand Canal to:

15. **the Soranzo villa,** a broad-fronted, white two-story building with six tall, arched windows in the center of its second floor, flanked on either corner by an additional round-arched window. Recently restored and absolutely shining, the Soranzo house is an example of a 16th-century Renaissance villa in its purest form. With its lacy balcony and once extensive orchards and pleasure gardens, this would have been an elegant summer retreat. The building is now used as a school.

Follow the Fondamenta Cavour to the point, where it curves leftward to become the Fondamenta Giustiniani.

After passing under another sotoportego, you'll arrive at the first of Murano's two main attractions the:

16. **Museo Vetrario** (Glass Museum), which is open April through October, Monday, Tuesday, and Thursday to Saturday from 10am to 5pm; the same days from 10am to 4pm in winter months; closed Wednesday and Sunday. Located in the Palazzo Giustiniani, the largest and most eminent house on the island, the Glass Museum is a treasure house of Murano's creations though the centuries. A visit here is an education in what to look for as you window shop and browse the glass showrooms of Venice and Murano. The building also offers a wonderful chance to explore a medium-size baroque palazzo, and to imagine what daily life inside these rooms might have been like. Originally a medieval house, in the late 1600s, the Palazzo Giustiniani became the episcopal residence of the Bishop of Torcello, and in 1707, it was renovated into a palazzo in the baroque style. If you go through the ground floor *androne*, and enter the rear courtyard, you'll see the medieval details of the building's earlier incarnation that have been left intact. The courtyard, overgrown with Virginia creeper, English ivy, oleander, loquat, and mulberry, is inhabited by a tribe of photogenic cats and dotted with a collection of Murano well heads and pieces of architectural sculpture. At the far end of the courtyard, an ornate wrought-iron gate, flanked by two figures in niches, opens to a view that once encompassed exquisite vineyards and orchards.

In 1861, at the time Murano's tradition of artistic glassware was being revived, the building was given to the Museo Vetrario, which had recently been founded under the guidance of Vincenzo Zanetti, the island's leading historian.

The ground floor houses a collection of glass from Roman times. In Case 30, there is a small 2nd-century dish made of melted glass canes and beads, strikingly contemporary in its striped and circular designs of mustard, navy, ochre, white, and olive. Case 13 holds a wine-colored dish composed of melted beads and is clearly the ancestor of modern *millefiori* glass.

When you reach the second floor, to the left you'll find an exhibit on the raw materials, processes, and tools of glassmaking. To the right is the airy grand sala, with its windows overlooking the canal. On the ceiling of the grand sala is *The Apotheosis of St. Lorenzo Giustiniani*, by Francesco Zugno. Set off in a corner of the room you'll find a counter displaying a good assortment of books on Venetian glass in all price ranges.

The rooms off the grand sala house collections from Murano's great centuries leading up to the fall of the Republic. The pure shapes of enameled and painted vessels from earlier centuries give way to diamond-point engraved crystal and the swirling stripes of filigree plates and goblets. Later come the ornate baroque configurations of the 17th and early 18th centuries. Among the most famous pieces to look for are the Barovier Wedding Cup, painted and gilded with lyrical, romantic scenes, and the miniature glass fantasy garden complete with its own fountain (an extravagant genre often produced by Murano artisans). Especially interesting is the museum's baroque drawing room, beautifully furnished and filled with examples of Murano glassware as they would have been displayed and used in the 18th century.

In the attic-like top floor, you'll find the work of glassblowers from the period of Murano's revival in the mid-19th century. Although glassmaking on Murano had virtually stopped for almost a century, the family names of many of these artisans reflect long ties to the island and to the art of glassmaking; in some cases, descendants of these craftspeople are still creating Murano glass today. Cases 3 to 9 display glass laced with multi-colored spiraling designs by Petro Bigaglia from the 1840s, as well as the marbleized glass of Lorenzo Radi (1856) and the Victorian creations of the famous Salviati workshops that led the Murano revival. (Salviati & Company's landmark palazzo on the Grand Canal in Venice, built in 1924 and faced with glistening glass mosaics, is located between the Salute and the Peggy Guggenheim Collection.) In Cases 22 and 23, Vincenzo Moretti's plates, created from the fusing of melted beads and glass canes, are a garden of multi-colored flowers. You'll see many interesting *millefiori* creations based on this technique in shops throughout Venice, but nothing will match these in size or intricacy.

Case 25 contains a *millefiori* mosaic plate that is clearly related to the mosaic dishes in the ancient glass room on the first floor. To complete the circle of history, by the 1890s, Salviati & Co. was producing a variety of perfume containers and vessels that echoed designs from antiquity.

An annex to the Glass Museum, at 3 Fondamenta Manin, near the Colonna Actv Stop, contains a collection of 20th-century glass. If the annex is open, your ticket receipt will admit you to both parts of the museum.

Exit the museum, turn left onto the Fondamenta, and you will quickly arrive at Campo San Donato, dominated by Murano's greatest architectural treasure, the:

17. **Basilica of Santa Maria and San Donato** (open daily, 8am to noon and 4 to 7pm). The beautiful arcaded apse of the church, overlooking the canal, is a tour-de-force of pattern and texture in brick that was heavily (and perhaps overly) restored by the Austrians in the 19th century. Founded in the 7th century by refugees from the mainland, and originally dedicated to the Virgin, the basilica's dedication was expanded in 1125 to include the relics of St. Donetus of Euboea, captured in a raid (Venetians could never resist a good relic raid) and interred here along with the bones of a dragon killed by the saint's potent and miraculous spit—the four very impressive dragon bones now hang behind the baroque altar in the apse. The most famous element of the interior is the mosaic floor, dated 1141. It incorporates pieces of ancient glass to create a carpet of abstract patterns and mysterious symbolic creatures. Two roosters bear a fox on a pole, and an eagle carries off a lamb. The apse mosaic of the Virgin alone in prayer against a golden background is also from the 12th century. The interior of the basilica is beautifully proportioned, covered by a 15th-century ship's-keel ceiling. The 2nd-century Roman sarcophagus in the baptistery came from Altinum, and was used as a font.

After visiting the basilica, cross the Ponte San Donato and turn left for a short stroll up this side of the canal, where you see wonderful views of the basilica. Then retrace your steps back to the foot of the bridge and continue straight along the Fondamenta Andrea Navagero. At:

18. **ALT,** 32 Fondamenta Navagero, you'll find a company that manufactures *millefiori* paperweights. Depending on circumstances, you may be able to see a range of ALT's creations and methods of production.

    At 34 Fondamenta Navagero, you'll notice:

19. **Palazzo Trevisan,** a faded, rather tall, severe structure that was a glittering architectural gem during the time when Murano was a center of culture and intellectual life. Many attribute this building to the great architect, Andrea Palladio (note the Palladian window and classical pediment in the center of the balconied *piano nobile*). Built in 1558, the facade was covered with frescoes by Prospero Bresciano, and the principal rooms frescoed by Veronese, who turned his attention here after finishing his brilliant trompe l'oeil paintings inside the Villa Barbaro at Maser on the mainland.

    Immediately after the Palazzo Trevisan is:

20. **Palazzo Pesaro,** with a broad 16th-century facade and ten windows across its *piano nobile*. Its size and proportions hint at its origins as a country villa, and like its neighbor, the Palazzo Pesaro was decorated inside and out with frescoes by the major artists of the time. The building was used as a barracks during the insurrection of 1848–49, and is now owned by a glassmaking consortium. Behind the house, a once famous botanical garden is now occupied by furnaces and storage sheds.

    The next house:

21. **Palazzo Capello,** seems less imposing. Its facade has suffered alterations and deterioration since its time of glory in 1574, when King Henry III of France lodged here during a state visit to Venice. The king's inspection of the island's glassworks was commemorated by a special Muranese coin, valued at 200 sequins, with a portrait of Henry III on one side and a view of the Capello house on the other.

    Down an alleyway just before 47 Fondamenta Navagero is:

22. the company of **Ercole Moretti** (at 42 Fondamenta Navagero), perhaps the most respected producer of glass

mosaic beads, jewelry and *millefiori* objects. *Millefiore* items from this workshop sold throughout Venice will have the signature of Ercole Moretti in the glass itself. In the same style, look for the *millefiore* work of Ragazzi, which is also labeled, and can be seen in many shops. A bit less expensive and less prestigious, Ragazzi claims to be "the cultural heir of Vincenzo Moretti," whose 19th-century masterworks are displayed in the Glass Museum. Ragazzi's products are always interesting.

As you continue to browse along the Fondamenta, you'll pass under the arcade of:

23. the vast brick **villa of Andrea Navagero,** at nos. 60 and 62, a noted 16th-century scholar who was ambassador to Spain. The villa was rescued from total decrepitude by a restoration in 1985. (To get a really good look at this imposing building, you will have to take a lengthy trek back and across the canal.) The Villa Navagero had an extensive garden and arboretum in back, running all the way to the shores of the lagoon.

If you'd like to end your tour of Murano now, check here at the Navagero Actv stop next to the villa for information on the somewhat erratic schedule of vaporettos back to Venice from this point. You might also want to continue to the point at the end of the Fondamenta Navagero, with its view across the lagoon.

The final part of this walk will backtrack to the Rio dei Vetrai and take in some glass showrooms on the Fondamenta Manin. We'll retrace our way back to the Grand Canal, across the Ponte Vivarini and onto the Fondamenta dei Vetrai, at which point we will cross the:

24. **Ponte San Pietro Martire** and walk along the Fondamenta Manin for a bit more glass hunting before taking the vaporetto back to town from the Actv Colonna stop. Among the most interesting workshops on this side of the Fondamenta is:

25. **S.A.L.I.R.,** 78 Fondamenta Manin, famous for engraved and etched glass and for reproductions of antique mirrors. Crystal vessels with ethereal 1930s engraved art deco designs were once the specialties of this studio.

For those going on to Burano and Torcello at the end of this walk, this is a good time to check the vaporetto schedules. Boats from Murano to these islands depart from the Faro Actv stop rather than from Colonna, where we disembarked. Just after no. 63 Fondamenta Manin, turn left onto the broad Viale Giuseppe Garibaldi, and continue straight to the end where you can inquire at the Faro Actv stop. En route, on the left, you'll come to the:

26. **Ospedale Briati,** a tiny baroque oratory with wonderful angels ornamenting its curved roof pediment. It stands in the midst of a block of charitable almshouses built in 1752 for the widows of glassworkers. This neighborhood is composed largely of simple terrace cottages built for working class families.

  After planning your schedule, return to the Fondamenta Manin to continue the walk. At:

27. **Bisazza,** 40 Fondamenta Manin (through the sotoportego and down an alleyway off the Fondamenta near no. 43) if you're in luck, you'll find an array of solid glass aquariums filled with exotic glass fish and fantasy under seascapes. Continuing straight on the Fondamenta Manin, after passing under the sotoportego of the gothic Obizzi and Sodaci houses that we viewed from across the canal at the start of this walk, you'll come to the:

28. **Museum of Contemporary Glass,** just after 6 Fondamenta Manin, a very worthwhile exhibit that is often closed. If it is open, remember that your receipt from the Museo Vetrario at the Palazzo Giustiniani includes entrance to this annex. At 3 Fondamenta Manin, is:

29. **the workshop of Carlo Moretti,** one of the most elegant contemporary designers on the island (New York's Museum of Modern Art has included his octagonal and oval vases and drinking glasses in its Industrial Design collection). In Venice, L'Isola, a sleek gallery at Campo San Moise 1468, near San Marco, handles Carlo Moretti's line of mouth-blown lead-free crystal.

  This walk ends at Ponte S. Chiara, in the heart of the glass bazaar, where you can continue your own personal exploration of the showrooms before returning to Venice.

Glass Shops in Venice

In addition to the many temptations of Murano, I recommend looking into the glass shops in Venice. Be sure to check out the tiny studio of **Amadi** (Calle Saonero 2747, San Polo), where you can see the artist himself blowing lighter-than-air dragonflies and incredibly realistic seashells, slices of glass sausage, and other creations that combine wit, skill, poetry, and magic. **Pagnacco** (San Marco 231, in the pricey and touristy Merceria), is a landmark for miniatures. **Paolo Rossi** (Campo San Zaccaria 4685), is the artist's own showroom for his beautiful and very reasonably priced reproductions of ancient glass. Also look into the new **Galleria Marina Barovier** (Calle della Bottegha 3127, San Marco), run by a descendant of the venerable Muranese family that created the 15th-century Barovier Wedding Cup. This gallery sells collector pieces from 1910 to 1960 by Murano's greatest glassmakers of that period. Finally, a visit to the workshop of **Gianfranco Penzo** (Campo Ghetto Novo 2895) is an exceptional excursion for lovers of glass. Mr. Penzo does custom-ordered, hand-painted glass designs, often based on illuminated medieval manuscripts. He has also created a repertoire of his own classical and art deco designs in diamond-point engraved crystal. Some of Mr. Penzo's work involves Judaica, but a good portion of his designs are of a non-religious nature.

ESSENTIALS & RECOMMENDED READING

Venice lies in the center of a lagoon, 2^1/$_2$ miles from the Italian mainland and 1^1/$_2$ miles from the sandy barrier beach of the Lido that separates the lagoon from the open seas of the Adriatic. Most visitors to Venice don't realize that in addition to the canal-laced islets and tidal flatlands that form the substructure of Venice, the lagoon contains an archipelago of some 117 islands, including Murano (10 minutes from Venice by vaporetto and famous for its glass), Burano, with its picturesque village (40 minutes by boat), and Torcello, with its beautiful Veneto-Byzantine cathedral. Dozens of other islands dot the lagoon. Some support small communities or isolated monasteries; others remain in their wild state or contain ruins of abandoned habitations. The ecosystem of the lagoon has a rich tapestry of tidal vegetation and shelters an amazing number and variety of shore birds.

CITY LAYOUT

The city of Venice is bisected by the S-shaped $2^1/_2$-mile-long Grand Canal, or "Canalazzo," that many consider to be the most magnificent boulevard in the world. This waterway is the main transportation route through the city. It is spanned by three bridges: the Scalzi Bridge near the railway station, the Rialto Bridge at the center of the city, and the Accademia Bridge, closer to the mouth of the Grand Canal. There are only very limited stretches of the Grand Canal along which you can actually walk. However, vaporettos, the buses of Venice, run along the length of the waterway. A ride down the Grand Canal on a slow vaporetto is never less than dazzling. Many of the so-called streets of Venice are actually canals, or *rios*, 150 in all. A total of 400 bridges span these smaller canals.

Venice is divided into six quarters that local residents call *sestieri* (singular *sestiere*)—three on each side of the Grand Canal. These include the most frequented sestiere, San Marco, which shares its side of the Grand Canal with the sestieri of Castello and Cannaregio.

Across the canal you'll find the sestiere of Dorsoduro, with the Accademia at its heart, San Polo, with its markets, and Santa Croce, which is full of wonderful scenes of everyday Venetian life. Each sestiere has its treasures and its own special character. The walks in this book give you a chance to sample each fascinating quarter.

South of the main part of Dorsoduro (which is south of the Grand Canal), you'll find another major channel, Canale della Giudecca, that separates Dorsoduro from the large island of La Giudecca. At the point where Canale della Giudecca meets the lagoon opposite San Marco, you'll spot the landmark Isola di San Giorgio Maggiore, a small island dominated by a classic white Palladian church.

Finding an Address The buildings in each sestiere are numbered, starting with civic number 1, and going well into the thousands. Unfortunately, the persons who first assigned numbers to the buildings several hundred years ago had to wend their way through the labyrinth of the city's passages, with the routes criss-crossing and retracing themselves unavoidably in many places. A building may have been assigned no. 213, and around the corner, a building nearby may be 3391. Worse yet—as each sestiere has its own set of civic numbers—if a calle crosses from one sestiere to the next, the sequence of numbers will suddenly change. So before you set out on a journey to a specific place, get detailed instructions and mark your map. Instead of depending on street numbers, locate the reference to the nearest cross street or campo, and, once there, look for signs posted outside a museum, building, or restaurant. You might also ask for the nearest church—locations are often given by parish (*parocchia*). When looking for a shop, remember that for esthetic reasons, the city of Venice does not encourage major signs, and many shops are only identifiable by civic number and what's in the window.

Street Maps If you are touring Venice and want to find that little hidden trattoria on a nearly forgotten street, you might as well abandon any map that doesn't detail every street and have an index in the back so you can find what you're looking for. One of the best is the pocket size **Falk** map of Venice. It details everything and is sold at many news kiosks and at all bookstores. The most complete and accurate guide, if you're staying in Venice for some time, is the book *Calli, Campielli e Canali: Guida di Venezia e delle sua Isole* by G. Paolo Nadali and Renzo Vianello (Venice: Edizioni Helvelia). The maps are in Italian, but easily deciphered.

GETTING AROUND

On Foot Since you can't hail a taxi, at least not on land, what you do in Venice is walk. This is the only way to explore Venice unless you plan to see it from a boat on the Grand Canal. Everybody walks in Venice. Distances between major sites in the city are not great, and you'll find there's a special pleasure in exploring a city unmarred by cars, buses, or thoroughfares created for vehicular traffic. The hardest thing for visitors to adapt to is climbing up and down the steps leading to the city's many bridges. You'll find your leg muscles will be reactivated, and you'll also notice that Venetians seem to be among the most agile, fit urban dwellers in Europe! Take things slowly at first. Remember that the steps on bridges can be very slippery when wet! In summer, the overcrowding in the San Marco area is so severe that some streets are designated one-way only.

By Public Transportation The water buses, or vaporetti, provide inexpensive and frequent, if not always rapid, transportation in this canal-riddled city. The average fare on an *accelerato* (which makes every stop) is 2,500 lire ($1.50), and it will take you from St. Mark's to the Lido. The average fare on a *diretto* (only express stops) is 3,500 lire ($2.10) for a trip, say from the railway station to the Rialto Bridge. In summer, the vaporetti are often fiercely crowded. Pick up a map of the system from the tourist office. The vaporetto system links Venice to the Lido and Murano; larger vaporetti, departing from the Fondamenta Nuove on the northern edge of the city will take you to the islands of Burano and Torcello. Service is daily from 7am to midnight, then hourly between midnight and 7am.

Discount Passes   A 24-hour, 14,000-lire ($8.40) *biglietto turistico*, or tourist ticket, allows you to travel all day on any of the many routes of the city's boat services. This all-inclusive ticket, also valid for service to Burano and Torcello, is a bargain, as is the three-day ticket allowing travel for 20,000 lire ($12). Students should inquire at the Tourist Information Office about discount passes coupled with guided itinerary pamphlets and museum discounts that may be in effect.

By Traghetto   Traghetti are open, gondola-like boats that Venetians use as short-cut ferries straight across the Grand Canal. There are seven traghetto ferries. Departure of the traghetto often depends on when enough customers have arrived. Passengers generally stand in the center of the boat for the one-minute ride across the canal; fare is 500 lire (about 35¢) each way. Among the most popular traghetto ferries are those connecting the Pescheria and Santa Sofia, and the one between Santa Maria del Giglio and the Salute Church on Dorsoduro. Some lines end service by 1:30 or 2pm; a few continue until 6 or 7pm.

By Water Taxi/Motor Launch   Private motor launches, called *taxi acquei*, cost more than public vaporettos. You always have to negotiate the fare before getting in, but begin at 27,000 lire ($16.20) for seven minutes, plus an 8,000-lire ($4.80) supplement from 10pm to 7am and a 9,000-lire ($5.40) surcharge on Sunday and holidays. To their credit, the captains of Venice's motor launches are usually adroit about depositing you within a short walking distance of your destination. You can call for a *taxi acquei*. Try **Radio Taxi** (tel. 523-2326).

By Gondola   Alas, the gondolas have become a luxurious and romantic anachronism in Venice. When arranging a ride in a gondola, three major agreements have to be reached—the price of the ride, the itinerary of special places you may want to pass, and the length of the trip. There is an accepted official rate schedule of about 70,000 lire ($42) for up to 50 minutes, but the rate is somewhat out-of-date, and most gondoliers will ask *at least* double the official rate, and may reduce your time aboard to 30 or 40 minutes. Prices go up after 9pm. If you decide to invest in a gondola ride, remember to schedule your trip when the tide is high and the level of the gondola is close to that of the land; otherwise, as you glide along, you'll have an eye-level view of the scum and gunk on the sides of the canals, exposed by low tide. A route that includes a section of the Grand Canal will enable you to see some of your favorite sites up close, but traffic on the Grand Canal can also make for a choppy voyage. Take advantage of your gondola rental to explore some of the smaller canals that cannot be viewed from a vaporetto.

Two major stations at which you can hire gondolas include Piazza San Marco (tel. 52-00-685) and Ponte Rialto (tel. 522-4904).Gondola ride tourist packages are offered by travel agencies in Piazza San Marco—including *serendades*!

SPECIAL VENETIAN FESTIVALS

Carnival   In February, for 10 days before the beginning of Lent, Venice attempts to revive something of the spirit of the 6-month-long Carnival of the 18th century. You may spot some masked, costumed revelers en route to a private ball as well as many younger people in full-blown punk attire. However, the movement to revive Venetian Carnival, which began in the 1980s, is still in its early stages.

La Sensa   In May, on the Sunday after Ascension Day, a pale reenactment of the once famed ritual of the Marriage of Venice to the Sea is performed by municipal authorities. On the same day, the vast *Vogalonga,* or long row is held. This is an exciting 32km race to Burano and back, open to all comers. Participants reach the San Marco basin between 11am and 3pm.

Feast of the Redentore   On the third Saturday night in July, half of Venice picnics aboard boats and gondolas and watches spectacular fireworks on the greatest of Venetian holidays, marking the end of the plague of 1576. A bridge of boats spans the Giudecca Canal and connects Dorsoduro to Palladio's Church of the Redentore on the island of Giudecca.

Venice Film Festival   Held at the Lido in late August or early September. Some films are occasionally screened for the public in the campos of Venice.

Regatta Storica   On the first Sunday in September, the Grand Canal is filled with a monumental pageant of historical vessels and crews decked out in Renaissance costumes. A series of gondola races is part of the spectacle.

Feast of the Madonna Della Salute   For approximately 24 hours on November 21, a pontoon bridge spans the Grand Canal to the great baroque Church of Santa Maria della Salute for a religious procession commemorating the deliverance of Venice from the plague of 1630–31.

FAST FACTS   Venice

Acqua Alta   If you are planning to be in Venice from October through March, high boots can be useful. The canals flood due to a combination of the tides and the winds. If a flood is expected, a warning siren will be sounded one hour before crest so people can get home. The city puts out boardwalks (*passarelle*) along major routes. Acqua alta generally lasts only about 2 or 3 hours at a time.

Area Code   The telephone area code is 041.

Consulates   There is no **U.S. Consulate** in Venice; the closest is in Milan, at Largo Donegani 1 (tel. 290-018-41). The **British Consulate** is at Dorsoduro 1051 (tel. 522-7207), open Monday through Friday from 9am to noon and 2 to 4pm.

Currency Exchange   There are many banks in Venice where you can exchange money. For example, try the **Banca d'America e d'Italia,** San Marco 2216 (tel. 520-0766). Many travelers find that **CARIPLO (Cassa di Riparmio di Lombardin)**, San Marco 1289 (tel. 520-8711), offers the best rates in Venice.

Emergencies   Phone numbers are 113 for **police,** 523-0000 for an **ambulance.** For first aid, call 520-3222 or go to **Ospedale Civile**, Pronto Soccorso.

Fax   The post office has a 24-hour fax service.

Floods   See "Acqua Alta," above.

Holidays   Offices and shops in Italy are closed on the following dates: January 1 (New Year's Day), Easter Monday, April 25 (Liberation Day), May 1 (Labor Day), August 15 (Assumption of the Virgin), November 1 (All Saints' Day), December 8 (Feast of the Immaculate Conception), December 25 (Christmas Day), and December 26 (Santo Stefano). Closings are also observed in Venice on April 25, the feast day honoring St. Mark, its patron saint.

Information   Visitors can get information at the **Azienda di Promozione Turistica,** piazza San Marco 71C (tel. 522-6356). It's open Monday through Saturday from 8:30am to 6:45pm. However these hours are not always consistent. There's also a tourist office in the train station.

Lost Property   The central office for recovering lost property is the **Ufficio Oggetti Rinvenuti**, an annex to the Municipio (town hall) south of the Rialto Bridge on the San Marco side at San Marco 4134 (tel. 788-225), on calle Piscopia o Loredan, lying off riva del Carbon on the Grand Canal. Open Monday, Wednesday, and Friday from 9:30am to 12:30pm.

Luggage Storage/Lockers   These services are available at the main rail station, **Stazione di Santa Lucia** (tel. 715-555).

Police   Dial 113. Also see "Emergencies," above.

Post Office   The major post office is at Fondaco dei Tedeschi (tel. 528-62-12), in the vicinity of the Rialto Bridge. It's open Monday through Saturday from 8:15am to 7pm.

Restrooms   These are available at **piazzale Roma** and various other places in Venice, but not as plentiful as they should be. Often you'll have to rely on the facilities of a cafe, although you should always at least order a coffee, as commercial establishments reserve their toilets for customers only. Most museums and galleries have public toilets. You can also use the acceptable public toilets at the Albergo Diurno, on via Ascensione, just behind piazza San Marco, or at the Accademia Bridge (under steps), Accademia side. Remember, *Signori* means men and *Signore* for women.

Safety   The curse of Venice is the pickpocket artist. Violent crime is very rare. But because of the overcrowding in vaporetti and even on the small narrow streets, it's easy to pick pockets.

Taxes   A 19% value-added tax (called IVA) is added to the price of all consumer goods and products and most services, such as those in hotels and restaurants.

Useful Telephone Numbers   To check on the time, call 161; for the weather, 191.

RECOMMENDED READING

The following is a selection of some of the most readable and evocative of the many books published about Venice.

Albrizzi, Alessandro, and Mary Jane Pool, *The Gardens of Venice* (New York, Rizzoli, 1989). This extensively photographed book helps you to find and appreciate the green places that are often not readily apparent in the dense urban structure of Venice.

Brodsky, Joseph, *Watermark* (New York, Farrar, Straus & Giroux, 1992). Observations by the Nobel Prize–winning author.

Canal, Antonio, called Canaletto, *Views of Venice by Canaletto,* with an introduction and descriptive text by J. G. Links (New York, Dover Publications, 1971). A selection of work by the most famous 18th-century Venetian landscape painter with commentary by a well-known writer on Venetian topics.

Curiel, Roberta, and Bernard Dov Cooperman, *The Venetian Ghetto* (New York, Rizzoli, 1990). A coffee table–size survey and history of the Jewish community in Venice with top-notch photographs and illustrations.

Franzoi, Umberto, and Mark Smith, *The Grand Canal* (New York, Vendome, 1994). A lavishly photographed guide to what many consider is the most magnificent waterway in the world and the grandest boulevard of Europe.

Hibbert, Christopher, *Venice, the Biography of a City* (London, Grafton Books, 1988; New York, Norton, 1989). A definitive and highly readable history filled with anecdotes and illustrations. The detailed appendix on buildings and works of art is a real plus.

James, Henry, *The Wings of the Dove* (New York, Charles Scribner's Sons, 1909). A novel partly set in a Venetian palazzo that draws upon the author's experiences as a guest at the Palazzo Barbaro.

Jong, Erica, *Serenissima* (New York, Houghton Mifflin, 1989). A novel in which an actress attending the Venice Film Festival, falls through the Venetian looking glass into Shakespeare's world of *The Merchant of Venice.*

Lauritzen, Peter, *Venice Preserved* (New York, Adler and Adler, 1986; published in Great Britain by Michael Joseph Ltd.). A documentation of the most important internationally backed restoration projects completed in Venice during the first fifteen years after the *acqua alta* of 1966. The intelligent text and fine photographs by Jorge Lewinski and Mayotte Magnus illustrate what has been accomplished, and the magnitude of what must be done to save Venice.

Lauritzen, Peter, and Alexander Ziecke, *The Palaces of Venice* (New York, Viking, 1979). This is a carefully photographed architectural survey that includes anecdotes and information about the histories of the city's great houses.

Mann, Thomas, *Death in Venice* (first published in 1912; many editions available). A novel set in the Hotel des Bains on the Lido, evocative of this once elegant resort and the romantic, decaying world of Venice at the turn of the century (also beautifully realized in a film by Visconti).

Masson, Georgina, *Courtesans of the Italian Renaissance* (New York, St. Martin's Press, 1976). A look at the lives of some of the most cultivated and talented women of their era, and the position Italian society assigned to them.

McCarthy, Mary, *Venice Observed* (New York, Harcourt Brace Jovanovich, 1963). A lively, intelligent survey of Venetian history, art, and culture.

Modena, Leone, *Haye Yehuda; the Autobiography of a 17th Century Venetian Rabbi: Leon Modena's Life of Judah,* translated and edited by Mark R. Cohen (Princeton, Princeton University Press, 1988). A carefully presented autobiography of the Venetian Ghetto's most famous and flamboyant rabbi.

Ritter, Dorothea, *Venice in Old Photographs 1841–1920* (London, Laurence King, 1994). An extensive and carefully chosen collection of photographs that will help you to look at many Venetian sites with a fresh eye.

Rolfe, Frederick (Baron Corvo), *The Desire and Pursuit of the Whole* (first published in 1909; many editions availble). This scalding satiric novel caused a scandal inside the English-speaking community of Venice because many of its members recognized portraits of themselves among the book's characters. The writing is uneven, but many of the descriptions of Venice are very knowing and beautiful.

Rosenthal, Margaret F., *The Honest Courtesan: Veronica Franco, Citizen and Writer in 16th Century Venice* (Chicago, University of Chicago Press, 1992). The life of perhaps the most famous, and talented woman in the history of Venice.

Ruskin, John, *The Stones of Venice* (first published in 1853; numerous abridged and later editions in print). Opinionated and extensive in its survey of the art and architecture of Venice, this classic was the first analysis of the Venetian cultural heritage in English in modern times.

Vitoux, Frederic, *Venice, the Art of Living* (New York, Stewart, Tabori & Chang, 1991). Beautifully photographed book on Venetian style, decor, and the pleasures of living in Venice, with an elegant, evocative text.